READING
SRI AUROBINDO

ADVANCE PRAISES FOR THE BOOK

'The most attractive, even unique, feature of this book is that it is a collection of volume-by-volume introductions to Sri Aurobindo's *Complete Works*. Written by the who's who of scholars of Sri Aurobindo and practitioners of his Integral Yoga, this anthology of readings is a fitting tribute to the master on his 150th anniversary, which also coincides with India@75'—Makarand R. Paranjape, MA, PhD (Illinois), and professor of English, Jawaharlal Nehru University

'Sri Aurobindo's 150th birth anniversary falls on 15 August 2022. One of the world's greatest philosophers, his voluminous writings collected in thirty-six volumes, represent a massive contribution to the wisdom of humanity. I congratulate the editors of *Reading Sri Aurobindo* for having produced a collection of perceptive essays by scholars of Sri Aurobindo and practitioners of his Integral Yoga. This is a brilliantly encapsulated introduction to the work of a truly great genius whose writings, including poems, cover a vast canvas of political, sociological and spiritual areas that reflect his integral approach to the individual and collective challenges faced by humanity'—Dr Karan Singh, former member of the 16th Lok Sabha

'This book fills a huge vacuum; in that it brings together, for the first time, in one volume the kernel and essence of Sri Aurobindo's ideas in an original rendering. What I find remarkable is that it makes Sri Aurobindo accessible to the first-time reader while retaining the subtle depth, richness and complexity of his manifold vision and work. The editors and scholars have done a fine work'—Ameeta Mehra, chairperson and founder-trustee of The Gnostic Centre

'The modern rishi Sri Aurobindo has been critical to the revival of Dharma in the modern day. Most have heard of him, but many would not have read his works. The thirty-six volumes are a daunting task for any lay reader. That is what makes Gautam and Devdip's book so important, helping more people access the profound thoughts of Sri Aurobindo. Few understand completely the scholarship of this multifaceted Indian sage whose writings on politics, scriptures and human evolution are transforming those who have internalized them. His writings show a new pathway to understanding the transitional nature of this creation called the universe in general and its human factor in particular. *Reading Sri Aurobindo* is the ideal introduction to those who want to access Sri Aurobindo's works but don't know where to begin their journey from the thirty-six volumes he has written'—Amish Tripathi, author

READING SRI AUROBINDO

Edited by
GAUTAM CHIKERMANE
and DEVDIP GANGULI

EBURY PRESS
An imprint of Penguin Random House

EBURY PRESS
USA | Canada | UK | Ireland | Australia
New Zealand | India | South Africa | China

Ebury Press is part of the Penguin Random House group of companies whose addresses can be found at global.penguinrandomhouse.com

Published by Penguin Random House India Pvt. Ltd
4th Floor, Capital Tower 1, MG Road,
Gurugram 122 002, Haryana, India

Penguin Random House India

First published in Ebury Press by Penguin Random House India 2022

10 9 8 7 6 5 4 3 2

ISBN 9780670097036

Typeset in Minion Pro by MAP Systems, Bengaluru, India
Printed at Thomson Press India Ltd, New Delhi

www.penguin.co.in

MIX
Paper
FSC FSC® C010615

To Sri Aurobindo and the Mother

Contents

Introduction: The Supramental Sage

Gautam Chikermane

My meeting with Sri Aurobindo began on the mental plane, through abstract ideas that explored the various aspects of Indian spiritual and philosophical traditions. I already had a working knowledge of the concepts, partly as a seeker and partly as a traveller, through the works and paths of other Indian philosophers and spiritual leaders to whom I was exposed to during my school days, college life and early career as a writer. It was not until I turned thirty that destiny placed me before Sri Aurobindo. More accurately, I was ready to receive his deep, wide and puissant ideas. This was no coincidence; it was the decisive tread of time that has irreversibly changed my life.

Since then, I have embarked on a journey that has gone beyond the mental. Or let us say, the mental has been enriched by the emotional-vital, which in turn has been deepened by the psychic, with all three held together by the spiritual. Sri Aurobindo's influence on every aspect of my life, from the way I think to the manner in which I express myself, has been, like his yoga, integral.

The Integral Yoga is a process by which not just the soul but the body, right down to the cells, is transformed through the union of two powerful forces—the human aspiration from below, and the divine grace from above. There is no single method, mantra, practice or process that the Integral Yoga professes; the journey and the resultant transformation of each individual soul is unique.

This transformation is destined. The Integral Yoga, according to Sri Aurobindo, accelerates what nature has preordained through evolution. To clarify, the Integral Yoga is not an admixture of Karma Yoga, Bhakti Yoga or Jnana Yoga (the yogas of Works, Devotion, and Knowledge). It is not a collection of ideas and words fused together by language. Sri Aurobindo's synthesis of yogas is wider than an agglomeration of extant schools, deeper than the living philosophical traditions and higher than the spiritual milestones mapped thus far. It is not an easy path. It requires grit, sincerity and the constant fire of aspiration.

The Integral Yoga begins where other yogas end. For Sri Aurobindo, dissolving into the Brahman is not the ultimate spiritual goal. His yoga attempts to transform the earth. Where other yoga paths find fruition in merging with the Absolute, Sri Aurobindo sees this union as an intermediate step. Divinisation of matter and not dissolution of consciousness is his destination, the transformation of humanity and not merely the individual his aim. Science may place homo sapiens at the pinnacle of evolution. But for Sri Aurobindo, this species is a transitional being, whose evolution is not yet over. Just as life entered matter, and mind entered life, both mind and matter await the descent of the spirit—the Supramental consciousness. Any transformation without the transformation of the body will remain incomplete. Life on earth has to be divinised. Life and afterlife are both here and now. The two are one.

'Sri Aurobindo does not believe in salvation,' his spiritual collaborator Mirra Alfassa, better known as the Mother, said. 'For us salvation is a meaningless word.'[1] Although his work is rooted in Hindu philosophy—or to put it more accurately, in

Sanatana Dharma, itself a wide spiritual rather than a narrow religious endeavour, and where even religious activities such as rituals have deeper meanings—through the Integral Yoga, Sri Aurobindo has taken Indian spiritual traditions several steps forward.

But neither the divinisation of matter, nor the transfer of consciousness, transformation and evolution, nor aspiration and grace are easy concepts to understand. 'Sri Aurobindo came upon earth to teach this truth to men,' wrote the Mother, combining all three concepts (man as a transitional being, the Supramental consciousness, and the transformation) elegantly. 'He told them that man is only a transitional being living in a mental consciousness, but with the possibility of acquiring a new consciousness, the Truth-consciousness, and capable of living a life perfectly harmonious, good and beautiful, happy and fully conscious. During the whole of his life upon earth, Sri Aurobindo gave all his time to establish in himself this consciousness he called supramental, and to help those gathered around him to realise it.'[2]

Despite the wide range of themes he engaged with, the essence of Sri Aurobindo's writings remained spiritual. Be it nationalism or freedom, poetry or drama, analysis or record, the Vedas or the Upanishads, science or metaphysics, all his writings are rooted in spirituality. What makes reading Sri Aurobindo challenging is the interpretations of ideas like surrender, equanimity or grace, when placed within the wider context of the Integral Yoga. Making the intellectual climb even steeper are other related ideas that we meet on the path—man as a divine potential, containing within himself a *swabhava* that translates into his *swadharma* to surpass matter, mind and soul. Add to this the layers of the being, the knowledge universes from the physical mind to the Overmind, or the ascent of consciousness meeting the descent of grace, and every book of

Sri Aurobindo becomes a self-contained force-field comprising a highly-specialized interplay of understandings, experiences and realizations. You can't read Sri Aurobindo only with the eyes of the mind. Even the reading has to be integral. The spiritual collaboration of the vital, the psychic and the physical is necessary to reach the depths he envisions. When some readers say they sense a presence while reading his works, we can empathise with what is going on behind the mind.

As far as words go, Sri Aurobindo is as much at ease with poetry as with prose, with philosophy as with politics, with dramas as with stories. His writings, as a prisoner or professor, a leader of revolutionaries or a resident of solitude, resonate with force and depth. I find his writings mantric; his words express Truth in sound. The mantra has to be read not just by the mind, but sensed by the being through words. 'The Mantra,' he wrote in *The Future Poetry with On Quantitative Metre* (See Chapter 22), one volume of his collected works, 'is born through the heart and shaped or massed by the thinking mind into a chariot of that godhead of the Eternal of whom the truth seen is a face or a form.'[3] This Truth reaches the deepest recesses of our souls.

These truths resonate in different ways. His revolutionary writings, particularly the ones that explore nationalism, make you sit up. His analytical writings, on silence or science, for instance, cut through all surfaces and bring Truths to you. His philosophical writings get to the core of issues in ways that make traditional philosophers look like amateurs grappling with ideas, which in turn are toying with them. Sri Aurobindo's mantric style is ancient *and* modern, Vedic *and* contemporary; it is integral across time, space and ideas, and as all Truths are—eternal.

Above all, every aspect of his writings, from education to freedom, psychological to physiological, physical to mental, the Vedas to the Upanishads to the Gita, is powered by a spiritual force whose presence is perceptible. His insights into political events of the day contain a vision for India that goes beyond it becoming a superpower; his vision of nations and global affairs raises the field of geopolitics to levels unseen; his engagement with culture and knowledge systems infuses a spiritually refined perspective into the subject. The manner in which he holds forth on Indian scriptures or Greek poetry, the way he contextualises them into disparate but unified conversations, the treatment he gives to his Sanskrit and Bengali writings showcase him as a literary genius with no equal.

The integral span of his work is not merely philosophical; it is equally scientific and spiritual. Take the 'hard problem' of consciousness. In a single chapter titled, 'The Science of Consciousness,' in *Essays Divine and Human*, Sri Aurobindo explained, and in the process bridged science and spirituality, psychology and yoga. 'Body, brain, nervous system are instruments of consciousness, they are not its causes,' he wrote. 'Consciousness is its own cause, a producer of objects and images and not their product.' He concluded by saying, 'It is through consciousness, by an instrumentation of consciousness only that the nature and laws and movements of consciousness can be discovered—and this is the method of Yoga.'[4]

Sri Aurobindo's mission was to begin the process of spiritualising the earth. His work re-examines the Indian spiritual traditions afresh and reaches a higher plane to open out a rope-ladder that other seekers may use to climb. His writings opened out the secret and occult pathways for disciples that began with a handful in Pondicherry, his 'cave of tapasya,' and are now dispersed across the world. He wrote political essays and spiritual chapters, threads of philosophy and streams of culture. Understanding the source code of his works required a higher intellectual level and broader requirement from sadhaks. Thus, there are letters he wrote to them from his tower of solitude, where he closed himself for twenty-four years, from

1926 to 1950. These letters are more intimate, simpler, each addressing a particular aspect of a sadhaka's question. But all are equally intense with insights for general readers. Finally, those who find even the letters difficult to engage with, there are conversations with the Mother, the spiritual mother to their disciples and devotees.

* * *

In this volume, we offer an introduction to all of Sri Aurobindo's ideas through all his books. These comprise essays and chapters, poetry and plays, translations, speeches and letters. While some have been conceptualised and written as books, others have been collected by editors at the Sri Aurobindo Ashram to whom we credit the classification. This was not an easy task. In fact, the putting together of *The Complete Works of Sri Aurobindo* by the editors at the Archives and Research Department of Sri Aurobindo Ashram in Pondicherry is in itself an intellectual adventure not merely in terms of categorization but equally in deciphering his handwritten words, with several corrections across every page. Broadly, there were four challenges while compiling Sri Aurobindo's works.

First, the several idea-streams of Sri Aurobindo, each of which has been refined to perfection, all facts and views taken into account. Every word Sri Aurobindo wrote has passed through the fire of rigour, inner and outer, and is synthesised by the power of knowledge, experience and realization. As a result, engaging with the grammar of his ideas, and the complexities of his nuanced vocabulary is like entering a new field, where every step has to be taken with great care.

Second, the humongous body of his work. Each volume is between 400 and 1600 pages. The shortest books are *The Future*

Poetry (415 pages) and *The Renaissance in India and Other Essays on Indian Culture* (484 pages), while the longest are *Record of Yoga* (1529 pages) and *Bande Mataram* (1206 pages). Altogether, Sri Aurobindo's work is printed across more than 21,000 pages and adds up to almost 6 million words. Recording these words, checking for accuracy, page by page, line by line was not an easy task.

Third, trying to decipher the handwriting of Sri Aurobindo. Apart from the readings, this volume also contains thirty-one of his handwritten manuscripts. You only need to go through them to see the challenges of transcribing his words from the original to the final. The pages may or may not be the final; Sri Aurobindo often made several changes. There are several levels of complexity here. For instance, if you examine the original manuscript page preceding *Collected Poems* (See Chapter 2), *Letters on Yoga* (See Chapter 24) or *Autobiographical Notes and Other Writings of Historical* Interest (See Chapter 31), the words are clear and easy to read, and hence, transcribe. But try to figure out the words in the manuscripts preceding *Essays in Philosophy and Yoga* (See Chapter 10), *The Synthesis of Yoga* (See Chapter 19) or *Letters on Poetry and Art* (See Chapter 23) and the corrections are such that only a professional and dedicated editor with grit and stamina can decode. As you read the manuscript pages, you will also note Sri Aurobindo's changing pens, inks and pressures. Spend time with them—they will bring you closer to him, mentally as well as in deeper domains.

And fourth, the classification across publication history. Here, editors have placed the thirty-six volumes of his work across three categories.

One, single and long works that Sri Aurobindo revised and published during his lifetime. These include four titles published across seven volumes—*Essays on the Gita* (See Chapter 16 by Monika Halan); *The Life Divine* (See Chapter 18 by Matthijs Cornelissen); *The Synthesis of Yoga* (See Chapter 19 by Debashish Banerji); and *Savitri: A Legend and a Symbol* (See Chapter 29 by Richard Hartz).

Two, collections of short- or medium-sized works that were published by Sri Aurobindo in some form during his lifetime, with or without revisions. There are five titles in this — *Essays in Philosophy and Yoga* (See Chapter 10 by Gautam Chikermane); *The Secret of the Veda* (See Chapter 12 by Anuradha Choudry); *The Renaissance in India and Other Essays on Indian Culture* (See Chapter 17 by Devdip Ganguli); *The Human Cycle* (See Chapter 20 by Anuradha Agrawal); *The Ideal of Human Unity*, and *War and Self-Determination* (See Chapter 21 by Devdip Ganguli); and *The Future Poetry with On Quantitative Metre* (See Chapter 22 by Karen Ecke).

And three, works of various lengths in different genres and on various topics, many not published during Sri Aurobindo's lifetime, and which have been compiled and arranged. There are eighteen titles across twenty-four volumes in this category—*Early Cultural Writings* (See Chapter 1 by Gautam Chikermane); *Collected Poems* (See Chapter 2 by Matriprasad); *Collected Plays and Stories I and II* (See Chapter 3 by Thirthankar Chakraborty); *Translations* (See Chapter 4 by Richard Hartz); *Bande Mataram* (See Chapter 5 by Anirban Ganguly); *Karmayogin* (See Chapter 6 by Matriprasad); *Writings in Bengali and Sanskrit* (See Chapter 7 by Sampadananda Mishra); *Record of Yoga* (See Chapter 8 by Richard Hartz); *Essays Divine and Human* (See Chapter 9 by Uday Arya); *Vedic and Philological Studies* (See Chapter 11 by Richard Hartz); *Hymns to the Mystic Fire* (See Chapter 13 by Pranjal Garg); *Isha Upanishad* (See Chapter 14 by Debashish Banerji); *Kena and Other Upanishads* (See Chapter 15 by Anshul Sinha); *Letters on Poetry and Art* (See Chapter 23 by

Patrick Beldio); *Letters on Yoga I, II, III and IV* (See Chapters 24 and 25 by Larry Seidlitz, Chapter 26 by Georg Stollenwerk, and See Chapter 27 by Payal Adhikari); *The Mother and Letters on the Mother* (See Chapter 28 by Gautam Chikermane); *Letters on Himself and the Ashram* (See Chapter 30 by Peter Heehs); and *Autobiographical Notes and Writings of Historical Interest* (See Chapter 31 by Peter Heehs).

The contributors in this book introduce each of these volumes to you and give you a taste of what they contain. All situate Sri Aurobindo from their positions of thought and action. Each of them has studied Sri Aurobindo from several books, but brought their expertise into one. For someone who has not engaged with the depth of Sri Aurobindo's works, these chapters provide a starting point.

This book has been conceptualised as a sacrifice, though not in the modern understanding of the word as a loss. This sacrifice is an offering. We are the wood, we the ghee. We are the mantras, we the fire. With all we have and all we are, we have given ourselves to this sacrifice. The words and the ideas that will finally make this book are an outer manifestation of what we offer from within. Into this book we have poured ourselves. We hope some of this pouring, this sacrifice, will become a bridge that will lead you to your own reading of Sri Aurobindo's works in the original.

* * *

Finally, as editors, Devdip and I approach Sri Aurobindo from two different worlds, but are integrally united by his ideas. Devdip is a second-generation student of the Ashram School and a fourth-generation resident of the Sri Aurobindo Ashram; I a first-generation devotee of Sri Aurobindo. Devdip chose to remain in the Ashram after he graduated; I stand rooted in what is known as the 'real' world. He not only serves the Ashram but is also a writer and speaker on Sri Aurobindo and a teacher to undergraduate students; I work at a think tank and contribute to the Ashram whenever I'm in Pondicherry. He engages with my world through the prism of Sri Aurobindo; I work with his from the vantage point of an outsider-insider. That said, both of us are rooted in the philosophy and spiritual paths of Sri Aurobindo's Integral Yoga.

In this volume, we bring a diverse set of devotees to our pages, and despite differences, find harmony and resolution between the external and the internal, the scholar and the doer, the witness and the actor. In doing so, we realize how Sri Aurobindo's integrality sweeps across geographies, times, and beings, unites them in a sublime harmony, and allows each to evolve in his unique manner.

Is there a 'favourite' book, a book that resonates more with me than others? Try as hard as I can, but the answer is 'no'. At different times, I have followed several streams of Sri Aurobindo's thoughts through different books. Sometimes, the same thought is expressed across varied volumes. I found analyses of the Bhagavad Gita in *Essays on the Gita*, of course; but there are deep references and intense chapters on the subject in *The Synthesis of Yoga*, *The Life Divine*, *Vedic and Philological Studies*, apart from shorter gleanings in several *Letters on Yoga*. Or take ideas such as the Integral Yoga, surrender, and the Supramental, which find space across several books such as *Essays Divine and Human*, *The Secret of the Veda*, and *Letters on Himself and the Ashram*. In fact, one way to read Sri Aurobindo is to follow one idea across various books.

The one book that accompanies me everywhere, from home to office, in India or abroad, while working or travelling, is *The Mother*. In six concise chapters, Sri Aurobindo brings home his core philosophy. The chapter on money, alone, can question the world of economics and finance and challenge our set ideas about it in a single line, 'Money is the visible sign of a universal force.'[5] The other book I often return to is *Essays on Philosophy and Yoga*. The one essay I read at least twice a year, and find new insights from it on every reading, is the 'The Bourgeois and the Samurai,' now a chapter in *Bande Mataram*. The first time I read it, it felt like Sri Aurobindo was giving me an intellectual lashing; now, I have reconciled to my failings and I dare say changed a bit. But I read it repeatedly—it keeps me grounded. In our loud world of noise, another chapter I repeatedly read is 'The Strength of Stillness', in *Essays in Philosophy and Yoga*: 'Silence prepares, speech creates. Silence acts, speech gives the impulse to action. Silence compels, speech persuades.'[6]

On the other hand, the one book I have never been able to finish or even progress beyond a canto is his epic, *Savitri*. Sri Aurobindo worked on this book first in 1916 and last in 1950. It has been stitched to perfection and is undoubtedly his greatest work. I find this poem so intense that it is difficult to comprehend it beyond a few lines. The reading of this book has been a journey for me. It began on the mental plane and now in the psychic. There is a mantric quality to *Savitri*'s verses that the mind cannot understand; it has to be read by the heart, in silence, with full concentration, calmness. 'Then,' the Mother said in a conversation with a disciple, 'the words, rhythms, vibrations will penetrate directly to this white page, will put their stamp upon the brain, will explain themselves without your making any effort.' *Savitri*, she says, is a book that can help aspirants climb the highest peaks: 'He has crammed the whole universe in a single book.'[7]

How, for instance, do you even begin to grapple with these lines:[8]

> Then something in the inscrutable darkness stirred;
> A nameless movement, an unthought Idea

Insistent, dissatisfied, without an aim,
Something that wished but knew not how to be,
Teased the Inconscient to wake Ignorance.

Savitri remains a height I still need to climb, an intellectual-psychic adventure I still need to embark on.

When we place ourselves in the ocean of his writings as humans that are still evolving and our current status transitional, reading Sri Aurobindo becomes an even more exciting voyage. Two persons reading the same text will emerge with different perspectives. This is not surprising—each individual is unique and the information, knowledge and experiences with which one reader absorbs and engages with the same truths will naturally be different from another. But what makes it a constant quest is that even the same reader reading the same book of Sri Aurobindo at two different times will read the truths differently. Not just the book, even a chapter or a few verses will impact the reader in different ways at different points of evolutionary journey.

Reading Sri Aurobindo is like entering a textual truth universe that spans the past, founds the present and envisions the future. *Savitri*, for instance, is a journey towards a future destined, a future where matter has been divinised, spiritualised. As we aspire to enter this future, we 'know' that future lies within us. We are the matter, we the mind, we the psychic, we the spiritualised. The universe, therefore, comprises outer worlds as well as inner countries. The integrality of his yoga thus transcends matter, life, mind and spirit, and points to a Supramentalised universe of space as well as time. The body is where the yoga happens, it is the playground of psychic growth, a bridge that carts the evolutionary cycle forward. Not in afterworlds, not in post-death…evolution happens in this universe, on this planet, through this body.

* * *

The twenty-one contributors in this volume have engaged with these texts for a long time, evolving with them. Some of them are teachers, some writers, politicians, thinkers, editors. All of them explore Sri Aurobindo from their respective vantage points and evolutionary states of being. Their perspectives and insights are only a starting point for your own journeys. When you embark on this adventure of reading Sri Aurobindo, it will be an experience unique to you, chiselled and driven by you. Despite having almost read all the books here, when I read some of the chapters by the contributors, they forced me to rethink what I know, got me to revisit my own reading of the text, and in an integral synthesis, expanded my outlook. In other words, reading Sri Aurobindo is like reading the scriptures.

This scriptural force will enrich the experience of the reading. In that context, this book is a starting point to understand the work of this modern sage and, in my opinion, the world's widest, deepest and loftiest thinker of the twentieth century. It is a handbook for humanity to negotiate the future centuries, living in the present, both of which are anchored in timeless principles—in his writings, the three are one, seamless. From the individual to the collective, inner journeys to historical ones, cultural aspects to global expressions, religion to spirituality, consciousness to the Supramental realization, if you think you resonate with the ideas of one book or one idea across several books, explore them in greater detail in his books.

We hope the ideas in *Reading Sri Aurobindo* find a home in your hearts, minds and bodies and you carve out your own paths, climb your own heights, explore your own depths…all within the context of integrality. That would be our reward and offering to our guru, the Supramental Sage, the messenger of the future, Sri Aurobindo.

* * *

1

Early Cultural Writings

Reading by Gautam Chikermane

Three major themes make up the first volume of Sri Aurobindo's complete works—one, a series of essays on education;[1] two, the examination of literature through the works of Bankim Chandra Chatterji, Kalidasa and Ved Vyasa;[2] and three, Sri Aurobindo's ideas on art, his reviews and his speeches.[3] Together, these pieces span the three decades between Sri Aurobindo at age nineteen, when he wrote the incomplete 'The Sole Motive of Man's Existence',[4] and forty-nine, when he authored *A Preface on National Education*.[5] Without exception, all remain relevant to the twenty-first-century Indian. Besides this, the volume contains his views on other issues—language, for instance. 'Sanskrit ought still to have a future as a language of the learned and it will not be a good day for India when the ancient tongue ceases entirely to be written or spoken,' he wrote in a March 1916 critique in *Arya*, the monthly periodical brought out by Sri Aurobindo between 1914 and 1921 from Pondicherry, in which many of his major works were first published.[6] 'But if it is to survive,' he continued, 'it must get rid of the curse of the heavy pedantic style contracted by it in its decline with the lumbering impossible compounds and the overweight of hair-splitting erudition.'

More than a century after Sri Aurobindo articulated them, his ideas on education have withstood the test of time as far as citizens are concerned, but have failed the exam of India's education policy. For instance, his perception of education being one where the individual's central objective would be the development of their deepest faculties, the nation's purpose would be the preservation and enrichment of its own dharma, and where both individual and nation will come together and become part of the ascending life and mind of humanity as a whole, is an intellectual vacuum in India's education system. To the philosopher, education was an individual enterprise. The educationist, he wrote, has to work in the 'elusive substance of mind and respect the limits imposed by the fragile human body',[7] not shape a masterpiece of academic excellence out of wood or stone.

In the essay 'The Human Mind',[8] Sri Aurobindo established three principles that form the core of his ideas on education. All three are steeped in an atmosphere of freedom, absolute consent and a gradualism from the tangible to the abstract. First, nothing can be taught—the teacher is not an instructor but a helper, a guide rather than a taskmaster; his job is to enable the student to acquire knowledge.[9] Second, education has to be in tune with the student's *swabhava*, the student's own nature and temperament. 'Every man has in him something divine, something his own, a chance of strength and perfection,' he wrote.[10] 'The task is to find it, develop it, use it.' And third, education must begin from the near to the far. That is, the education must start from heredity, the land and its people, culture and 'his soul's past'.[11] If it's done otherwise, imported from outside, for instance, the student's learning would become empty and artificial as it would be disconnected from his lived experience. 'The past is our foundation, the present our material, the future our aim and summit. Each must have its due and natural place in a national system of education.'[12]

His writings on education were political as well. In 'A Preface on National Education', published in the last two issues of *Arya* in 1920 and 1921, he wrote that education must be in tune with the *swabhava* and the *swadharma* (true way of being) of India. It must record and strengthen 'in man the individual a soul, a portion of the Divinity enwrapped in mind and body, a conscious manifestation in Nature of the universal self and spirit.'[13] Spiritual seeking must underline the quest for knowledge, and knowledge in turn must power the seeker's path:[14]

> It must be an education that for the individual will make its one central object the growth of the soul and its powers and possibilities, for the nation will keep first in view the preservation, strengthening and enrichment of the nation-soul and its dharma and raise both into powers of the life and ascending mind and soul of humanity. And at no time will it lose sight of man's highest object, the awakening and development of his spiritual being.

An emphasis on original thinking naturally followed from Sri Aurobindo's ideas on education. In 'Originality in National Literatures',[15] a short chapter he wrote between 1906 and 1908, he examined this idea across geographies and timelines. He believed that because the science of spirituality originated and was nurtured on Indian soil, the resultant thought-streams too were influenced by and carted on it. Few cultures, nations and civilizations have been able to develop a consistently original and self-revealing literature. The literatures of a few nations have been able to express original thought for short periods. These include the works of the Italians (Petrarch, Machiavelli, Cellini, and Castiglione), the Spaniards (Calderon and Cervantes), the sagas of the Scandinavian people, Germany's Nibelungenlied, and 'the extraordinary picture of Mahomedan civilisation of which the Thousand and One Nights are the setting'.[16] In these, he said, 'We have the picture of an age, not the spiritual and mental history of a nation.' The literature of only five nations—the ancient Greeks, the modern English and French, the Chinese and the Indians—he believed, would survive 'immortally before the eyes of posterity'.[17]

> Of all these the Hindus have revealed themselves the most perfectly, continuously and on the most colossal scale, precisely because they have been the most indomitably original in the form & matter of their literature. The Vedas, Upanishads & Puranas are unique in their kind; the great Epics in their form and type of art stand apart in the epic literature of the world, the old Sanscrit drama has its affinities with a dramatic species which developed itself in Europe more than a thousand years later, and the literary epic follows laws of form and canons of art which are purely indigenous.

Of all the original Indian literature that Sri Aurobindo explored, I find the Mahabharata to be the most fascinating. If there is any rebel text, it is the Mahabharata, which uses the form of storytelling to offer every listener-reader insight into the most profound knowledge systems of India. The Bhagavad Gita, for instance, conveys the essence of Indian spirituality through this unassuming format. Within the context of a story, this great text explores everything, from geography and statecraft to psychology and philosophy, all underlined by dharma. Approaching this text from a hermeneutics of respect rather than suspicion opens up every philosophical aspect of India.

Sri Aurobindo critiqued and translated parts of the epic in two pieces he wrote in 1902, 'Notes on the Mahabharata'[18] and 'Notes on the Mahabharata [Detailed]'.[19] The critique was in response to an article published in *The Indian Review of Madras* by Velandai Gopala Aiyer, where the author put forth the view that the Mahabharata comprised 8,000 verses. Spanning the limitations of Western literary methods, Sri Aurobindo offered in these essays the hypothesis that 'the original epic was something over 24,000 and under 26,400 slokas'. He gave insights into the story and the time period. He propounded that India was driven by two political forces—the centripetal force of the Kuru empire that attempted to bring scattered kingdoms under a singular emperorship and a centrifugal force that drove the smaller kingdoms into independent sovereigns.[20] Even within the story, his analysis of the underlying politics is unique:[21]

> But Bhishma & Drona must have perceived that behind the Pandavas were the Panchalas & Matsyas. They must have suspected that these nations were supporting Yudhisthere not out of purely disinterested motives but with certain definite political objects. Neither Drupada nor Virata would have been accepted by India as emperors in their own right, any more than say Sindhia or Holkar would have been in the last century... It can hardly be supposed that Bhishma and the Kuru statesmen of his party were autonomists; they must have been as eager for a Kuru empire as Duryodhana himself.

Accompanying these political hypotheses, is an exploration of the poetic style of its author: 'Vyasa is the most masculine of writers.'[22] He acknowledged the intrusion of Valmiki's style, but noted that it 'belongs to a less powerful intellect, duller poetical insight and coarser taste, which has yet caught something of the surge and cry of Valmekie's Oceanic poetry'.[23] The two poets, Vyasa and Valmiki, he wrote, stood on two opposite ends. The latter embraced the universal genius, the former enjoyed his own 'heaven of golden clearness'.[24] Valmiki dealt with drama and ornate speeches, Vyasa with silences; Valmiki was a painter, Vyasa a sculptor; Valmiki captured the waves of the oceans,

Vyasa chiselled on mountains; Valmiki was flamboyant, Vyasa was restrained; the long speeches of Valmiki flowed from the heart, Vyasa's flowed from an austere mind with the force of intellectuality:[25]

> The style of this powerful writer is perhaps the one example in literature of strength in its purity; a strength undefaced by violence & excess yet not weakened by flagging and negligence… Vyasa takes little trouble with similes, metaphors, rhetorical turns, the usual paraphernalia of poetry; nor when he uses them, is he at pains to select such as shall be new & curiously beautiful; they are there to define more clearly what he has in mind, and he makes just enough of them for that purpose, never striving to convert them into a separate grace or a decorative element.

The genius of the young Sri Aurobindo flowed from the ancient to the modern, from literature to economic policy, with effortless ease. For policymakers, Sri Aurobindo left a message in 'The Revival of Industry in India', a speech he wrote for the Maharaja of Baroda at the opening of the Industrial Exhibition held in Ahmedabad on 15 December 1902, in conjunction with the 1902 session of the Indian National Congress.[26] Sri Aurobindo was thirty then. The speech addressed all the issues—manufacturing, agriculture, trade, wealth, knowledge, technology, protectionism—that the world, from the US to China to India, can be seen grappling with today. Sri Aurobindo pointed out that there was no shortage of capital in the country (this is applicable to India today too), but there was a dearth of risk-taking and lack of self-confidence. 'Without self-confidence you can never do anything; you will never found an industry or build up a trade, for you have nothing to carry you through the first anxious years when the only dividend is hope, and the best assets are unfaltering courage and faith in oneself. And without confidence in one another you will never have a credit system, and without a credit system no modern commerce can exist.'[27] These insights should be a part of every textbook on the economic history of India, and the paragraph below should be the defining thought for economic administrators and all those who swear by the public sector:[28]

> My experience teaches me that it is very difficult for Government to provide industries for its people in the absence of a real business spirit amongst the people themselves. It is very difficult for so impersonal an entity as Government to get capable managers or to supervise its enterprises properly… A State fund for the advance of capital and other assistance to manufacturers also failed. I found that the managers were not sufficiently interested in the scheme and not impartial in the working of it. I am convinced, however, that the fault lay not with the industries themselves but in the fact that they were State enterprises.

As Sri Aurobindo's mind expanded, a courageous intellectual honesty underlined his approach to ideas and writings. 'I have not intended to republish these articles as they were written when I had just recently come from England,' he said in 1950, regarding his remarks in an 1894 essay on Bankim Chandra Chatterji.[29] 'They contain some very raw matter such as the remarks about Indian art which I no longer hold.' Anyone making such a confession today would be publicly discredited. The pressure to deliver absolute and consistent truths from the first piece of writing to the last is a huge weight on the writers who embark on exploring the world through words today. Reading Sri Aurobindo's writing gives us the strength to write our truths with confidence, have the intellectual humility to be proven wrong and the courage to change our mind. In the six-decade-long literary output of Sri Aurobindo, the essays mentioned in this book were the green shoots that grew into the trees of nationalism, philosophy and spirituality.

* * *

2

Collected Poems

Reading by Matriprasad

Sri Aurobindo was a born poet. Turning to poetry at a very young age, he did not cease to write until his passing away in 1950. From his response to a query by one of his disciples, we gather that one of his poems was published in a local magazine even before he had turned twelve. Relying on this circumstantial evidence, researchers first believed that they had unearthed his earliest published poem. Subsequently, however, a chance discovery of an earlier publication of the same piece and some further investigation into the matter made them conclude that the poem was written by Sri Aurobindo when he was only a small boy; and the poem published in the magazine referred to by him, must have surely been another one, which remains untraced. Much of the juvenilia has not survived and we may perhaps never be able to lay our hands on the early creations of this prolific poet, but it is inconceivable that there would not have existed a much larger body of work in English, as also in the classical tongues, from his younger days.

The philosopher's father had desired that his sons should have a proper British education. In the year 1879, at the age of seven, Sri Aurobindo, along with his two elder brothers, was transported to an alien land so that he may pursue his studies there. He spent his childhood in Manchester, later studied at St Paul's in London, and finally went to Cambridge in 1890.

As a result, apart from his command over the English language, Sri Aurobindo gained mastery over the European classical tongues, namely Greek and Latin. A small fragment of one of his early creations in Greek, in the form of an epigram, survives.

Sri Aurobindo also had a good command over French and two small pieces of prose-poems in the language were discovered in his manuscripts. Moreover, in later years, after his return to India, he mastered Sanskrit and Bengali. Although there exists a small body of his poetic works in these two languages, those pieces have been published in a separate volume (See Chapter 4),[1] just as his translations into verse from Sanskrit and Bengali and other languages have been compiled in yet other volumes of his Complete Works[2] (See Chapter 7). Similarly, his magnum opus, the epic *Savitri*[3] (See Chapter 29), also forms a part of another volume and has not been included in *Collected Poems*.

For Sri Aurobindo, the calling of a poet was a serious pursuit. In the present age, where there is a general tendency to give primacy to the mastery of sciences, the study and the cultivation of poetic art and sensitivity is relegated to a rather subsidiary role. The pursuit of poetry is considered to be a frivolous enjoyment, an unnecessary element for an individual's development. At best, giving oneself to poetic pursuits is looked upon to be an ostentatious ornament in an educated and cultured person. An indulgence in the realm of imagination and make-believe, poetry is a condonable pastime as long it does not interfere in the more serious pursuits. In Sri Aurobindo's words, 'To us poetry is a revel of the intellect and fancy, imagination a plaything and caterer for our amusement, our entertainer, the nautch-girl of the mind.'[4]

One of the most influential thinkers of the twentieth century, Sri Aurobindo's prolific contributions encompass such varied themes as philosophy, literary criticism, Vedic and philological studies, Indology, Yogic traditions, study of the evolution of human society with an attempt to forecast its possible future developments, critiques of contemporary political events and their evaluation from a historical perspective and translations from great literary works of the past. His voluminous correspondence cover topics of every hue, from the most sublime and intellectually challenging to the ticklishly humorous and the mundane. Given his extraordinarily eclectic personality, it is only natural that his poetical creations are also extremely varied with regards to their themes, forms and styles. He had that remarkable capacity to convert every personal experience, idea and incident in his life into material for poetic creation.

Take, for instance, the sonnet entitled 'The Godhead'. It was occasioned by a real-life experience that Sri Aurobindo had gone through: once, during a carriage ride, the horse had panicked. Under usual circumstances, this incident could have led to a fatal tragedy but, as it happens for a person whose life was touched by miracles, the situation was brought under instant control. Sri Aurobindo believed that a greater divine power, with the capacity to move and alter the destinies of men, intervened in that moment. He captured this incident in a sonnet that ends with magical lines, overwhelming in their unadorned simplicity and directness:[5]

> The moment passed and all was as before;
> Only that deathless memory I bore.

Similarly, in the sonnet entitled 'Adwaita', Sri Aurobindo refers to a spiritual experience that engulfed him during his trip to

Kashmir, after he had climbed a hill in the vicinity of Srinagar, popularly known as Takht-i-Sulaiman or Shankaracharya's Hill:[6]

> A lonely Calm and void unchanging Peace
> On the dumb crest of Nature's mysteries.

Although it is understandable that many of his spiritual experiences are captured in his poems, what takes one by surprise is the fact that even in the midst of dangerous crises and in times of imminent peril, poetic expression came so easily and naturally to him. During the almost year-long spell when he was incarcerated on charges of sedition and the Alipore Bomb Trial was in progress, a young co-accused, hoping to get Sri Aurobindo to recall for him some passages from celebrated English poets, had bemoaned the fact that life in prison had deprived him of the pleasures of English poetry. The next day, Sri Aurobindo presented him with a poem, composed by him, even though he was awaiting the outcome of a trial where a conviction would have resulted in capital punishment. The awareness of the background enhances our appreciation of lines such as these in the poem titled 'Invitation':[7]

> Not in the petty circle of cities
> Cramped by your doors and your walls I dwell;

The poem culminates in an ecstatic and triumphant cry:[8]

> I am the lord of tempest and mountain
> I am the Spirit of freedom and pride.

On his return to India, Sri Aurobindo plunged himself into the nationalist movement. At a period in history when the banners of imperial armies fluttered all over the globe and held in thrall the native populations everywhere, when the world was gobbled up by empires that ruled it from the distant capitals of just a few nations, Sri Aurobindo believed that the Age of Imperialism was moving towards its demise. Hence, some of his early poems celebrated the resistance that a nation like Ireland offered to the overbearing British rule. Later, after his return to India, in narrative poems like 'Baji Prabhou',[9] he evoked the same spirit of defiance to foreign rule by extolling the intrepid virtues of those who fought to preserve their independent vitality and distinct identity rather than consent to be absorbed into larger imperial aggregates:[10]

> One look he cast upon the fallen men
> Discernible by their attire, and saw
> His ranks not greatly thinned, one look below
> Upon the hundreds strewing thick the gorge,
> And grimly smiled; then where the sun in fire
> Descending stooped, towards the vesper verge
> He gazed and cried: 'Make iron of your souls.

His poems advocated that imperialism was fast becoming an anachronism, and he wrote satirical verse about those who were willing to be the servitors of the Raj in India.

As regards the form of poetry, Sri Aurobindo's poetic works include lyrics and narratives of several kinds. He even indulged himself in amusingly nonsensical verses, imitating in a mocking way the surrealist movement in fashion at the time. Sri Aurobindo believed that although there is a genuine level of dream-consciousness that seeks to express itself through the poetic form, mere lack of cohesion and cultivation of deliberate absurdity and incomprehensibleness did not necessarily touch upon that level of consciousness. A poem does not necessarily become inspired or profound simply by virtue of it being meaningless. A section of this volume—'Nonsense and "Surrealist" Verse'—puts together such poetry.[11]

The poet seemed to have a strong proclivity for the sonnet as a structure. His poetic output is replete with sonnets and he freely used both the Petrarchan and the Shakespearean formats. The iambic foot, one of the most widely used in English, seems to be the natural movement for the English language, and was used extensively by both these poets as well. Most of Sri Aurobindo's poems also use the iambic foot as the basic building material. But, given the fact that he had a strong grounding in Greek, he often experimented with exotic feet and meters borrowed from the classical tongues.

One of the classical meters for which he had great admiration was the hexameter. But he faced the usual difficulty which one encounters in trying to replicate the rounded sonority and the grandiose resonance of the hexameters of the classical tongues within the structure of English. This is even more so if one remains anchored to the iambic foot. For in English prosody, feet are based upon the interplay of stressed and unstressed syllables while in classical languages the length of the vowels and the weight of the voice in uttering the syllables forms the basis of the meter. After extensive research into this hitherto perceived incompatibility, Sri Aurobindo developed his own theory of quantitative hexameters in which he proposed to use the dactylic movement as the fundamental building block of the hexameter integrating into it the play of quantity while not discounting stress as the determining characteristic of English prosody. To demonstrate the validity of his theory, he wrote a long poem, 'Illion', where he recreated in English the Homeric vibrations of austerity with such resonant lines as:[12]

> Eviller fate there is none than life too long among mortals.
> I have conversed with the great who have gone, I have fought in their war-cars;
> Tros I have seen, Laomedon's hand has dwelt on my temples.

And:[13]

> Dream, when Virtue departs, that Wisdom will linger, her sister!
> Wisdom has turned from your hearts; shall Fortune dwell with
> the foolish?

Although a heroic theme forms the usual context to employ the classical hexameter, what is remarkable is that Sri Aurobindo could also mould this hexameter into a delicate lyrical sweetness, such as in 'Ahana':[14]

> Sun-drops flake from thy eyes and the heart's caverns packed
> are with pleasure
> Strange like a song without words or the dance of a
> measureless measure.

While Sri Aurobindo the poet was very much a representative of the present age, he was also a votary of an ancient wisdom that assigned a sublime function to poetry, '...to men of old, the poet was a seer, a revealer of hidden truths, imagination no dancing courtesan but a priestess in God's house, commissioned not to spin fictions but to image difficult and hidden truths...' Since such was the role and function that he assigned to poetry, it should come as no surprise to us that even as a very young man who had not yet returned to the land of his birth, he would pen such lines as:[15]

> When earth is full of whispers, when
> No daily voice is heard of men,
> But higher audience brings
> The footsteps of invisible things,
> When o'er the glimmering tree-tops bowed

The night is leaning on a luminous cloud,
And always a melodious breeze
Sings secret in the weird and charmed trees,
Pleasant 'tis then heart-overawed to lie
Alone with that clear moonlight and that listening sky.

Shakespeare once wrote:[16]

And as imagination bodies forth
The forms of things unknown, the poet's pen
Turns them to shapes and gives to airy nothing
A local habitation and a name.

Sri Aurobindo may not have quite agreed with this. The 'unknown' is not necessarily the 'unknowable'—what remains invisible to our so-called normal consciousness may yet reveal itself if we open our doors to a heightened and greater perception. And consequently, the poet gives shape not to an 'airy nothing' but rather, he seeks to manifest a body of Truth that lies beyond the truth. It was in this sense that Sri Aurobindo resurrected in modern times the Vedic notion of *kavi* (poet) as one who sees and hears the Truth that lay beyond our ordinary perceptions. The poet's mission is to make visible the invisible worlds, and in *Collected Poems*, Sri Aurobindo fulfilled this deeper purpose.

* * *

3

Collected Plays and Stories I and II

Reading by Thirthankar Chakraborty

The two volumes, *Collected Plays and Stories I and II*,[1] comprise Sri Aurobindo's five complete and seven incomplete plays, and one complete and five incomplete stories. These were mainly written before 1915, initially in Baroda and then in Pondicherry, when Sri Aurobindo was between twenty and forty-three years of age. They reveal not only his vast reading of prominent pieces of world literature, from *The Arabian Nights* and the *Kathasaritsagara* to the works of Frenchman Pierre Corneille, but also his knowledge and insight into world languages and cultures, from the Greek myths to the histories and legends of Norway and India. Out of these, he wove together tragedies, romances and short fiction that reflected intense human emotions—love, pleasure, jealousy, anger and the thirst for power.

If we regard Sri Aurobindo's oeuvre as a temple that guides us from the periphery to the innermost reaches of our soul, his theatrical works can be seen as the intricate and sensuous sculptures that make up the carvings around the outer precincts. They represent an unabashed depiction of life, teeming with thoughts, emotions, instincts and habits that constitute the human being. This chapter explores some of the predominant themes of the plays and stories put together in these two volumes, while presenting a broad overview of his literary accomplishments.

Sri Aurobindo's five complete plays in the collection are *The Viziers of Bassora*,[2] *Rodogune*,[3] *Perseus the Deliverer*,[4] *Eric*,[5] and *Vasavadutta*.[6] Amongst these, the first two were published over fifty years after their writing, as their manuscripts were seized by the police when Sri Aurobindo was arrested in connection with the Alipore Bomb Case in 1908. *Perseus the Deliverer* was the only play published in Sri Aurobindo's lifetime. It was brought out serially in *Bande Mataram*[7] (See Chapter 5), the weekly newspaper edited by Sri Aurobindo during his revolutionary period, in 1907.

The plays reveal Sri Aurobindo's keen insight into human emotions. Amongst these, love is the most prevalent, from Nureddene's love for Anice-Aljalice in *The Viziers of Bassora*, to the love shared between Rodogune and Antiochus in *Rodogune*, Perseus and Andromeda in *Perseus the Deliverer*, Eric and Aslaug in *Eric*, Vasavadutta and Vuthsa in *Vasavadutta*, Melander and Alaciel in *The Witch of Ilni*,[8] Ismenia and Antonio in *The Maid in the Mill or Love Shuffles the Cards*,[9] and Bappa and Comol Cumary in *The Prince of Edur*.[10] Through each of these pairs, Sri Aurobindo explores different forms of love that reveal the unique attributes of the characters—like gallantry, entitlement, romanticization and selfless love. The earliest of Sri Aurobindo's incomplete plays, *The Witch of Ilni*, written as an undergraduate at the University of Cambridge in 1891, describes the sensuous relationship between Melander, a sylvan poet, and Alaciel, the witch of Ilni. With echoes of the love shared between the four lovers in Shakespeare's *A Midsummer Night's Dream*, the romance between these two is garbed in their verbal exchanges. When contrasted with the cynical attitude of other characters, these lines reveal an evident romanticization that could either end in heartbreak, or as a dream with a touch of magic, as the play's subtitle suggests. Other expressions of love in Sri Aurobindo's plays bear a clear resemblance to the figures of speech used by the Romantic poets. For instance, when describing Vasavadatta's love for Vuthsa, Munjoolica, a captive princess serving Vasavadutta, herself the daughter of the King of Avunthy, says: 'Vustha, she loves thee as the half-closed bud / Thrills to the advent of a wonderful dawn,'[11] drawing on nature to portray the intensity of emotion.

Love in Sri Aurobindo's plays also lead to conflict and power struggles. In *Viziers of Bassora*, after purchasing Anice-Aljalice, a Persian slave-girl for his king, Chief Vizier Ibn Sawy finds his son Nureddene deeply in love with her. Although he is severe and chastises his son, familial love and his partiality towards Nureddene leads to a rivalry between him and Almuene Bin Khakan, second vizier to the king of Bassora, whose son was also in love with the Persian slave. The play reaches its climax when the falsely accused Nureddene is about to be killed, and the caliph Haroun Alrasheed's army comes to intercept the execution with a message to crown the condemned prisoner as the king. Love changes the course of politics in *Eric* and *Vasavadutta* as well. Instead of slaying the usurper Eric, who was crowned as the King of Norway, Aslaug, the sister of Swegn Olafson, who she believes is the rightful heir to the throne, falls in love with Eric, which leads to her captivity along with her friend Hertha. As a result, her brother Swegn Olafson is forced to bend his knee and agree to the conditions that Eric sets out for him, which he does with grace. Likewise, Vasavadutta's love for Vuthsa, the king of Cowsamby, foils the initial plan of her father, King Mahasegn of Avunthy, and his son Gopalaca to force Vuthsa into allegiance. Instead, it is the mutual love shared between the two that promises to bring together the kingdoms of Cowsamby and Avunthy in peaceful unison.

The struggle between love and power is also a central theme in *The Prince of Edur,*[12] where Rana Curran, the prince of the Rathore clan, plots to marry his daughter off to Toraman, the prince of Cashmere. His wife Ménadevi's plans, however, override the prince's intentions, since she hopes that Pratap, Rao of Ichalgur, a Chouhan noble, will marry her daughter instead. This politicizing of the family dynamics finally ends when the daughter, Comol Cumary, is captured by Bappa, the ruler of the Bheels. The plot twists when Comol falls in love with Bappa, who defeats Pratap and keeps her as his captive, free to roam around the boundless forests. *Rodogune*, a tragedy in five acts, sees Timocles' unlawful ascension to the throne, despite being the younger of the two sons of Cleopatra. As the title suggested, however, it is Rodogune who is the central character in this play with her selfless love for Antiochus, the older son of Cleopatra, which ultimately results in their calamitous deaths.

When considering his later works, one could surmise that Sri Aurobindo kept returning to the theme of love because love conquered not just evil, but made human beings exceed themselves. Hence, in *Perseus the Deliverer*, love is portrayed as being more powerful than the gods. When Perseus the Greek demi-god and Andromeda the daughter of the king of Syria finally meet with their common purpose, not even Polydaon, the priest inspired by the god Poseidon, can stop the two from saving the sacrificial victims who crossed the sea and transgressed into foreign territory. As if in response to Andromeda's verdict against heartless men with cruel gods, Perseus concludes the play with a powerful message:[13]

> [...] the blind nether forces still have power
> And the ascent is slow and long is Time.
> Yet shall Truth grow and harmony increase:
> The day shall come when men feel close and one.
> Meanwhile one forward step is something gained,

Since little by little earth must open to heaven
Till her dim soul awakes into the Light.

As a matter of fact, even in his earliest plays, Sri Aurobindo represented this yearning within human beings to exceed their mortal limitations in order to evolve. For instance, when Nureddene meets Ajebe, who was forced into following his uncle Almuene Bin Khakan's orders, he speaks without anger, 'Man / Is not ignoble, but has angel soarings, / Howe'er the nether devil plucks him down.'[14]

Sri Aurobindo's sense of humour speaks through several of his plays. The interaction between Basil, the nephew of King Philip of Spain, and Brigida, a noblewoman, in *The Maid in the Mill or Love Shuffles the Cards*, like the comic parley between Benedict and Beatrice in Shakespeare's *Much Ado About Nothing*, shows the quick wit of Sri Aurobindo's characters. The duo's infatuation is masked behind words that flirtatiously criticize one another, with Brigida firmly in control of Basil's outpouring of self-love and masculinity. Moreover, influenced by ancient Greek and pre-Christian notions of anthropomorphic gods, some of Sri Aurobindo's comic characters are near blasphemous. On seeing Perseus in *Perseus the Deliverer*, for instance, Poseidon's servant, Cireas, says, 'I pray thee, my good bright darling Zeus, do not come in the way of my earnings. Do not be so cantankerously virtuous, do not be so damnably economical.'[15] When asked whether he fears Poseidon for his betrayal, he replies: 'Oh, the blue-haired old bogy there? I have lived eighteen years in this temple and seen nothing of him but ivory and sapphires. I begin to think he cannot breathe out of water; no doubt, he is some kind of fish and walks on the point of his tail.'[16]

Fine instances of wordplay that lighten the intensity of the drama pepper Sri Aurobindo's works. For instance, again in *Perseus the Deliverer,* when Praxilla, head of the palace household, playfully takes the words of Andromeda's servant and playmate Diomedes literally when she brings news about Perseus at the start of the play, Diomedes retorts, 'A plague! can you not appreciate a fine metaphor when you hear it? I never saw so prosaic a mortal. The soul in you was born of a marriage between a saucepan and a broomstick.'[17] This self-reflexive mix of metaphysical and materialistic words playing with the dramatic conceit of the scene draws the sort of laughter that only a master in his craft can successfully effectuate without losing focus on the plot.

Besides humour, the plays also have moments of seriousness. Sri Aurobindo mastered the art of retelling historical events from an imaginary perspective, as we find in the incomplete story of *The Devil's Mastiff*,[18] where political upheavals from the times of Cromwell and Charles Stuart play a central role. *The House of Brut*,[19] another example, begins with a boisterous scene where Humber, the king of Norway, boasts of his victories and plans to rename all his conquered territory as Humberland. The astute character study, much like Robert Browning's dramatic monologues, reveals Sri Aurobindo's insight into the power-hungry mindset of a ruler and politician. At the same time, some of Sri Aurobindo's aristocratic characters also reveal a longing for the common life that those in power might never experience. In *The Maid in the Mill*,[20] for instance, King Philip of Spain says ruefully:[21]

> Is not a peasant happier than a king?
> For he has useful physical toil and sleep
> Unbroken as a child's. He is not hedged
> By swathing ceremony which forbids
> A king to feel himself a man.

With power comes responsibility, which can only be assumed by eminent rulers when their actions are in accordance with the will of the gods. King Cepheus in *Perseus the Deliverer* is acutely aware of this, when he utters words that echo Sri Aurobindo's own realization when fighting for the freedom of India:[22]

A nation's happiness was my only care:
I made the people's love my throne's sure base
And dreamed the way I chose true, great, divine.
But the heavenly gods have other thoughts than man's;
Their awful aims transcend our human sight.

While Cepheus' speech ends in despair, Sri Aurobindo's turn to yoga from an early career steeped in literature and politics was driven by an absolute faith in the divine will that would eventually fulfil India's destiny as an independent country.

If Sri Aurobindo's plays are more to do with emotions, his short story *The Phantom Hour,*[23] set in London, describes a surreal and fatalistic experience of one Sturge Maynard that drives him to kill Frenchwomen Renée Beauregard's lover and assassin. The second story, *The Door at Abelard,*[24] is a classic gothic tale depicting the fatalistic incidents that takes place in the ancestral house of Abelard where, each time a male heir is born, the mother and child die mysteriously. The story is largely narrated from the perspective of a Dr Armand Sieurcaye, husband to Aloÿse, who is the younger daughter of Stephen Abelard, last male heir to the house. Dr Armand Sieurcaye is witness to a gruesome murder where, possessed by the spirit of one Bertha Abelard, Richard Lancaster kills his own wife, the older daughter of Stephen Abelard and his son, before shooting himself through the heart. Like Edgar Allan Poe's tales of horror, the haunting of the Abelard house is not so much depicted through a devilish spirit manifesting itself, but through an unsaid narrative about the mysterious family madness, which is steeped in the very bricks of the ancestral mansion.

The variety of cultures and subjects that Sri Aurobindo wrote about in his plays and short stories reveals the wide-ranging appeal his works carry. Out of the handful of short stories that survive, mostly in fragments, it is easy to discern a talented writer of exceptional merits, especially when they are seen in combination with his poems and his magnum opus, *Savitri*[25] (See Chapter 29). From romance to tragedy, comedy, history, and gothic horror, the wide gamut of his writings are products of an imaginative genius. Had Sri Aurobindo not become a yogi, he may well have been remembered as a writer and a dramatist who explored universal themes and topics. These dramatic compositions bear a prescient vision of his future work, with evident traces of a self-conscious spirit capable of delving into a tumult of emotions while maintaining the calm and poise of an enlightened being.

* * *

4

Translations

Reading by Richard Hartz

Throughout his life, Sri Aurobindo took a keen interest in the art of translation. Multilingual as he was, he not only grappled with problems of translation from a theoretical point of view, but applied his theories to the rendering of works in several Indian and European languages, both ancient and modern. He placed a high value on literary translation as a means of bringing the people of the world together through mutual appreciation of the beauty and riches of each other's cultures. Moreover, in an age when people were 'turning away from the study of the great classical languages', he considered translation to be important for keeping alive 'the ennobling influences spiritual, romantic and imaginative' of older literatures.[1]

Translations, the fifth volume of Sri Aurobindo's complete works, contains English translations from five languages: Sanskrit, Bengali, Tamil, Greek and Latin. It does not include his translations from the Rig Veda[2] (See Chapters 11, 12 and 13) and Upanishads[3] (See Chapters 14 and 15), which can be found in the volumes dealing with those subjects. Also published elsewhere in *The Complete Works of Sri Aurobindo* are his translations from French into English of selected *Prayers and*

Meditations of the Mother[4] (See Chapter 28) and renderings of Sanskrit texts into Bengali[5] (See Chapter 7). Some of the translations in the volume under discussion here are in prose, but much of it illustrates Sri Aurobindo's approach to the problem of poetic translation, as it evolved from the 1890s to the 1940s. A poet himself, his translations often read like original poetry. This book is closely related, therefore, to his *Collected Poems*[6] (See Chapter 2) and *Collected Plays and Stories*[7] (See Chapter 3).

Having received most of his education in England, Sri Aurobindo grew up speaking English. Early in life, he learned French, Greek and Latin, as well as some Italian, German and Spanish. His interest in languages at this stage was mainly literary. His knowledge of Bengali and Sanskrit was acquired largely on his own, after his return to India at the age of twenty. The last language to receive his serious attention was Tamil, which he studied after moving to Pondicherry. Sri Aurobindo began translating Sanskrit literature soon after he came back to India in 1893. His last translations in the 1940s included some from Greek and Latin, which he had learned as a student in England. Thus, this volume represents his creative engagement with the art of translation over a period of more than fifty years.

Sanskrit was the language from which he translated most extensively. His translations from Sanskrit account for well over half of the present volume, as well as most of the translations that appeared in other volumes of *The Complete Works*. His early translations of several adhyayas, chapters, of the Sabha Parva of the Mahabharata use rhymed couplets, an experiment he never repeated. A few years later, he captured the style of the Sanskrit epic poetry more successfully in the blank verse renderings of passages from the Ramayana with which this volume begins. He also experimented with prose for translating the Mahabharata and the Ramayana. But the challenge that attracted him most persistently, in part because of its seeming intractability, was the translation of poetry into poetry. This problem has frequently been declared to be insoluble. But difficulties, as Sri Aurobindo remarked in an essay on translating Kalidasa, 'are after all given us in order that we may brace our sinews by surmounting them'.[8]

His major achievement in this respect is *Vikramorvasie or The Hero and the Nymph.*[9] In the original play by Kalidasa, prose dialogue—partly in Sanskrit, partly in Prakrit—alternates with Sanskrit verses in many different metres. Sri Aurobindo translated this inimitable form into blank verse for the most part. But he also made effective use of prose in speeches by some of the minor characters.

More typical of Kalidasa's style is the stream of imaginative language that flows from the lips of Pururavas, especially in the fourth act where the poetry reaches its height. Here, the king wanders in the forest, driven to the brink of madness by the disappearance of his beloved Urvasie. At one point, he accuses a cloud of carrying her off:[10]

> Halt, ruffian, halt! Thou in thy giant arms
> Bearest away my Urvasie! He has
> Soared up from a great crag into the sky
> And wars me, hurling downward bitter rain
> Of arrows. With this thunderbolt I smite thee.
> *He lifts up a clod and runs as to hurl it;*
> *then pauses and looks upwards.*
> (*pathetically*)
> Oh me, I am deceived! This was a cloud
> Equipped for rain, no proud and lustful fiend,
> The rainbow, not a weapon drawn to kill,
> Quick-driving showers are these, not sleety rain
> Of arrows; and that brilliant line like streak
> Of gold upon a touchstone, cloud-inarmed,
> I saw, was lightning, not my Urvasie.

The first five and a half lines of this speech are in prose in the original. The rest is the translation of a verse in the *harini* metre, consisting of four lines of seventeen syllables each with a complex pattern of long and short syllables. It is impossible to imitate such a form in English. But even if it could be done, duplicating Kalidasa's alternation of prose and poetry in English would, as Sri Aurobindo pointed out, 'result in opera rather than in drama'. For this reason, he 'thought it best, taking into consideration the poetical feeling and harmonious flow of Kalidasa's prose, to use blank verse throughout varying its pitch according as the original form is metrical or prose and the emotion or imagery more or less exalted'.[11]

While Sri Aurobindo brought his gifts for epic and dramatic poetry to translating Sanskrit literature, when it comes to his translations from Bengali, what strikes one most is his mastery of the lyrical style. A notable contribution is the manner in which he made the beauty of Vaishnava bhakti poetry accessible to the reader of English. This included the poetry of Vidyapati (c. 1352–1448). The poet Vidyapati lived in what is now Bihar and wrote in a form of Maithili closely related to the Bengali of his time, but had a broad influence on the early development of the literatures of eastern India. Sri Aurobindo read Vidyapati's *Padavali* in the 1890s in the context of the Bengali tradition and translated selections from it into exquisite English verse. Here Radha speaks of falling hopelessly in love with Krishna; in the last couplet, the poet consoles her:[12]

I know not what this lovely thief
Did to me in that moment brief.
Surely such craft none yet possessed!
He robbed my heart out of its nest
Only with seeing, and gone is he
Taking my poor heart far from me.

And ah! his eyes did then express
Such tenderness, such tenderness,
The more I labour to forget
My very soul remembers it.
Mourn not, sweet girl, for thy heart's sake;
Who took thy heart, thyself at last shall take.

More modern Bengali poetry and prose also received Sri Aurobindo's attention. The most important work of modern literature he translated was the famous novel by Bankim Chandra Chatterji, *Anandamath*.[13] Sri Aurobindo regarded Bankim as 'a seer and nation-builder', the rishi 'who gave us the reviving mantra which is creating a new India, the mantra *Bande Mataram*'.[14] His translation of *Anandamath* was left unfinished, as he was in the midst of serialising it in weekly instalments in *Karmayogin*, the journal edited by Sri Aurobindo (See Chapter 6), when he abruptly left Calcutta in February 1910, never to return. Fortunately, the chapters he completed include the one containing the words to 'Bande Mataram', the song that played such a conspicuous role in the Indian freedom struggle. Sri Aurobindo's poetic rendering of this song is undoubtedly his most widely read translation. Besides its occurrence in the narrative setting of the tenth chapter of the novel,[15] it is also reproduced separately along with a more literal prose version.[16]

Sri Aurobindo took advantage of moving to south India in 1910 to further enrich his linguistic versatility with a knowledge of Tamil. He could not continue his study long enough to achieve the same level of proficiency as in the other languages. But, in 1915, with help from his friend Subramania Bharati, the Tamil poet, he published translations of a few poems of Vaishnava saints of the eighth and ninth centuries in *Arya*. A little later, he rendered into English a chapter and a half of the classic text on ethics and morality, the *Kural,* written by the ancient poet and philosopher Tiruvalluvar. The flavour of these translations into poetic prose is illustrated in the following lines from the ancient Vaishnavite poet-saint Nammalwar's 'Hymn of the Golden Age':[17]

> 'Tis glory, glory, glory! For Life's hard curse has expired; swept out are Pain and Hell, and Death has nought to do here. Mark ye, the Iron Age shall end.... (1)
>
> We have seen, we have seen, we have seen—seen things full sweet for our eyes. Come, all ye lovers of God, let us shout and dance for joy with oft-made surrenderings.... (2)
>
> The Iron Age shall change. It shall fade, it shall pass away. The gods shall be in our midst. The mighty Golden Age shall hold the earth and the flood of the highest Bliss shall swell.... (3)

Sri Aurobindo's translations from Greek and Latin take up only a few pages at the end of this volume. But spanning half a century as they do, they show his growing mastery of these two languages, and include some remarkable examples of the art of poetic translation. For the opening passages of the Iliad and the Odyssey, he used Homer's own metre—the dactylic hexameter—whose successful handling had defied the efforts of a number of well-known English poets. His translation of the beginning of the Iliad, dating from around 1901, shows the possibilities of rendering Homer into English hexameters without entirely fulfilling them. But by the time he translated the opening of the Odyssey, around 1913, he was already working on *Ilion*, his original epic in the Homeric style and metre.[18] By then, he was on the way to perfecting his technique and capturing the surging rhythmic movement that has earned Homer a place among the world's supreme poets. Future translators of the blind bard might do well to find inspiration in lines such as these:[19]

> Sing to me, Muse, of the man many-counselled who far through the world's ways
> Wandering was tossed after Troya he sacked, the divine stronghold,
> Many cities of men he beheld, learned the minds of their dwellers,
> Many the woes in his soul he suffered driven on the waters,
> Fending from fate his life and the homeward course of his comrades.
> Them even so he saved not for all his desire and his striving;
> Who by their own infatuate madness piteously perished,
> Fools in their hearts! for they slew the herds the deity pastured,
> Helios high-climbing....

Translations is a volume which can easily be overlooked. Yet, Sri Aurobindo engaged with translations throughout his life on several levels, from the most technical to the most philosophical. 'Your life on this earth,' he wrote in an essay, 'is a divine poem that you are translating into earthly language.'[20] In this sense, his whole philosophy could be explained in terms of the translation of the divine into the human. More pragmatically, he recognized the growing importance of translation between languages at a time when humanity was being drawn together as never before. Unity among humans requires communication, but Sri Aurobindo regarded the preservation of diversity as equally essential. Translation mediates between these two needs, encouraging and enabling mutual appreciation of the great variety of ways in which cultures in the East and West, from ancient to modern times, have expressed our common humanity.

Much of Sri Aurobindo's specific contribution was to translate classical literature in India into English. If these literatures are to occupy the place they deserve in world literature, there must be translations that bring them to life for a global readership.

Recognizing their importance, Sri Aurobindo applied all his skill to producing translations that can be enjoyed in their own right, while giving an authentic taste of the distinctive qualities of the original works. Collected in a single volume, they represent a significant part of his literary achievement, reveal a deep understanding of the translator's craft, and form an appealing introduction to a broad sample of Indian and world literature.

* * *

5

Bande Mataram: Political Writings and Speeches, 1890–1908

Reading by Anirban Ganguly

The two volumes under this heading include all of Sri Aurobindo's surviving political writings and speeches from the years before his arrest in May 1908. The bulk of these volumes comprises articles published in the newspaper *Bande Mataram*, the English language weekly newspaper published from Calcutta, from 1906 to 1908. The volumes also include his speeches, unpublished writings and documents related to the nationalist movement of this period.

Sri Aurobindo's editorials and articles in *Bande Mataram*, which he wrote almost daily between 1907 and 1908, are a comprehensive indicator and schema of his early political activism, its trajectory and thinking. They provide the reader with an insight into the nationalist political discourse of the era, and also the evolution of the nationalist movement, especially of the early phase. Often referred to as the pre-Gandhian phase, this was a time of political developments that laid the foundations on which the nationalist movement would later be broadened.

Bande Mataram came into action at a time when the advanced group within the Congress, or the 'New Party' as Sri Aurobindo termed it, was struggling to gain political control and ascendancy against the party's old guards, known as the Moderates. As one of the principal leaders of the 'New Party', Sri Aurobindo felt the need for an English daily, through which the ideas and policies of the new nationalist group could be broadcast among the educated sections in Bengal and the rest of India.

George Curzon had partitioned Bengal in 1905. It was, as Sri Aurobindo told the British journalist and author Henry Nevinson, 'the greatest blessings that had ever happened to India', since 'no other measure could have stirred national feeling so deeply or roused it so suddenly from the lethargy of previous years'.[1] Sri Aurobindo saw *Bande Mataram* as a vehicle through which those feelings could be fomented and channelized across the country.

The early phase of the Indian freedom struggle had two distinct dimensions to it—one was public political action and the other was secret revolutionary activities aimed at violently overthrowing British rule. Sri Aurobindo saw the need for combining both these dimensions. In his short but intense period of political action, he succeeded, to a certain degree, in synergizing the two. *Bande Mataram* emerged as the ideational platform for articulating and spreading the political philosophy and policies of his 'New Party'. It soon acquired wide popularity. Read throughout India, it came to be identified with Sri Aurobindo's politics, and the politics of the Extremists:[2]

> *Bande Mataram* was almost unique in journalistic history in the influence it exercised in converting the mind of a people and preparing it for revolution.

Sri Aurobindo's editorials in *Bande Mataram*, articulating the policies and political stance of the new party, were both intense and well-argued; and were read and appreciated even by his political opponents and the British. The call for revolt in his columns was masterly couched in symbolism, the demand for non-cooperation astutely argued, making it difficult for the colonial censors to clamp down on the paper for sedition. *Bande Mataram*, as Sri Aurobindo observed, 'was never prosecuted for its editorial articles'.[3] In fact, there were complaints against its highly skilled messaging:[4]

> The editor of the Statesman complained that they were too diabolically clever, crammed full of sedition between the lines, but legally unattackable because of the skill of the language. The Government must have shared this view, for they never ventured to attack the paper for its editorial or other articles, whether Sri Aurobindo's or from the pen of his three editorial colleagues. There is also the fact that Sri Aurobindo never based his case for freedom on racial hatred or charges of tyranny or misgovernment, but always on the inalienable right of the nation to independence. His stand was that even good government could not take the place of national government,—independence.

S.K. Ratcliffe, a veteran British journalist with nationalist sympathies who had edited the *Statesman* for a while, described *Bande Mataram* in a letter to the *Manchester Guardian* in December 1950, decades after the paper had shut shop. He remembered how the daily had 'struck a ringing new note in Indian journalism'.[5] He gave a precise description of how *Bande Mataram* actually looked:[6]

> It had a full-size sheet, was clearly printed on green paper, and was full of leading and special articles written in English with brilliance and pungency not hitherto attained in the Indian

> press. It was the most effective voice of what we then called nationalist extremism.

The pages of *Bande Mataram* abounded with articles on 'Swaraj, Swadeshi, Boycott, National Education'—the four-fold programme on which the Extremist school based its politics. After much struggle behind the scenes, the Moderate leaders were obliged to incorporate these principles in the resolutions of the 1906 annual session of the Congress held in Kolkata.[7] This was the first major political victory of the new party within the Congress. In the following months, Sri Aurobindo's increasing involvement and gradual control of *Bande Mataram* would see the daily emerge as the mouthpiece of the new group.

Bipin Chandra Pal, one of the leading lights of the 'new school', had started *Bande Mataram* in 1906 with 'only 500 rupees in his pocket'.[8] Pal's invitation to Sri Aurobindo to join the venture in support, and to write a lead article every day for the daily, saw ready consent from the latter. He wrote, 'Sri Aurobindo saw his opportunity for starting the public propaganda necessary for his revolutionary purpose.'[9] The name chosen for the new daily signified both devotion to the motherland and defiance of the British authorities.

Though the daily was an immediate success, it soon ran into financial difficulties.[10] Over the next few months, Sri Aurobindo 'took up the joint editorship of the journal, edited the paper during Bipin Pal's absence and induced the Nationalist Party to take it up as their organ and finance it'.[11] Sri Aurobindo's proposal to set up *Bande Mataram* as a joint-stock company to ensure its financial viability saw the Kolkata-based industrialist with Swadeshi sympathies, Subodh Chandra Basu-Mullick, and his brother, Nirodh, support the venture. A close collaborator of Sri Aurobindo and an insider of the secret revolutionary network, Subodh not only financed the newspaper and provided for its office, but was also a benefactor of the national education movement. By late 1906, the circulation of *Bande Mataram* 'was ever on the increase and its popularity was the envy of the pro-colonial or Anglo-Indian press'.[12] Soon, Sri Aurobindo was practically in full control of the policy of the paper till his own arrest in the Alipore Bomb Case in 1908.[13]

The year 1907, when Sri Aurobindo churned out most of the pieces for the newspaper, was also the fiftieth anniversary year of the revolt of 1857—suggestive of the vortex and ferment of Indian politics of that time. His articles in *Bande Mataram* give an insight into the problems and the politics of the period.

Sri Aurobindo's range in *Bande Mataram* was phenomenal. He wrote on social and economic issues, education, self-help, self-reliance, agriculture, the need to return to the land, rural empowerment, village organizations, national education, communal issues, riots and resistance and the Swadeshi movement—educational and commercial. He was caustic of moderate politics, inveterately aggressive towards the British and their supporters in the Anglo-Indian press, discussed the need for broad-basing the movement and repeatedly wrote of freedom and complete freedom. It was in the columns of *Bande Mataram* that Sri Aurobindo articulated his famous demand for absolute independence:[14]

> The Congress has contented itself with demanding self-government as it exists in the Colonies. We of the new school would not pitch our ideal one inch lower than absolute Swaraj—self-government as it exists in the United Kingdom. We believe that no smaller ideal can inspire national revival or nerve the people of India for the fierce, stubborn and formidable struggle by which alone they can again become a nation.

'The Doctrine of Passive Resistance',[15] serialized in the pages of the newspaper between 11 and 23 April 1907, was the first public statement of an idea and method that would become the principal method of the national movement only after 1919, applied as 'satyagraha' by the Congress under Mahatma Gandhi.[16] No one before Sri Aurobindo, in the Indian political context, had examined the method of passive resistance and its applicability and suitability to the struggle for freedom as he did in these columns. Before him, none had enunciated in such bold and clear terms the objectives, the methods and limitations of passive resistance. Sri Aurobindo called for complete freedom:[17]

> But if the subject nation desires not a provincial existence and a maimed development but the full, vigorous and noble realization of its national existence, even a change in the system of government will not be enough; it must aim not only at a national Government responsible to the people but at a free national Government unhampered even in the least degree by foreign control.

He continued:[18]

> We desire industrial expansion, but Swadeshi without boycott... has no attractions for us, since we know that it can bring no safe and permanent national gain; that can only be secured by the industrial and fiscal independence of the Indian nation. Our immediate problem as a nation is not how to be intellectual and well-informed or how to be rich and industrious, but how to stave off imminent national death, how to put an end to the white peril, how to assert ourselves and live. It is for this reason that whatever minor differences there may be between different exponents of the new spirit, they are all agreed on the immediate necessity of an organized national resistance to the state of things which is crushing us out of existence as a nation and on the one goal of that resistance,—freedom.

Similarly, the article titled 'Shall India be Free' also forcefully advocated the need for complete independence:[19]

> Liberty is the first requisite for the sound health and vigorous life of a nation. A foreign domination is in itself an unnatural condition, and if permitted, must bring about other unhealthy and unnatural conditions in the subject people which will lead to fatal decay and disorganisation. Foreign rule cannot build up a nation—only the resistance to foreign rule can weld the discordant elements of a people into an indivisible unity.

Sri Aurobindo's vision of a new nationalism may be understood more deeply from an unpublished but seminal essay, 'The Bourgeois and the Samurai', written between 1906 and 1907 (whether intended to be published in *Bande Mataram* or not, we will never know). Here, Sri Aurobindo called for the democratisation of the nationalist movement, for making it inclusive. Sri Aurobindo wrote that this new nationalism's scope and ambit cleared every barrier:[20]

> The new overleaps every barrier; it calls to the clerk at his counter, the trader in his shop, the peasant at his plough; it summons the Brahmin from his temple and takes the hand [of] the Chandala in his degradation; it seeks out the student in his College, the schoolboy at his books, it touches the very child in its mother's arms & the secluded zenana has thrilled to its voice; its eye searches the jungle for the Santal and travels the hills for the wild tribes of the mountains. It cares nothing for age or sex or caste or wealth or education or respectability; it mocks at the talk of a stake in the country; it spurns aside the demand for a property qualification or a certificate of literacy. It speaks to the illiterate or the man in the street in such rude vigorous language as he best understands, to youth & the enthusiast in

> accents of poetry, in language of fire, to the thinker in the terms of philosophy and logic, to the Hindu it repeats the name of Kali, to the Mahomedan it spurs to action for the glory of Islam. It cries to all to come forth, to help in God's work & remake a nation, each with what his creed or his culture, his strength, his manhood or his genius can give to the new nationality.

The same fiery tone of Sri Aurobindo's writings in *Bande Mataram* extended into his speeches of that period. Among his better known speeches was the one he gave to the students of the Bengal National College in Calcutta on 23 August 1907. Learning that he was about to be arrested for sedition, and not wanting to embarrass the institution of which he was the principal, Sri Aurobindo resigned from his post. A few weeks later, he was invited for a photograph on the college premises and was requested to speak a few words to the assembled students. His words to the young students of the college ring with truth and power, and speak to us as vividly as they would have over a century ago:[21]

> When I come back I wish to see some of you becoming rich, rich not for yourselves but that you may enrich the Mother with your riches. I wish to see some of you becoming great, great not for your own sakes, not that you may satisfy your own vanity, but great for her, to make India great, to enable her to stand up with head erect among the nations of the earth, as she did in days of yore when the world looked up to her for light...There are times in a nation's history when Providence places before it one work, one aim, to which everything else, however high and noble in itself, has to be sacrificed. Such a time has now arrived for our motherland...If you will study, study for her sake; train yourselves body and mind and soul for her service. You will earn your living that you may live for her sake. You will go abroad

> to foreign lands that you may bring back knowledge with which you may do service to her. Work that she may prosper. Suffer that she may rejoice. All is contained in that one single advice.

In the winter of 1907–08, Sri Aurobindo undertook a trip to western India as a part of his political work. After attending the historic Surat session of the Indian National Congress (which led to the split of the Congress between the Moderates and the Extremists), Sri Aurobindo went to Baroda, and then, starting with a speech at the house of Bal Gangadhar Tilak in Pune, went on to give at least fourteen speeches in various towns of modern-day Maharashtra, including in Bombay (now Mumbai), Nasik, Amravati and Nagpur. The speeches dealt with the situation and experiences of the nationalists in Bengal and the programmes put forth by Sri Aurobindo to carry forward the movement.

It is evident from these speeches that Sri Aurobindo would have left an incredible mark wherever he spoke. His words are full of an intense and absolute devotion to the motherland. To read them is to understand and feel, at least to some extent, the passion that flowed in the veins of the revolutionaries of this period. Let us take, for example, this passage from a speech titled 'The Present Situation', delivered in Bombay on 19 January 1908, at a time when the British government was coming down heavily on the revolutionary movement in Bengal:[22]

> You call yourselves Nationalists. What is Nationalism? Nationalism is not a mere political programme; Nationalism is a religion that has come from God; Nationalism is a creed in which you shall have to live. Let no man dare to call himself a Nationalist if he does so merely with a sort of intellectual pride… You must remember that you are the instrument of God for the salvation of your own country. You must live as the instruments

> of God...By what strength are we in Bengal able to survive? Nationalism has not been crushed. Nationalism is not going to be crushed. Nationalism survives in the strength of God and it is not possible to crush it, whatever weapons are brought against it. Nationalism is immortal; Nationalism cannot die, because it is no human thing. It is God who is working in Bengal. God cannot be killed, God cannot be sent to jail.

Such is the inspiring and insightful material available in this volume, which is a record of the absolutely central role played by Sri Aurobindo in India's freedom struggle. The essence and spirit of Sri Aurobindo's early political thought and action, which permeates and radiates through the pages of *Bande Mataram*, essentially describe and shape a new nationalism, a nationalism that would drive India's quest for selfhood over the decades, long after Sri Aurobindo had physically withdrawn from the movement.

***

6

Karmayogin: Political Writings and Speeches, 1909–1910

Reading by Matriprasad

There comes a time when a person reaches a fork on the path of life; from that point onwards, their life moves on an identifiably divergent arc. Usually, the milestone indicating such a junction is important at a very personal level—an event that could be either deeply inspiring or disturbingly shattering. For Sri Aurobindo, one such determining occurrence was the period from May 1908 to May 1909.

By 1906–07, Sri Aurobindo was acknowledged as one of the most influential and outstanding leaders of the radical faction of the political movements of the time. He spoke, wrote and inspired large masses of people by expounding compellingly the creed of complete independence for India. Many of the ideas that are accepted as self-evident today were considered somewhat impractical in the early twentieth century. Colonialism was an established fact, and the contemplated emancipation of subject nations was considered to be the pipe dream of a few demented people. It was at this juncture that Sri Aurobindo advocated forcefully that for India, *swaraj* (complete freedom) was the only ideal worth pursuing and, further, that each nation had an inherent right to self-determination and to fashion its own destiny.

Naturally, the Raj chose to strike back. In May 1908, Sri Aurobindo was arrested and charged with sedition for daring to wage war against the King-Emperor. For about a year, he endured incarceration as an under-trial prisoner. The conditions of life in a colonial prison were starkly dehumanizing and often left prisoners scarred and broken at the psychological level. However, for Sri Aurobindo, the period triggered an ascent to a higher level of self-actualization.

The prison doors that fenced him off from the world, mysteriously or, rather, miraculously, opened his eyes to a higher level of freedom. While the world outside was full of anxiety and sensation with regards to the outcome of his trial, he himself was totally unconcerned about the flow of events in the courtroom, since he was having, by his own account, splendid spiritual experiences during those prison days. From then onwards, the idea of attaining political freedom for India, although always implicit in his vision, was supplemented by a broader outlook. Henceforth, he advocated that India's philosopher's stone would be the emergence of a spiritual consciousness in his countrymen, and that its touch would not only bring about the political freedom of the country but also elevate national life to a new level of self-fulfilment.

Consequently, after Sri Aurobindo was acquitted, he started two journals: *Karmayogin* (June 1909-February 1910) in English and *Dharma* (1909–1910) in Bengali (See Chapter 7). What did Sri Aurobindo seek to achieve by launching *Karmayogin*? He wanted to awaken his countrymen to the need for a greater ideal than mere political freedom:[1]

> The task we set before ourselves is not mechanical but moral and spiritual. We aim not at the alteration of a form of government

> but at the building of a nation. Of that task politics is a part, but only a part.

This volume takes up the articles published in *Karmayogin*. The choice of the title (meaning, divine worker) indicates the shift in emphasis, to the pursuit of a more conscious and explicit practice of attaining a greater spiritual ideal at a national level. The cover page of every issue of *Karmayogin* carried a picture of Shri Krishna as the charioteer of Arjuna, when the hero rode into battle. Below the picture would be a shloka from the Bhagavad Gita—Shri Krishna exhorting Arjuna to remain rooted in a spiritual state, calm and free from desires, and yet, while remaining thus, to plunge himself into the valiant and relentless action of the battle, offering everything, including his actions and the result of his actions, to the Divinity within himself.

It is also worth noting that at the bottom of the cover page, the journal proclaimed the contributors as 'Aurobindo Ghosh and others'. Although the journal did carry articles from others, a good portion of the material published therein was by Sri Aurobindo.

To emphasize the power and the necessity of the emergence of this greater idea, Sri Aurobindo turned to his own epiphany. The very first article in this volume is the text of a speech he gave at Uttarpara, a suburb of Calcutta (now Kolkata). The event took place just after his release, consequent to his acquittal, and it was, in fact, his first public appearance after his release from prison. It was also the first and the last event where Sri Aurobindo spoke in public about his own personal spiritual experiences. He recalled the circumstances of his arrest and the 'realization in jail, of God within us all, of the Lord within the nation'.[2] He recollected how the secret Divinity that inhabits the hearts of men had revealed itself to him and had assured him of the protection extended to him. He said, 'I knew I would come out. The year of detention was meant only for a year of seclusion and training.'[3]

He was invited to speak at Uttarpara by the Society for the Protection of Religion. Indeed, he declared the pursuit of such an aim to be the work ahead. But what was this religion to which Indians must dedicate themselves? He said, 'That which we call the Hindu religion is really the eternal religion, because it is the universal religion which embraces all others. If a religion is not universal, it cannot be eternal.'[4]

He did speak about nationalism, but there was a clear shift in emphasis henceforth: previously, he might have said that nationalism had to be pursued like a religion; now, it was the dedication of oneself to *Sanatana Dharma* (the universal religion) that itself constituted the only true nationalism, its very heart.[5]

> I say no longer that nationalism is a creed, a religion, a faith; I say that it is the Sanatana Dharma which for us is nationalism. This Hindu nation was born with the Sanatana Dharma, with it moves and with it grows. When the Sanatana Dharma declines, then the nation declines, and if the Sanatana Dharma were capable of perishing, with the Sanatana Dharma it would perish. The Sanatana Dharma, that is nationalism.

Later, he urged Indians not to abandon old programmes like Swadeshi and boycott:[6]

> The one message we can give to you, under such circumstances, is the message to hold firm. If you cannot progress see that you have not receded. Hold firm to the Swadeshi, hold firm to your refusal to the recognition of the Partition, hold firm to the national movement which is uplifting India.

But to these stirring words and emotions was now added a new catalyst, a kind of fervour that enlivens only those who perceive the working of a hidden hand behind the turn of events:[7]

> If we look higher, if we look to the deeper significance of this movement, remember that whenever a subject nation arises it is by the will of God. If only we are true and hold firm, everything in this God-given movement will help towards the goal. As favourable circumstances help us so also will unfavourable circumstances help us.

For too long, religion has, fairly or unfairly, been associated with a seclusion, if not a revulsion, from the flow and stress of external life, a withdrawal of interest from everything perceived to be outward and worldly. The Sanatana Dharma that was preached through the articles of *Karmayogin* was in sharp contrast to this attitude:[8]

> God does not want falterers and flinchers for his work, nor does he want unstable enthusiasts who cannot maintain the energy of their first movements.

In keeping with this spirit of resurgence of the totality of national life, *Karmayogin* covered a wide variety of topics such as philosophy, art, literature, current events and politics. It evaluated the special appeal that some paintings emerging from the Bengal School of Art evoked. It deeply appreciated the work of those artists who no longer copied the styles and techniques of the European masters that they had been taught to imitate in art schools established by the government, but who now ventured into new approaches and practises, seeking inspiration from various art forms in the indigenous traditions.

Sri Aurobindo, who had earlier mastered Sanskrit all by himself, was deeply influenced by great works in that classical tongue. *Karmayogin* also carried essays by him on the poems of Kalidasa, and his translations of the Upanishads, two of which, *Isha Upanishad* (See Chapter 14) and *Kena and Other Upanishads* (See Chapter 15), make up full-fledged volumes in his *Complete Works*.

As noted earlier, in this emerging vision of Sri Aurobindo, true spirituality implied that raising one's consciousness and being engrossed in elevated preoccupations did not imply a disregard and rejection of the more mundane issues that beset our daily lives. So, for example, apart from dealing with highly philosophical subjects in the magazine's pages, he also dealt with such worries as the ordeals of managing worldly matters.

In the 7 August 1909 edition of the magazine, Sri Aurobindo published an appeal by the promoters of the Swadeshi Steam Navigation Company. The British had a monopoly over the highly lucrative maritime trade in the Indian Ocean. V.O. Chidambaram Pillai, a pleader from Tuticorin who argued for self-reliance, had floated a joint-stock company to challenge this monopoly. The objective of the company was to run a ship between Tuticorin and Colombo, and train Asians in the art of navigation and shipbuilding. Pillai had formed this company not for profit but to forward the ideals of nationalism. Any Asian was permitted to subscribe to the shares of the company. For a time, the operations of the Swadeshi Steam Navigation Company had posed a real threat to the profits of the British interests controlling maritime trade—that is, until the British government misused the regulatory machinery under its command to bankrupt the company. It is when the company was in this dire strait and starved of resources that the Swadeshi Steam Navigation Company had appealed for funds.

The columns of *Karmayogin* not only published this appeal, but Sri Aurobindo himself commented upon it in the journal and, extolling the boldness of this enterprise, declared in no uncertain terms:[9]

> The Company represents an output of patriotic effort and self-sacrifice such as no other has behind it and it would be a public disgrace if its appeal went unheard.

It is also interesting to observe on the very same day the emphasis of Sri Aurobindo on self-sufficiency in manufacturing in the columns of the *Karmayogin.* He lamented that some companies were selling '…Swadeshi umbrellas although these are Swadeshi only so far as the labour of fitting the parts together is concerned'.[10] At the same time, he lauded in the same piece the sincerity of an umbrella manufacturer in Poona (now Pune) who was manufacturing almost all the components of the umbrella locally, and praised the people of Bombay and Poona who were willing to buy such umbrellas, notwithstanding their higher price tag.

Thus, in one sweep, Sri Aurobindo dealt in the columns of this journal with topics of high sublimity, as also routinely commonplace matters. Indeed, there was no topic or issue that could be deemed to be either too metaphysical and ontological or too mundane and banal to be discussed in the pages of *Karmayogin.* As he himself wrote in a poem entitled 'Who' (which was also first published in the journal):[11]

> The hand that sent Jupiter spinning through Heaven,
> Spends all its cunning to fashion a curl.

From its very first issue, *Karmayogin* was financially self-sustaining, as an enthusiastic public ensured that all the issues were sold out. Subscribers enrolled from distant places such as Madras (now Chennai) and Bombay. Hindi and Tamil editions were started, and even a Marathi edition was planned. The magazine ran from June 1909 till April 1910. In mid-February 1910, Sri Aurobindo left Calcutta for good to go to Pondicherry, 'his cave of tapasya',[12] as he described it. Sister Nivedita (Margaret Noble) took up the editorship of the newspaper. He had left behind a few articles that were intended for publication, and those appeared in the issues following his departure. Two months later, the journal stopped publication.

In the pages of *Karmayogin,* we can discern the gradual but compelling transition of its editor from nationalist political leader to spiritual seer and master—Aurobindo Ghosh of Calcutta on his way to becoming Sri Aurobindo of Pondicherry.

* * *

7

Writings in Bengali and Sanskrit

Reading by Sampadananda Mishra

I have always been amazed that Sri Aurobindo, who had almost no contact with any Indian language before he returned to India after fourteen years in England, mastered Bengali and Sanskrit in such a short time. *Writings in Bengali and Sanskrit*[1] is a testimony to this achievement. This volume compiles writings by Sri Aurobindo in these two languages, published together for the first time.

The Bengali writings of Sri Aurobindo cover a wide range of formats: poems, essays, translations, letters, stories, prayers and editorials. These are related to his own life, social and political topics, religion, yoga, spirituality, tradition and nationalism. The writings belong to different time periods, from 1893 to the 1930s. Many of these pieces were published during Sri Aurobindo's lifetime, while the rest were published later. The Bengali weekly *Dharma*, which Sri Aurobindo launched and edited in 1909–10, carried most of these essays. As for the letters, they were written predominantly in the 1930s, when he corresponded in Bengali with some of his disciples residing in his ashram in Pondicherry.

The volume begins with 'Hymn to Durga' (দুর্গা-স্তোত্র),[2], an inspiring invocation in the context of the fervour for freedom he was striving to ignite in order to destroy the spell of inertia and selfishness that had caught hold of the people. This powerful prayer invoked the Divine Mother for the protection of Bharata. Even today, it is recited by thousands of devotees of Sri Aurobindo. Patriotism, faith and force, all come together in thirteen short but forceful stanzas such as this one:[3]

> মাতঃ দুর্গে! অন্তঃস্থ রিপু সংহার করিয়া বাহিরের বাধাবিঘ্ন নির্মূল কর। বলশালী পরাক্রমী উন্নতচেতা জাতি ভারতের পবিত্র কাননে, উর্বর ক্ষেত্রে, গগন-সহচর পর্বততলে, পূতসলিলা নদীতীরে একতায় প্রেমে, সত্যে শক্তিতে, শিল্পে সাহিত্যে, বিক্রমে জ্ঞানে শ্রেষ্ঠ হইয়া নিবাস করুক, মাতৃচরণে এই প্রার্থনা, প্রকাশ হও ॥
>
> MOTHER DURGA! Slay the enemy within, then root out all obstacles outside. May the noble heroic mighty Indian race, supreme in love and unity, truth and strength, arts and letters, force and knowledge ever dwell in its holy woodlands, its fertile fields, under its sky-scraping hills, along the banks of its pure-streaming rivers. This is our prayer at the feet of the Mother. Make thyself manifest.[4]

One of the most significant turning points in Sri Aurobindo's life was his incarceration in Alipore Jail in 1908–09 while he was in the thick of organizing the revolutionary movement against the British in Bengal. It is during this time that he underwent a transformative experience and realized concretely the immanent divinity in all beings, an experience he mentioned in his famous Uttarpara Speech (See Chapter 6). *Tales of Prison Life* (কারাকাহিনী),[5] is a rare and remarkable autobiographical document that not only provides a lively presentation of his life in Alipore Prison during his trial, but also brings out many facets of the case. Sri Aurobindo's sarcasm and wit are evident throughout the book. In one of the most poignant passages of this text, beyond its light-heartedness, it is painful to read about the dehumanizing manner in which political prisoners in general, and Sri Aurobindo in particular, were treated in British jails:[6]

> থালা হইতে বাটীটীই আরও প্রিয় ও উপকারী জিনিষ ছিল। ইহা জড় পদার্থের মধ্যে যেন ব্রিটিশ সিভিলিয়ান। সিভিলিয়ানের যেমন সর্ব্বকার্য্যে স্বভাবজাত নৈপুণ্য ও যোগ্যতা আছে, জজ, শাসনকর্তা, পুলিস, শুল্কবিভাগের কর্ত্তা, মিউনিসিপ্যালিটির অধ্যক্ষ, শিক্ষক, ধর্ম্মোপদেষ্টা, যাহা বল, তাহাই বলিবামাত্র হইতে পারে, – যেমন তাহার পক্ষে তদন্তকারী, অভিযোগকর্তা, পুলিস বিচারক, এমন কি সময় সময় বাদীর পক্ষে কৌসিলীরও এক শরীরে এক সময়ে
>
> But more dear and useful than the plate was the bowl. Among inert objects it was like the British civilian. Just as the civilian, ipso facto, is fit and able to undertake any administrative duty, be it as judge, magistrate, police, revenue officer, chairman of municipality, professor, preacher, whatever you ask him to do he can become at your merest saying—just as for him to be an investigator, complainant, police magistrate, even at times to be the counsel for defence, all these roles hold a friendly concourse in the same hospitable body, my dear bowl was equally multipurpose. The bowl was free from all caste restrictions, beyond discrimination, in the prison cell it helped in the act of ablution, later with the same bowl I gargled, bathed, a little later when I had to take my food, lentil soup or vegetable was poured into the same container, I drank water out of it and washed my mouth. Such an all-purpose priceless object can be had only in a British prison. Serving all my worldly needs the bowl became an aid in my spiritual discipline too. Where else could I find such an aid and preceptor to get rid of the sense of disgust?[7]

The next section of the book has six small write-ups under the title 'Dharma' (ধর্ম্ম),[8] in which Sri Aurobindo outlines a few ideas and concepts pertaining to Sanatana Dharma. The tone in these writings is influenced by the inspired nationalistic fervour of this period in his life:[9]

> দেশ জাতীয়তার প্রতিষ্ঠা, জাতি নহে, ধর্ম্ম নহে, আর-কিছুই নহে, কেবল দেশ। আর-সকল জাতীয়তার উপকরণ গৌণ ও উপকারী, দেশই মুখ্য ও আবশ্যক। অনেক পরস্পরবিরোধী জাতি এক দেশে নিবাস করে, কখনও সদ্ভাব, একতা, মৈত্রী ছিল না, কিন্তু তাহাতে ভয় কি? যখন এক দেশ, এক মা – একদিন একতা হইবেই হইবে, অনেক জাতির মিলনে এক বলবান অজেয় জাতিই হইবে।
>
> The country and nothing but the country is the foundation of Nationalism, neither the nation, nor religion, nothing else matters. All other elements are secondary and contributory, it is the country alone that is primary and essential. Many mutually exclusive races live in the land, perhaps there never was enough goodwill, unity or friendliness. What is there in that to worry about? When it is one country, one Mother—there is bound to be unity one day, and out of the union of many races shall emerge a strong and invincible nation.[10]

The fourteen articles published under Nationalism (জাতীয়তা)[11] throw much light on his political ideology, the true meaning of nationalism, freedom, fraternity and India's national resurgence. These need to be read together with the twenty-three editorials from *Dharma* ("ধর্ম" পত্রিকার সম্পাদকীয়,)[12] and are a record of Sri Aurobindo's original thoughts with regard to the problems of India at many levels and their possible solutions. These essays contain a potent message for the people of India:[13]

> ভগবান যখন ভারতকে জাগাইলেন, তখন সেই জাগরণের প্রথম আবেগে জাতীয়ভাবের উদ্দীপনার জ্বালাময়ী শক্তি জাতির শিরায় শিরায় খরতরবেগে

> বহিতে লাগিল। তাহার সহিত স্বদেশপ্রেমের উন্মদকর আবেগ যুবকবৃন্দকে অভিভূত করিল। আমরা পাশ্চাত্যজাতি নহি, আমরা আসিয়াবাসী, আমরা ভারতবাসী, আমরা আর্য্য। আমরা জাতীয়ভাব প্রাপ্ত হইয়াছি, কিন্তু তাহার মধ্যে স্বদেশপ্রেমের সঞ্চার না হইলে আমাদের জাতীয়ভাব পরিস্ফুট হয় না। সেই স্বদেশপ্রেমের ভিত্তি মাতৃপূজা। যেদিন বঙ্কিমচন্দ্রের 'বন্দেমাতরম্ গান বাহ্যেন্দ্রিয় অতিক্রম করিয়া প্রাণে আঘাত করিল, সেইদিন আমাদের হৃদয়ের মধ্যে স্বদেশপ্রেম জাগিল, মাতৃমূর্তি প্রতিষ্ঠিত হইল। স্বদেশ মাতা, স্বদেশ ভগবান, এই বেদান্ত-শিক্ষার অন্তর্গত মহতী শিক্ষা জাতীয় অভ্যুত্থানের বীজস্বরূপ।
>
> When God roused India, in the first flush of her awakening the flaming power of the national consciousness began to flow swiftly in the veins of the nation. At the same time, a maddening emotion of patriotism enraptured the youth. We are not Europeans, we are Asiatics. We are Indians, we are Aryans. We have gained the national consciousness but unless it is steeped in patriotism our national consciousness cannot blossom. Adoration of the Mother must be the foundation of that patriotism. The day "Bande Mataram", the song of Bankimchandra, crossed the barrier of the outer senses and knocked at the heart, on that day patriotism was born in our heart; on that day the Mother's image was enshrined in our heart. The country is Mother, the country is Divine—this sublime precept which forms a part of the Upanishadic teachings is the seed of the national rising.[14]

Some articles focus on the basic features of the Integral Yoga and on human society, revealing further aspects of Sri Aurobindo's unique perspective that combined Indian spiritual concepts with modern social and political ideals. In 'The Chariot of Jagannatha' (জগন্নাথের রথ),[15] Sri Aurobindo holds that, 'আদর্শ সমাজ মনুষ্য-সমষ্টির অন্তরাত্মা ভগবানের বাহন, জগন্নাথের যাত্রার রথ। ঐক্য স্বাধীনতা জ্ঞান শক্তি সেই রথের চারি চক্র।' (The ideal society is the vehicle of the indwelling Godhead of a human aggregate, the chariot for the journey of Jagannath. Unity, Freedom, Knowledge and Power constitute the four wheels of this chariot.)[16]

While the volume *Essays on the Gita*[17] (See Chapter 16) provides a comprehensive commentary on the teachings of the Bhagavad Gita, a few articles in Bengali on the Gita[18] in this volume have many interesting points which address various questions in an insightful manner. For instance, the choice of Arjuna to receive the knowledge of the Gita, despite several other characters being apparently more ready to receive it:[19]

> অর্জ্জুন সমসাময়িক মহাপুরুষদিগের মধ্যে শ্রেষ্ঠ ছিলেন না। আধ্যাত্মিক জ্ঞানে ব্যাসদেব শ্রেষ্ঠ, সেই যুগের সর্ববিধ সাংসারিক জ্ঞানে পিতামহ ভীষ্ম শ্রেষ্ঠ, জ্ঞানতৃষ্ণায় রাজা ধৃতরাষ্ট্র ও বিদুর শ্রেষ্ঠ, সাধুতায় ও সাত্ত্বিক গুণে ধর্ম্মপুত্র যুধিষ্ঠির শ্রেষ্ঠ, ভক্তিতে উদ্ধব ও অক্রূ শ্রেষ্ঠ, স্বভাবগত শৌর্য্যে ও পরাক্রমে জ্যেষ্ঠ ভ্রাতা মহারথী কর্ণ শ্রেষ্ঠ। অথচ অর্জুনকেই জগৎপ্রভু বরণ করিয়াছিলেন, তাহারই হস্তে অচলা জয়শ্রী এবং গাণ্ডীব প্রভৃতি দিব্য অস্ত্র সমর্পণ করিয়া তাহার দ্বারা ভারতের সহস্র সহস্র জগদ্বিখ্যাত যোদ্ধাকে নিপাত করিয়া যুধিষ্ঠিরের অসপত্ন সাম্রাজ্য অর্জ্জুনের পরাক্রমলব্ধ দানরূপে সংস্থাপন করিলেন; উপরন্তু তাহাকেই গীতোক্ত পরম জ্ঞানের একমাত্র উপযুক্ত পাত্র বলিয়া নির্ণীত করিলেন।
>
> Arjuna was not the best among his great contemporaries. In spiritual knowledge, Vyasa was the greatest; in all kinds of worldly knowledge of that epoch, Bhishma was the best; in the thirst for knowledge king Dhritarashtra and Vidura led the rest; in saintliness and sattwic qualities Yudhishthira was the best; in devotion there was none equal to Uddhava and Akrura; his eldest brother Kama, the mighty warrior led in inborn strength and courage. And yet, it was Arjuna whom the Lord of the worlds elected; it was in his hands that He placed divine weapons like the Gandiva bow and gave to him eternal victory; it was through him that thousands upon thousands of India's world-renowned fighters were made to fall; and he founded for Yudhishthira his undisputed empire as a gift of Arjuna's prowess. Above all, it was Arjuna whom He decided as being the one fit recipient of the supreme knowledge given in the Gita.[20]

Though the bulk of his commentary on the Vedas is in English, Sri Aurobindo was keen to present his Vedic insights to Bengali readers as well. His writings on the Vedas and Upanishads[21] in this volume are a good introduction to these foundational texts of Sanatana Dharma.

Among the letters that Sri Aurobindo wrote in Bengali, the one to his wife, Mrinalini, (মৃণালিনীদেবীকে লিখিত)[22] is profound and deserves our special attention. It is here that Sri Aurobindo spoke of his 'three madnesses'—that all belongs to the Divine and therefore must be returned to him, that God must be experienced directly, and that the country must be known as the Mother and worshipped accordingly.

Sri Aurobindo's Bengali stories and poems have many inspiring elements in them. 'The Ideal of Forgiveness' (ক্ষমার আদর্শ)[23]is a finely written story that shows the importance of forgiveness through a tale involving the great rishis of yore Vashishtha and Vishvamitra. His Bengali poems also carry an echo of the force and sublimity we find in his English poetry, such as in his poem on the defeat of Ravana:[24]

ত্রিদিব পৃথিবী
জিনিয়াছি যুদ্ধে, বাঁধিয়াছি দেবগণে,
ভুঞ্জেছি অতুল্য যশঃ, বিশ্বচক্ষু পুড়ি।
সূর্য্য যেন জ্বলে নভে গ্রীষ্মের মধ্যাহ্নে,
উত্তাপে জগৎ ক্লিষ্ট রুদ্রদীপ্তি পূজে।
জ্বলিয়াছি ভূমণ্ডলে কিরণ প্রকাশি।
রঞ্জিয়া নিজ রুধিরে গগন-নীলিমা
সূর্য্য যেন অস্তাচলে ডোবে মহাতেজা,
ডুবিব মৃত্যুসাগরে। ছিলাম উদয়ে,
ভোগকালে উচ্চশির মহাতেজা। অস্তে
রহিব, মরণে, নাশে অজেয় তেজস্বী।

The three heavens with Earth I have won in battle,
I imprisoned all the gods, I enjoyed fame incomparable;

I am as though the all-enveloping world-eye of the Sun,
I burn at noon of mid-summer; afflicted by its heat
The world adores the scorching Fire.
As the sun reddens the blue of the firmament with its own blood
And goes down at setting in all its glory,
So shall I sink into the sea of Death.
I was at dawn, during my sway, head uplifted,
Fierce and radiant.
And at the setting I will be there still,
In death and destruction unconquerable, a fierce lustre and a mighty blaze.[25]

The awe-inspiring Bengali poetry of Sri Aurobindo finds resonance in his Sanskrit writings as well, compiled in the second part of the volume. Among his notable writings in Sanskrit are the patriotic poem *Bhavani Bharati* (भवानी भारती),[26] a philosophical work *Ekamevaadvitiyam Brahma* (एकमेवाद्वितीयं ब्रह्म),[27] a set of received mantras titled *Saptacatustayam* (सप्तचतुष्टयम्),[28] and an incomplete work on the Tantra—*Tantrikasiddhiprakaranam* (तान्त्रिकसिद्धिप्रकरणम्),[29] apart from a few smaller incomplete notes and verses. Though the volume of his Sanskrit writings is smaller than his output in other languages, it is still sufficient to reveal his poetic excellence and his remarkable command over the language.

'Bhavani Bharati' is a short poem written by Sri Aurobindo sometime between 1904 and 1908, during his days as a freedom fighter, and the only poem he wrote in Sanskrit. The ninety-nine verses of the poem—in three different eleven-syllabled meters—resound with patriotism. The poem was untitled when Sri Aurobindo wrote it. He could not revise the work, as it was confiscated by the Calcutta police in May 1908 when he was imprisoned. In 1985, the Sri Aurobindo

Ashram recovered the manuscript and published it under the title, *Bhavani Bharati*.

The theme of the poem is short and simple, but vigorous, powerful, inspiring and an embodiment of the spirit of the nation, the sense of the time. For Sri Aurobindo, the nation was the Mother of strength and so, *Shakti,* or the divine feminine principle of energy or strength of the nation has been invoked in this poem.

A poetic masterpiece, *Bhavani Bharati* occupies a special place among the heroic poems of the twentieth century. Apart from its intense subject matter, it is a unique creation from the point of view of poetic beauty. Sri Aurobindo presented the story in a *puranic* style, similar to what one would find in a traditional Sanskrit text, such as *Durga Saptashati* (also known as Shri Chandi) of the Markandeya Purana. Any perceptive reader can experience the simplicity and the power, and the rhythm and the soaring movement of the work. Take for example, these verses from the beginning of the poem, when the Goddess first appears before the writer in the terrifying form of Kali, seeking to banish the inertia and weakness of a nation that has resigned itself to colonial subjection:[30]

आलोलकेशैः शिखरान्निगृह्य करालदंष्ट्रैश्च विसार्य सिन्धून् ।
श्वासेन दुद्राव नभो विदीर्णं न्यासेन पादस्य च भूश्चकम्पे ॥८॥
उत्तिष्ठ देहीति पिपासुरम्बा दध्वान रात्रौ नगरे वितारे ।
सेयं स्तनन्ती रजनीं तमिस्त्रां बभौ समापूर्य मनंसि चार्या ॥९॥
भीतः समुद्विग्नमनाश्च तल्पादुत्थाय पप्रच्छ तमो नमस्यम् ।
का भासि नक्तं हृदये करालि कुर्वीय किं ब्रूहि नमोऽस्तु भीमे ॥१०॥
सिंहस्य सारावमुदीरयन्ती क्रूरस्य कुञ्जे भ्रमतो वधार्थम् ।
ससर्ज वाक्यानि करालमूर्तिर्यथा समुद्रस्तनितं शिलायाम् ॥११॥
मातास्मि भोः पुत्रक भारतानां सनातनां त्रिदशप्रियाणाम् ।
शक्तो न यान् पुत्र विधिर्विपक्षः कालोऽपि नाशयितुं यमो वा ॥१२॥

> The mountain-tops cowered beneath her dangling locks and the seas drew back from her awful fangs; her breath scattered the torn clouds and earth trembled at the fall of her feet.
> "Arise! Give!" The Mother's thirsting call resounded through the night in the starless city. Thundering, the noble goddess filled with her presence the night's blackness and the hearts of men.
> Alarmed and shaken in mind, I sprang from my couch and questioned that shape of darkness which compelled worship: "Who art thou who appearest to my heart in the night in thy terrible splendour? What must I do? Speak! Salutation to thee, O dreadful goddess!"
> Uttering a sound like the lion's roar when it roams ferocious in the jungle in search of prey, the goddess in her form of terror loosed forth words like the thundering of ocean upon the rocks: "I am the mother, O child, of the Bharatas, the eternal people beloved of the gods, whom neither hostile Fate nor Time nor Death has a power to destroy."

The philosophical work, *Ekamevaadvitiyam Brahma*, is in the Upanishadic style. This significant text was published separately under the title *Sri Aravindopanishad*[31] for the first time in 1987 by the Sanskrit Karyalaya of Sri Aurobindo Ashram in Pondicherry. This work captured Sri Aurobindo's philosophy in just twenty-seven lines. The essence of the text was summed up by the editors of the booklet as follows:[32]

> ब्रह्म सत्यं जगत् सत्यं सर्वं ब्रह्ममयं जगत् ।
> एकमेवाद्वितीयं तज्जीवो ब्रह्मैव नापरः ॥

> The Brahman is real, the Jagat is also real and the Jagat is fully pervaded by the Brahman who is one without a second, and the jiva himself is Brahman.

The entire thought, style and presentation of the text is poetic, aphoristic and philosophic, and is undoubtedly based on Sri Aurobindo's own spiritual experiences.

Saptacatustayam is another text by Sri Aurobindo with deep spiritual content. It comprises mantras received by Sri Aurobindo while he was imprisoned in Alipore jail in 1908–1909. These mantras were noted down by him afterwards. The text contains seven quartets, each expounding upon four aspects related directly to *yogic sadhan*, or the practice of yoga. The text is written in *sutra* style in original Sanskrit, while certain explanations for it in English may be found in *Record of Yoga* (See Chapter 8).

Sri Aurobindo intended to write a systematic book in Sanskrit on Tantra an esoteric Indian spiritual tradition, but the *Tantrikasiddhiprakaranam* was left incomplete. Written in a *sutra* style too, similar to Patanjali's *Yogasutras*, the text deals with the worship of Shakti, the divine feminine principle of energy. This, *upasana,* or worship, according to Sri Aurobindo, is the supreme accomplishment of a *sadhaka* (practitioner) of the Tantra method. He says that this worship may be of two types: worshiping Shakti with the sense of 'I am She', or with the sense that 'She is the Prakriti and I am the Purusha'. This worship then leads either to the state of the Goddess Kali, or to the state of *vibhuti*, the god in becoming.

But the principal instrument for both these forms of worship remains self-surrender. When the sadhaka arrives at this sense of total self-surrender, makes no effort and sits joyfully—leaving aside, or rising above, dharma and adharma, virtue and vice, good and bad, pleasant and unpleasant—then Goddess Kali enters their body. She removes *ahankara* or ego and makes the sadhaka stand above the three *gunas* or the modes of Nature. She removes all imperfect *samskaras,* or past impressions, and in this way the sadhaka attains *cittashuddhi*, or purification of mind, and finally becomes an accomplished Tantrika. In total there are thirty-seven *sutras* dealing with the Tantra. Although incomplete, the text reveals the fundamental secret of the Tantrik system of yoga.

Finally, the original mantras[33] at the end of this volume form part of the daily practice of many sadhakas of the Integral Yoga. For instance, this meditatation on the highest form of the Divine Mother:

ॐ आनन्दमयि चैतन्यमयि सत्यमयि परमे
Om anandamayi chaitanyamayi satyamayi parame
Om, She, the Delight
She, the Consciousness
She, the Truth
She, the Supreme.

But the most important and well-known among all the original mantras is undoubtedly Sri Aurobindo's 'Gayatri Mantra':

ॐ तत्सवितुर्वरं रूपं ज्योतिः परस्य धीमहि ।
यन्नः सत्येन दीपयेत् ॥
Om tat savitur varam rupam jyotih parasya dhimahi yannah satyena dipayet.
Let us meditate on the most auspicious form of Savitri, on the Light of the Supreme which shall illumine us with the Truth.

For the sadhakas of the Integral Yoga, the significance of this mantra is obvious. The light invoked here has the power to lead the sadhaka to the realization of the Supramental illumination.

Sri Aurobindo learned Bengali and Sanskrit largely through his own efforts—languages which were still mostly foreign to him when he returned to India after his education at Cambridge. And yet, the writings in this volume reveal to us the extent to which he mastered the two languages and made them powerful vehicles of his incredible creative and spiritual genius.

* * *

8

Record of Yoga

Reading by Richard Hartz

The central theme of Sri Aurobindo's writings is the possibility of a change of consciousness, individual and collective, leading to a transformation of our lives that will eradicate the causes of ignorance, disharmony and suffering. This is the message he offered to the world in *Arya*, the monthly philosophical review where he published most of his major works serially in their original form between August 1914 and January 1921. Beginning a few years earlier and continuing through the period of *Arya* and beyond, Sri Aurobindo also kept a diary, which he called the *Record of Yoga*.[1] First published in book form in 2001, this detailed documentation of the day-to-day progress of an advanced spiritual practitioner provides unique insights into the experiential foundations of his philosophy and teaching.

When Sri Aurobindo left politics behind him and arrived in Pondicherry in April 1910, he was heralded as the 'Yogi from the North'.[2] All evidence suggests that his spiritual development had already reached the point where, according to traditional ideas, there should have been little left for him to do in this world except to impart his knowledge and realizations to others.

But, in fact, his practice of yoga was just beginning. By around 1910, his exploration of the path to a profound transformation of human nature was entering hitherto uncharted territory. The *Record of Yoga* is an account of this adventure into the unknown.

Clearly, such a text is of unusual interest for the serious reader of Sri Aurobindo's works. It is also the most challenging of his writings. For one thing, the English is peppered with Sanskrit words (mostly in transliteration) and occasionally other languages, including French, Bengali and Greek. Keeping the diary for his own use, Sri Aurobindo made none of the concessions a writer would normally make to readers. The published text is as far as possible a verbatim transcript of the manuscripts. The following passage in the last entry of 1912, summing up the stage his yoga had reached at the end of that year, is a typical example:[3]

> It has been seen that in repose, in nivritti[,] in udasinata, perfect peace and ananda are possible; but the thing the Yoga has set out to establish is the perfect harmony of Nivritti & Pravritti… By the fulfilment or failure of this harmony the Yoga stands or falls. The siddhi has now reached a stage when the test of its positive worldward side has to be undertaken. Tyaga is finished; shama & shanti & udasinata have had their fulfilment; but in that resting place there can be no abiding. It is the starting point of the Lila, not its goal.

This is a key statement to understand how Sri Aurobindo saw his own yoga. In his view, spiritual life has all too often been identified with the path of withdrawal (*nivritti*) as an end in itself, at the expense of the capacity for action (*pravritti*). He did not underestimate the need to establish a deep peace (*shama*, *shanti*) in our whole subjective being, cultivate a philosophical indifference (*udasinata*) towards the vicissitudes of life, and achieve an inner renunciation (*tyaga*) of worldly desire as a motive force. These things belong to what he called the 'static half' of the work, but for him they were the easy part. To engage in the full, even heightened flow of pravritti without losing one's tranquillity was much harder, but no less necessary. This was the 'active half' of the work,[4] and it was his primary focus during the period covered by the *Record of Yoga*.

Sri Aurobindo's spiritual realizations led him to see the world not as an illusion (*maya*), but as the unfolding play (*lila*) of an infinite Being seeking the delight (*ananda*) of manifestation in the universe. But under the present troubled conditions of this half-evolved world, how is it possible to act dynamically from the undisturbed poise of an illumined consciousness? A basis of action other than our ordinary egoistic motives is required. Sri Aurobindo found it in the principle of tapas, the transcendent and universal Force or Will which channels its workings through the individual being (*jiva*). A month after the entry quoted above, he described what must be done. His use of the phrase *navadware pure*, 'in the nine-gated city' (Bhagavad Gita 5.13, where the gates are the openings in the body) indicated how far the Gita served as a point of reference for him:[5]

> Formerly life was regarded as a thing to be worked upon and worked out, by active mental will and bodily means.... The remnants of this way of seeing clung until now to the thought and action, but henceforth it is removed. Life is a great mass of existence, Sat, moulding itself through its own Tapas. All that has to be done is for the Jiva, the knowledge centre of this existence, to sit fast in his city, navadware pure, & allow the infinite Tapas to manifest through him... This must be the first principle of the new period of action.

But the infinite tapas can manifest freely through the jiva only if there is no ego to intercept it and deflect the workings of the Force to serve its limited personal ends. A decisive stage in the elimination of this distorting factor is noted in an entry in November 1913 under the heading '*Ahankara-Mukti-Siddhi*' (perfection of the liberation from ego). Here Sri Aurobindo distinguished several components of this liberation. Not only must the little ego (*aham*, the 'I') cease to be the doer (*karta*) of our actions, so that we become aware of the universal *brahman* as their doer (*kartri brahma*), but a similar substitution must take place in the ego's role as the knower (*jnata*), enjoyer (*bhokta*), upholder (*bharta*) and witness (*sakshi*) of the activities of Nature. The dissolution of the ego does not mean the disappearance of all individualization of action, knowledge and enjoyment (*bhoga*). The individual being still exists as a centre (*kendra*) of manifestation but, as is explained in *Essays on the Gita*[6] (See Chapter 16), it remains only as 'a centre of living spiritual consciousness whose circumference is lost in the infinite'.[7] What now thinks, acts and enjoys through this centre is *Kali*, the name used in the *Record of Yoga* for the universal Energy executing the supreme Will:[8]

> The aham karta is now replaced by the kartri brahma, so the aham jnata by the jnatri, the aham bhokta by the bhoktri, the aham bharta by the bhartri, the aham sakshi by the sakshi brahma. What is left of the aham is a kendra of action, a kendra of knowledge, a kendra of vision, a kendra of enjoyment. In this kendra Kali receives the will of God, thinks it out in the idea, fulfils it in action, watches its fulfilment and sends up the bhoga to God, becoming herself the will, the action, the vision, the bhoga, the knowledge.

Even this realization is not enough, however, so long as knowledge and action proceed through the instrumentality of the divided consciousness of the mental being (*manishi*, the thinker). Until that can be replaced by the supramental (*vijnanamaya*) harmony based on an awareness of the totality of existence, there must be an unshakable faith in the guidance of the Lord (*ishwara*) who is working upon us to transform our imperfection into the image of his own gnostic and beatific (*anandamaya*) nature. The elements and stages of the thoroughgoing transformation of human nature envisaged by Sri Aurobindo are enumerated in the system he explained in 'The Yoga of Self-Perfection', part four of his book, *The Synthesis of Yoga*.[9]

Each of the seven parts of this system is divided into four and therefore is called a *chatusthaya* (quartet). Since the entries in the diary constantly refer to this system as a framework by which to measure progress, mastery of its terminology as outlined in the introduction to the *Record of Yoga* is essential if one wants to understand this text. For example, the second chatusthaya (the shakti-chatusthaya or quartet of strength) is represented by faith, surrender, (*dasya*) and the divine Nature (*daivi prakriti*); the third (the *vijnana*-chatusthaya or quartet of the supra-intellectual faculty) by Knowledge and Power; and the sixth (the *brahma*-chatusthaya or quartet of Brahman) by *ananda brahman* (Brahman as the All-Blissful). Each chatusthaya is interconnected with the others:[10]

> The faith must be that it is the Ishwara, Anandamaya & Vijnanamaya who is the guide, although He still uses the impulsions & ideas of the Manishi & not yet the full Vijnanamaya harmony…

> Therefore it is an integral fulfilment that is being worked out & this aim prevents the separate perfection of each chatusthaya by itself without relation to the rest.
>
> Faith & Ananda Brahman are the two keys to the perfect internal state, with dasya as the joining point. Knowledge & Power are the two keys to the perfect external state, with Daivi Prakriti as the joining point.

The diary has occasional lighter moments; though here, too, there is an underlying seriousness of purpose. Sri Aurobindo was experimenting, for instance, with what he called the 'siddhis of power', constituting what parapsychologists now term 'distant mental influence'. These he first developed in the 'field of exercise', often meaning that they were tried out on animals or birds in the vicinity, before being applied to events of importance in India or abroad (the 'field of life'). *Record of Yoga* contains an account of one such experiment, in which he observed resistance to the exertion of the force:[11]

> A curious example shows how difficult the resistance now finds it to be effective; a crow sitting on a branch received the suggestion of going to the end of the branch, but the force in it was unwilling; it went a little way thence came rapidly back, & for some minutes began dancing on the branch this way & that, towards the end when the force was applied, away from it when it was relaxed, until it reached the point as if driven suddenly by physical force, seeming several times about to fall off the tree, & then fluttered off to another bough.

The *Record of Yoga* is a text that offers great rewards to readers who are already familiar with Sri Aurobindo's other writings on the subject and are prepared to grapple with its unusual challenges. Published in two large volumes and consisting of nearly 1250 pages of dated entries, preceded and followed by almost 250 pages of additional material, it is not a book which lends itself well to reading through from beginning to end. It has neither a logical nor a narrative structure, but a chronological organization. Yet, extraordinary glimpses of the inner life of a Yogi are buried in its pages, waiting to be unearthed by those who have the patience to find them. By immersing ourselves in this remarkable diary, we bring ourselves into the presence of one who showed by example what it means to say: 'All life is Yoga.'[12]

9

Essays Divine and Human

Reading by Uday Arya

After arriving in Pondicherry in 1910, Sri Aurobindo continued writing, bringing his profound insights to a wide array of subjects. *Essays Divine and Human*[1] includes essays, thoughts and aphorisms that will likely strike the reader as deeply uplifting and soul-stirring.

This volume is primarily a collection of essays—on philosophy, psychology and yoga. Sri Aurobindo wrote extensively on God, nature, man and superman, the science and problem of consciousness, and yoga as a change of consciousness. One of the refrains in this volume is that of man as a being of an intermediate nature:[2]

> Man is a transitional being, he is not final. He is a middle term of the evolution, not its end, crown or consummating masterpiece.

Most of the material that appears in Part One of this volume was written before he began his seminal work for *Arya*.[3] *The Life Divine*,[4] *The Synthesis of Yoga*[5] and his myriad letters on yoga[6] complement these earlier writings in this part of the book.

One of the most memorable short essays in this book is 'On Original Thinking'.[7] Powerful and evocative, it serves as a timeless exhortation 'to accept nothing, to question everything'[8] and to 'get rid of all unexamined opinions old or new'.[9] Sri Aurobindo's well-known quote on man and reason appears in a draft version of this essay:[10]

> Man may be, as he has been defined, a reasoning animal, but it is necessary to add that he is, for the most part, a very badly-reasoning animal. He does not ordinarily think for the sake of finding out the truth, but much more for the satisfaction of his mental preferences and emotional tendencies; his conclusions spring from his preferences, prejudices and passions; and his reasoning & logic paraded to justify them are only a specious process or a formal mask for his covert approach to an upshot previously necessitated by his heart or by his temperament.

Several shorter essays from the volume's first part, such as 'The Interpretation of Scripture',[11] 'Social Reform',[12] and 'Hinduism and the Mission of India'[13] shed profound insights on issues that continue to affect us today. In the last of these essays, he discussed the challenges facing India in engaging with its past in order to fashion its future, of the dangers of confusing Hinduism with conventionalism, and the limitations of modern solutions blindly imported from the West:[14]

> I write, not for the orthodox, nor for those who have discovered a new orthodoxy, Samaj or Panth, nor for the unbeliever; I write for those who acknowledge reason but do not identify reason with Western materialism; who are sceptics but not unbelievers; who, admitting the claims of modern thought, still believe in India, her mission and her gospel, her immortal life and her eternal rebirth.

'From Man to Superman',[15] the second part and a large chunk of *Essays Divine and Human*, overflows with the 'flamings of beauty into earthly shapes',[16] that he wrote about in his magnum opus, *Savitri*[17] (See Chapter 29). This portion of the book has 171 short pieces written by Sri Aurobindo over a thirty-five-year period, from 1912 to 1947. While these were not prepared by him for publication, each of them offers invaluable insights for those who are looking for answers to questions of existence and yoga. Consider, for example, the Upanishadic seeking: [18]

> Does universe ever end? Does it not exist eternally in God's total idea of His own being? Unless the Eternal is tired out by Time as by a load, unless God suffers loss of memory, how can universe cease from being?

Or the revelatory image:[19]

> The Suns are only physical concentrations of Light, but the splendour they concentrate for us is self-born and everywhere.

The section also includes a treatise[20] on one of the most pressing questions of modern society—what is consciousness? Tomes have been written on this one word, and the frontiers of modern science still grope in the dark for a handle on this elusive concept and secret to the riddle of existence. How are the nature and laws and movements of consciousness to be discovered within us? What we have within these fifty-odd pages is a progressive and systematic exploration of the subject, a grand tour of humanity's quest for self-knowledge. Every view, every objection and every denial has been taken into account, whether the fumblings of physical science, the myopic lens of illusionism, or the experiential advances of yogic seekers. Sri Aurobindo takes nothing for granted, and leads the reader logically towards what he refers to as a 'true scientific psychology'. What he means is that 'it is through consciousness, by an instrumentation of consciousness only that the nature and laws and movements of consciousness can be discovered—and this is the method of Yoga.'[21]

But what makes *Essays Divine and Human* a unique book to me, the part that I find myself returning to time and again, is the section on aphorisms.[22] In India, the more well-known term for an aphorism is the Sanskrit word *sutra*. For several millennia, evolved individuals in India and in other parts of the world have employed sutras to express profound ideas with great effect. Take, for example, 'the gods are mortals, men immortals.'[23] These penetrating and pithy phrases cast a deep impression on all who come in touch with them, undoubtedly lighting 'thoughts that glow through the centuries'.[24]

What is it about the method of embedding Truth into such phrases that give them such durability? In one of the essays in this book, Sri Aurobindo reveals:[25]

> The aphoristic method has great advantages. It prevents the mind from getting encrusted in details and fossilising there; it leaves a wide room & great latitude for originality & the delicate play of individuality in the details. It allows a science to remain elastic and full of ever new potentialities for the discoverer.

Around the year 1913, Sri Aurobindo penned hundreds of scintillating aphorisms on a vast range of topics. He grouped these in his notebook under the three classical paths of yoga—Jnana, Karma and Bhakti. In a way, these aphorisms constitute a synthesis of these paths of yoga, expressed in a manner, as the Mother (born Mirra Alfassa, the spiritual collaborator of Sri Aurobindo) reveals, 'always original and always unexpected'.[26] In content, however, there is almost nothing classical about these flashes of revelation. Consider the utterance:[27]

> God's laughter is sometimes very coarse and unfit for polite ears...

Or:[28]

> A God who cannot smile, could not have created this humorous universe.

These are radical departures from conventional images of a serious God, and introduce ideas that inevitably challenge our traditional beliefs and worldviews. Naturally, some of the earlier disciples had pressing questions on what Sri Aurobindo may have meant in these profound aphorisms and turned to the Mother for guidance. She was asked to help shed light on almost each of these gems, and her commentaries have been diligently recorded in *On Thoughts and Aphorisms.*[29] A single aphorism of Sri Aurobindo has an explanation ranging from a paragraph to several pages in this book—and that alone makes it an invaluable companion volume to *Essays Divine and Human.*

In one of her explanations, the Mother provided an insight into the nature of Truth, the limitations of our reasoning minds (when we do use our reason) and why Sri Aurobindo chose this particular method of expression:[30]

> Sri Aurobindo tells us that 'the reason trembles' because these higher truths always appear in the human domain as paradoxes, revelations contrary to reason; not because reason is incapable of understanding what comes from the higher regions, but because these revelations are always ahead of, very much ahead of, that which reason has understood or accepted. What the human reason of today finds reasonable has been paradoxical and mad in the past; and probably—one may say, certainly—these unexpected, paradoxical, revolutionary revelations which

> are manifesting now and making the reason tremble, will in time to come be very reasonable knowledge, which in turn will tremble before new revelations.
>
> It is this sense of something which is always moving, progressing, being transformed, that Sri Aurobindo is trying to give us with these compact phrases which for a time shake our understanding of things. It is to push us forward, to give us the sense of the complete relativity of all that manifests in the world, and of this universe which is always in motion, ever moving towards a higher and greater Truth.

Beyond the broad groupings of Jnana, Karma and Bhakti, Sri Aurobindo often classified the aphorisms by topic. So, for example, you will find his thoughts on history and historicity, or health and medicine grouped together. Each aphorism illuminates a different aspect of the subject, in unique and surprising ways. The Mother, in one of her responses to a question on these aphorisms, said of Sri Aurobindo:[31]

> ... he presents each problem, each question in all its aspects, showing the truth contained in each way of seeing things, and he explains that in order to attain the Truth you must realise a synthesis which goes beyond all mental notions and emerge into a transcendence beyond thought.

This many-sidedness of Truth is itself a theme in Sri Aurobindo's aphorisms, and each pithy expression has the potential to make you sit back and reflect. Every one of them offers us a chance to widen our outlook, and I can speak from my own experience—there is no going back once you have read them. As Sri Aurobindo wrote in one of his letters to a disciple:[32]

> Anything that carries the Word, the Light in it, spoken or written, can light this fire within, open a sky, as it were, bring the effective vision of which the Word is the body.

If one were to examine the record of Sri Aurobindo's commentaries on the sages of Greece, one would find that he has spent the majority of his time on the mystic Heraclitus—not Plato, Socrates or the Stoics, but an earlier aphoristic philosopher, whose thought comes down to us 'in detached aphoristic sentences aimed like arrows at truth'. They are not, Sri Aurobindo says, '... really scattered philosophical reflections. There is an inter-relation, an inter-dependence; they all start logically from his fundamental view of existence itself and go back to it for their constant justification.'[33]

This interrelation and interdependence are evident in Sri Aurobindo's aphorisms too—each of which is founded on his vast and all-encompassing experience of reality. In this volume, it is this beautiful tapestry, this profound and often uncommon groupings of ideas, images and symbols that give us contiguous glimpses of Sri Aurobindo's *divya-drishti* (divine vision), 'oceans of an immortal luminousness'.[34]

* * *

10

Essays in Philosophy and Yoga

Reading by Gautam Chikermane

Largely a collection of short essays written across forty-one years, from 1909 to 1950, and published during Sri Aurobindo's lifetime, *Essays in Philosophy and Yoga*[1] can be seen as a confluence of intellectual-spiritual tributaries. Ideas that evolved during this period, they may seem disparate when read in isolation, but flow seamlessly into some of his larger works. A few, notably 'Aphorisms', inform the works of, and have been expanded by, his spiritual collaborator, the Mother. Four of the five parts in this collection were first published in *Karmayogin*, *Arya*, *Standard Bearer* and *Bulletin of Physical Education*. The fifth part, 'The Yoga and Its Object', is a longer thesis and was part of a 1912 letter that was published as a booklet in 1921, with several editions.

The essays are short but that affects neither the intensity of ideas nor the integrality of the thoughts presented. In fact, one of the most impactful set of ideas sit under one of the shortest collections, 'Thoughts and Glimpses'.[2] In nine pages, Sri Aurobindo dissects concepts, disrupts predictable mass and shakes the ground under our feet to create a new thought universe that nudges us towards the transformation of reason into intuition, the limited and divided individual into a universal personality:[3]

> When we have passed beyond knowings, then we shall have Knowledge. Reason was the helper; Reason is the bar.
> When we have passed beyond willings, then we shall have Power. Effort was the helper; Effort is the bar.
> When we have passed beyond enjoyings, then we shall have Bliss. Desire was the helper; Desire is the bar.
> When we have passed beyond individualising, then we shall be real Persons. Ego was the helper; Ego is the bar.
> When we have passed beyond humanity, then we shall be the Man. The Animal was the helper; the Animal is the bar.

The word 'transformation' has a special place in India. Used in everyday vocabulary, transformation can mean several things—the development of a village, electrification of a district, or digitization of a nation. In the context of the inner realms, transformation has been described as creating a self-image and fitting into it, or changing the approach from religion to spirituality. For Sri Aurobindo, the idea of transformation held a deeper meaning that went beyond the senses or the mind. To him, transformation was an evolutionary concept, the creation of a new species, a gradation, an intermediary stage in the path from homo sapiens to a 'divinised manhood and the divine life'. In an August 1950 piece, which was part of an essay series called 'The Supramental Manifestation upon Earth' and is part of this volume, he defined the contours of what he called the 'Mind of Light':[4]

> A new humanity means for us the appearance, the development of a type or race of mental beings whose principle of mentality

> would be no longer a mind in the Ignorance seeking for knowledge but even in its knowledge bound to the Ignorance, a seeker after Light but not its natural possessor, open to the Light but not an inhabitant of the Light, not yet a perfected instrument, truth-conscious and delivered out of the Ignorance. Instead, it would be possessed already of what could be called a mind of Light, a mind capable of living in the truth, capable of being truth-conscious and manifesting in its life a direct in place of an indirect knowledge.

Simple but not simplistic, the essays in this volume form introductory ideas that help a reader get conversant with the basics of Sri Aurobindo's writings. They are also markers to understand his larger works. The seventeen essays under the head 'Arguments to *The Life Divine*' for instance, are intellectual synopses, windows to that monumental work (See Chapter 18). The chapter 'The Human Aspiration'[5] in *The Life Divine* is present here under the title 'The Human Aspiration: Argument in Brief: Shorter Synopsis of the Chapter,'[6] where Sri Aurobindo writes: 'The animal is a laboratory in which she has worked out man; man may be a laboratory in which she wills to work out the superman, the being of a divine nature.' Similarly, the single-page chapter, 'Death, Desire and Incapacity: Argument', feeds into the ten-page chapter 'Death, Desire and Incapacity' in *The Life Divine*:[7]

> Life, at first darkened, ignorant, divided and helplessly subject, seeks as it develops to become master and enjoyer, to grow in Power; but until it escapes from the bonds of individuality it must be subject to its three badges of limitation, Death, Desire and Incapacity.[8]
>
> Therefore growth by struggle is the third Law of Life. This strife again has to divinise itself and become the clasp of Love. Until

> then Death, Desire and Strife are and must be the triple mask of the divine Life-principle in its cosmic self-affirmation.[9]

To me, one of the most powerful pieces in *Essays in Philosophy and Yoga* is 'The Strength of Stillness', published in February 1910. Silence as a tool of spiritual growth binds several sages; Swami Vivekananda said, for instance: 'The ideal man is he who in the midst of the greatest silence and solitude finds the intensest activity, and in the midst of the intensest activity, the silence and solitude of the desert.'[10] Sri Aurobindo explored, expanded and expounded on this strength, differentiating it from the inaction of the tamasic man, characterized by inertia and indolence:[11]

> There are two great forces in the universe, silence and speech. Silence prepares, speech creates. Silence acts, speech gives the impulse to action. Silence compels, speech persuades. The immense and inscrutable processes of the world all perfect themselves within, in a deep and august silence, covered by a noisy and misleading surface of sound—the stir of innumerable waves above, the fathomless resistless mass of the ocean's waters below.[12]

And:[13]

> To be capable of silence, stillness, illuminated passivity is to be fit for immortality... The inaction of the tamasic man is a stumbling-block to the energies around him, the inaction of the Yogin creates, preserves and destroys; his action is dynamic with the direct, stupendous driving-power of great natural forces.

Silence, in fact, is an important and recurring theme in Sri Aurobindo's works. Take *The Synthesis of Yoga*[14] (See Chapter 19): 'In a complete silence only is the Silence heard; in a pure peace only is its Being revealed. Therefore to us the name of That is the Silence and the Peace.'[15] Or *Essays on the Gita*[16] (See Chapter 16): 'For the Gita insists that we can and should, while we live, be conscious in the self and its silence and yet act with power in the world of Nature.'[17] Or *Letters on Yoga II*[18] (See Chapter 25): 'It is in the silent mind that the true consciousness can be built.'[19] In this piece in *Essays in Philosophy and Yoga*, Sri Aurobindo takes this idea, translates it into an image, and transmutes it into our hearts. Permanently.

It is not easy to read Sri Aurobindo and nobody is more conscious of this fact than Sri Aurobindo himself, whose light-hearted and introspective introduction to *Arya*'s second year is as much an editor listening to his readers as it is a confession, 'We have been obliged in our first year for reasons we shall indicate in the preface to our August number to devote the Review almost entirely to high philosophy and severe and difficult thinking. But the object we had in view is now fulfilled and we recognize that we have no right to continue to subject our readers to the severe strain of almost sixty-four pages of such strenuous intellectual labour.'[20] That said, once a reader gets conversant with the vocabulary, the grammar and the sentence construction of Sri Aurobindo's writing, the path becomes easier. The sole requirement then is concentration. In a longer and deeper journey to Sri Aurobindo's philosophy, *Essays in Philosophy and Yoga* is a volume that a beginner can start with. The style of writing, the ideas they contain and the invisible heights they lead to, all are present here in what can be termed as an abridged form.

Sri Aurobindo's exploration of religion finds voice here. In 'Thoughts and Glimpses' he observed the functionality of six religious paths[21]—paganism, Christianity, Buddhism, Judaism, Islam and Hinduism—and wrote, 'A great thing would be done if all these God-visions could embrace and cast themselves into each other; but intellectual dogma and cult egoism stand in the way.'[22] He also carved the way forward:[23]

> All religions have saved a number of souls, but none yet has been able to spiritualise mankind. For that there is needed not cult and creed, but a sustained and all-comprehending effort at spiritual self-evolution.
>
> The changes we see in the world today are intellectual, moral, physical in their ideal and intention: the spiritual revolution waits for its hour and throws up meanwhile its waves here and there. Until it comes the sense of the others cannot be understood and till then all interpretation of present happening and forecast of man's future are vain things.

Here we find his thoughts on the strains of evolution and man as a transitional being, 'The gradual self-liberation from bondage to Nature is the true progress of humanity. The inert stone or block is a passive sport of natural laws, God is their Master. Man stands between these two extreme terms and moves upward from one to the other.'[24]

We also get a preview of his nationalism, 'Our aim will therefore be to help in building up India for the sake of humanity—this is the spirit of the Nationalism which we profess and follow.'[25]

And find his social criticism, '... afterwards it was the law of the Smritis which tried to do the same thing more roughly by classifying men according to the general classes of which the Vedas speak, the *caturvarnya*; today it is little more than blind mechanical custom and habitual social observance, a thing not sattwic but tamasic, not a preparatory discipline for liberation, but a mere bondage.'

Here we are introduced to his grand vision, the definition of his ideals:[26]

> Unity for the human race by an inner oneness and not only by an external association of interests; the resurgence of man out of the merely animal and economic life or the merely intellectual and aesthetic into the glories of the spiritual existence; the pouring of the power of the spirit into the physical mould and mental instrument so that man may develop his manhood into that true supermanhood which shall exceed our present state as much as this exceeds the animal state from which science tells us that we have issued. These three are one; for man's unity and man's self-transcendence can come only by living in the Spirit.

From explorations into the principle of evil[27] to the involution of spirit in matter as a precursor to the fullness of spiritual evolution,[28] this volume, like *Essays Divine and Human*[29] (See Chapter 9), not only gives us insights into the wide span of events, ideas and directions of Sri Aurobindo, it also tracks his journey as a writer, philosopher and sage.

* * *

11

Vedic and Philological Studies

Reading by Richard Hartz

For thousands of years, the Vedas have formed at one and the same time the most revered and, paradoxically, the least understood body of texts in India's long and rich spiritual tradition. Sri Aurobindo's efforts to rescue them from this sacred oblivion are among his major contributions to scholarship on Indian culture. A familiarity with his work on the Vedas is essential, besides, for a grasp of the central aspects of his own philosophy and yoga, including his explanation of the key term, Supermind or 'Truth-Consciousness'. Ideas drawn from his interpretation of the Vedas play a crucial role in volumes as diverse in their subject matter as *The Life Divine*[1] (See Chapter 18), *The Human Cycle*[2] (See Chapter 20), and *The Future Poetry*[3] (See Chapter 21).

Sri Aurobindo's writings on the Vedas fill three large volumes of *The Complete Works of Sri Aurobindo*. The most important of these are *The Secret of the Veda with Selected Hymns*[4] (See Chapter 12) and *Hymns to the Mystic Fire*[5] (See Chapter 13), which contain the latest results of his Vedic research, including all the translations and commentaries published during his lifetime. *Vedic and Philological Studies*,[6] on the other hand, consists of transcribed material from his personal manuscripts that supplements what he published on the Vedas, and shows the process through which his interpretations evolved and gives students of the Vedas access to many more hymns with the help of his translations. This volume also contains Sri Aurobindo's writings on the nature and origins of language. These writings, though incomplete, constitute his original contribution to linguistics, as well as illuminate the archaic vocabulary of Vedic Sanskrit and thus support his reading of the Vedas where it departs from received tradition.

Readers are likely to be most interested in Part One, 'Essays in Vedic Interpretation'.[7] Written over a period of two to three years before the launch of *Arya* in August 1914, most of these essays (many of them unfinished) can be regarded as sketches for the pieces that were published under the series 'The Secret of the Veda' as it appeared in print from *Arya*'s first issue. But since Sri Aurobindo made a fresh start for those pieces and there is no indication that he referred to what he had already written, the essays in *Vedic and Philological Studies* cannot be dismissed as mere drafts. They are full of passages that are of interest not only for a study of the development of his theory, but as part of the documentation of the period when his practice of yoga was 'spontaneously converging towards the ancient and now unfrequented paths followed by our forefathers'.[8]

The relationship between the essays published in *Vedic and Philological Studies* and writings which appear in *The Secret of the Veda* (See Chapter 12) can be illustrated by 'The Colloquy of Agastya and Indra'.[9] This commentary on the Rig Veda (1.170) has been reproduced in this volume from a notebook that Sri Aurobindo used around 1912. Two years later, when he began the series of 'Selected Hymns' which accompanied the pieces in 'The Secret of the Veda', he presented a new commentary on this hymn under the similar title 'The Colloquy of Indra and

Agastya'[10] as the first example of the results of his method of interpretation. But his earlier commentary contains valuable insights that he did not repeat and remains worth reading in its own right, especially for its observations concerning the anticipation of themes of the post-Vedic tradition.

The hymn opens, as Sri Aurobindo noted, with 'one of the most remarkable riks [hymns] in the whole Veda'. He translated it almost word for word, 'It is not now nor tomorrow; who knoweth that which is utterly wonderful? its movement has for its field the knowledge of another, but when it is approached, it disappears.'[11] Traditional and modern commentators alike have been led into extraordinary contortions in their forced attempts to reconcile this verse and those that follow with preconceived notions of Vedic ritualism. For Sri Aurobindo, the sense is perfectly straightforward:[12]

> What sublime & numerous echoes wake in our memory as we repeat this mantra. There comes to us… the solemn assertion of the Kena, na tatra vag gacchati no manah ["there speech travels not, nor the mind"];… vividly there comes the great fable of the mighty Yaksha who stood before the gods, the advance of this very Indra to know him, the vanishing of the Brahman as soon as approached….

Such echoes in the Upanishads are, in Sri Aurobindo's theory, among the most important clues to the real meaning of the Veda. But later and more popular traditions are also illuminated by this striking hymn, once it is correctly understood:[13]

> The hymn throws a flood of light on the persistent tales of the Purana & Itihasa in which Indra appears as the enemy of the Yogin, fearing to be overpassed, seeking to keep him by any means from conquering Swar and becoming too mighty for Indra himself. It is the Powers of mind that seek to preserve

> their activity in the human being, & do not wish him, stilling these activities, to pass into the silent Brahman. In the Vedic ideal Indra does not need to be an enemy, he is the best friend of the seeker, because the ideal of the Vedic Rishi is fulfilment & not cessation….

This and other items collected in 'Essays in Vedic Interpretation' open a window into the mind of Sri Aurobindo, the 'Yogi from the North',[14] the modern Agastya, during a decisive period of his spiritual development—when the light of the Vedic dawn had begun to break upon his consciousness.

Parts Two to Four of this volume—'Selected Vedic Hymns', 'Commentaries and Annotated Translations' and 'Vedic Notes'—provide abundant further material for a deeper study. Some of the pieces written as late as the 1940s, they show Sri Aurobindo's continued engagement with texts in which he believed he had discovered the secret of 'that knowledge and practice of a divine life to which the march of humanity, after long wanderings in the satisfaction of the intellect and senses, must inevitably return and is actually at the present dawn, in the impulses of its vanguard, tending more and more, but vaguely and blindly, to return.'[15]

Part Five of *Vedic and Philological Studies* is 'Essays and Notes on Philology'. The essays in this section consist of two drafts of an unfinished work entitled *The Origins of Aryan Speech* and a few shorter, related pieces. These are followed by a substantial section of philological notes, largely categorized lists of words and roots in Sanskrit, Greek, Latin and Tamil, which give a glimpse of how systematically Sri Aurobindo worked out the theory outlined in the essays.

At the time of Sri Aurobindo's research, the languages now referred to by linguists as 'Indo-European' were commonly called 'Aryan languages'. While he accepted this usage, Sri Aurobindo questioned 'the rigid philological divorce of the Dravidian & Aryan languages'[16] and excluded from his inquiry any notion of race and 'all ethnological conclusions, all inferences from words to the culture & civilisation of the men or races who used them, however alluring may be these speculations'.[17] Limiting himself to the history of words and their meanings, he focused strictly on the domain proper to philology in the older and British sense, encompassing what is now often called historical and comparative linguistics.

A key tenet of the science of 'linguistic embryology'[18] that Sri Aurobindo hoped his research might help to found was the 'superior importance of the root in early language to the formed word'.[19] Language 'in its first movement', he hypothesized, did not represent 'distinct ideas of the intelligence' so much as 'feelings, sensations, broad indefinite mental impressions.... The intellectual sense in its precision must have been a secondary element which grew more dominant as language evolved along with the evolving intelligence'. Linguistics, he believed, had till then been too preoccupied with this secondary element and insufficiently sensitive to 'an indefinable quality or property in the sound to raise certain vibrations in the life-soul of the human creature, in his sensational, his emotional, his crude mental being'.[20]

His theory is an intriguing and plausible one that deserves serious consideration from linguists and philosophers of language. Sri Aurobindo saw his theory of language as having the merit that 'it takes its stand on the two natural movements which constitute speech, the physical movements of articulation & the mental movement, partly sensational, partly discriminatory which attends the physical movements. And it seeks to establish itself by reducing the relation between these two motions to classified order & ascertained rule'.[21]

This innovative approach to understanding language and its development was not pursued to a final conclusion, as

Sri Aurobindo himself acknowledged. Writing as a scholar, he formulated hypotheses, collected data and drew reasoned conclusions, but was modest about the results of his work. He expressed the hope that one day it would stimulate others to follow this line of research, wherever it might lead:[22]

> If it does no more, it may possibly lead to a deeper & freer approach to the problem of the origin of speech, which, once undertaken in the right spirit and with an eye for the more subtle clues, cannot fail to lead to a discovery of the first importance to human thought & knowledge.

The scientist in Sri Aurobindo's temperament—the side of patient and meticulous attention to detail which he associated with the Mahasaraswati personality of the Shakti[23]—is on full display in both the Vedic and the philological material collected in this volume. Placed first in the triad of his Vedic writings, since much of it belongs to the period of preparation and exploration that preceded his first publications in this field, *Vedic and Philological Studies* is a book that should not be overlooked by students and scholars of Sri Aurobindo's writings and Indian culture. In view of the unique status of the Vedas as a founding text of Indian civilization, Sri Aurobindo's unravelling of the clues to the 'secret words' of the ancient Rishis is an achievement deserving of our special gratitude.

* * *

12

The Secret of the Veda

Reading by Anuradha Choudry

'Is there at all or is there still a secret of the Veda?'[1]

The Secret of the Veda's opening words invite readers to revisit Sri Aurobindo's reading of the mystic psycho-spiritual content of the Vedic hymns. This work is presented in four parts: 1) The Secret of the Veda; 2) Selected Hymns; 3) Hymns of the Atris; and 4) Other Hymns, followed by an appendix on the interpretation of the Veda. The first three parts compile his writings on and translations of the Rig Veda in the monthly review in *Arya* between 1914 and 1920. The fourth part consists of hymns that were not covered under the headings mentioned above.The oldest and most authoritative of the Sanatana Dharma sacred texts, the Vedas are considered to be primordial cosmic vibrations that were 'heard' by the inner ear of the ancient sages, or rishis, and cast in the form of a collection of hymns and passed down orally for millennia. The Vedas are composed of four individual texts—the Rig Veda, Sama Veda, Yajur Veda and Atharva Veda. Some of the important gods of the Vedas are Agni, Indra and Varuna. Scholars of comparative philology, comparative mythology and the science of comparative religion often argued that the Vedic hymns merely described the warring

Aryan and Dravidian tribes making offerings to propitiate Nature Gods, who granted boons to these barbaric primitive people in return for the oblations they received.

The objective of this essay is to closely examine these allegations and to identify the hymns' real purport. In the process, Sri Aurobindo unravels their underlying universal and eternal sense and spirit for aspiring seekers to use as a roadmap to lesser-explored inner pathways until they eventually succeed in releasing the 'hidden Sun from the dark Caves of their being'—an image that is symbolic of profound psycho-spiritual realizations, representing 'the transition of the human soul from a state of Death to a state of immortality by the exchange of the Falsehood for the Truth, of divided and limited being for integrity and infinity'.[2]

Sri Aurobindo proposes that the hymns in the Vedas, received by the rishis in the heights of their meditation, held scope for multi-layered interpretation owing to the 'living force'[3] of the Word in Vedic Sanskrit, which is 'a thing of power, creative, formative',[4] where 'sound determines sense'[5] and is 'itself the former of ideas' carrying 'within it the memory of its roots' and 'is still conscient of its history'.[6] The sound contains the sense, the sense leads us to the meaning of the word in a specific context:[7]

> I have continuously found that a sense thus restored illumines always the context wherever it is applied and on the other hand that a sense demanded always by the context is precisely that to which we are led by the history of the word.

Another remarkable feature of Vedic Sanskrit is 'the enormous number of different meanings of which a single word was capable and also the enormous number of words which could be used to represent a single idea'.[8] The term *ghrta*, for example, from the root 'ghr' can convey 'the idea of a strong brightness and heat such as that of fire or the summer sun' or 'to sprinkle or anoint, Greek *chrio*' or even 'any bright, thick liquid', which is the usual outward sense attributed to it, as in 'clarified butter in the sacrifice'. However, its association with the word *dhi* in several hymns allows for the possibility of an inward symbolic meaning where it represents 'a rich and bright state of activity of the brain-power, *medhā*, as basis and substance of illumined thought'. When this inner meaning is taken into account, it makes incoherent expressions like *dhiyam ghrtācī*, literally 'an intellect associated with clarified butter', reveal their couched psychological dimension—in this case, the implication of an 'intellect full of a rich and bright mental activity'.[9]

Having thus laid the foundations for a symbolic reading of the Vedas, Sri Aurobindo gives an outline of the arrangement of the ten Mandalas, or books, of the Rig Veda. In the following chapters, he analyses the first eleven *Suktas* (hymns) of the first Mandala, to reveal the psycho-spiritual dimension of some important godheads like Agni and Varuna-Mitra, and their relationship with Truth, the Ashwins, Indra and the Vishwadevas, and the goddess Saraswati and her consorts, Ila, Bharati and Mahi, respectively. He achieves this by comparing his interpretation with that of the most authoritative commentator of the Vedas, Sayana.

Sri Aurobindo draws parallels between the ancient Greek gods and their Vedic counterparts, to establish their 'psychological complexion'. Whereas the Greek gods were attributed distinct psychological symbolism with the passage of time, this evolution was not considered as a possible development in the case of the Vedic gods. For example, in the fifth verse of the first hymn, Agni is referred to as *citrasravastama*. Sayana renders the term *sravas* as 'fame', implying that 'Agni has an exceedingly various renown'. Sri Aurobindo, on the other hand, prefers to grant the word the sense of 'wealth', associating Agni with 'the most varied wealth',[10] thus widening the expression in its psychological context. According to him, Agni is much more than the ritual fire; he symbolically represents 'the divine will perfectly inspired by the divine Wisdom, and indeed one with it, which is the active or effective power of the Truth-Consciousness'.[11] This inner psychological interpretation is also clearly indicated by another epithet accorded to the god—*kavikratuh,* implying 'he whose active will or power of effectivity is that of the seer', who works with the knowledge that 'comes by the Truth-Consciousness and in which there is no misapplication or error'.[12]

On a similar note, when discussing the psychological significance of the duo Varuna-Mitra, Sri Aurobindo lays down the grand psycho-spiritual scheme of the Vedas and univocally declares that:[13]

> (...) the Gods in the Veda represent universal powers descended from the Truth-Consciousness which build up the harmony of the worlds and in man his progressive perfection, so the influences that work against these objects are represented by hostile agencies, Dasyus and Vritras, who seek to break up, to limit, to withhold and deny.

In this context, Varuna becomes 'a power of wideness and purity' and Mitra 'a power like Varuna of Light and Truth (representing) Love, Joy and Harmony, the foundations of Mayas, the Vedic beatitude'.[14]

The Secret of the Veda goes on to unravel the hidden dimension of godheads like the Ashwins, Indra and the Vishwadevas. The two Ashwins, the 'Riders on the Horse',[15] are compared to the characters of Castor and Polydeuces from Mediterranean mythology.[16] As riders on the horse, the ashwa, that are 'symbolic of force and especially of life-energy and nervous force, the Prana', are often invoked as 'gods of enjoyment, seekers of honey'. They are the Vedic physicians who 'bring back youth to the old, health to the sick and wholeness to the maimed'. In short, the special function of the twin divine powers is to establish perfectly the course of action and enjoyment in the vital and nervous aspects of the human personality. [17]

To Sri Aurobindo, Indra, one of the most important Vedic godheads, represents Mind-Power.[18] He was 'the power of pure Existence self-manifested as the Divine Mind'.[19] Agni is the upward rising Force of knowledge rising from earth to heaven, while Indra is the descending principle of the Light instinct with force.[20] This dual movement of Agni and Indra enables the aspiring soul to rise beyond the two firmaments of earth, representing the body, and heaven, symbolising the mind.

The Vishwadevas, literally 'all the gods or the all-gods', are regarded by Sri Aurobindo as 'the universal collectivity of the divine powers'. They are generally associated with the performance of the sacrifice or offering as *omas ascarsanidhrto*—'fosterers or increasers of man and upholders of his labour and effort in the work, the sacrifice'.[21] He then identifies several other characteristics that are common to all the gods who collaborate with man in order to lead him to the 'streams of Truth'.[22]

Following this, Sri Aurobindo elaborates on another very important godhead, Saraswati. He states categorically, 'Saraswati is not only the goddess of Inspiration, she is at one and the same time one of the seven rivers of the early Aryan world'.[23] He goes on to show how this dual association is possible, marrying the literal physical sense with its psycho-spiritual symbolic one, the physical river and the psychological inspiration, and highlights the need to recognize her strong association with her consorts, the other rivers, who also have the same symbolic nature. Thus, Saraswati represents the truth-audition, *sruti*, which gives the inspired word, and Ila represents *drsti*, the truth-vision.[24] These are the two powers of the rishis. Bharati or Mahi is the largeness of the Truth-Consciousness which dawns upon man's limited mind and invites the two sister powers.[25] These three, he says, in later times merged into the single form of Saraswati, the goddess of knowledge. In this manner, Sri Aurobindo leads his readers into the esoteric realms of the externalized representations of the Vedic lore.

The next few chapters of this volume reveal the essence of Vedic symbolism. A recurring image is the quest to retrieve the Lost Sun and Lost Herds of the Dawn, in the Cow and the Angirasa Legend. The Sun or Surya is the Lord of the Truth[26] and the cows, said to be its rays, are symbols of the physical light, a figure of the mental and spiritual, of knowledge and of an inner illumination[27] that are stolen by the Panis, the Bargainers. These have to be won back with the help of Indra, the gods and the Hound of Heaven, Sarama. Dawn or the goddess Usha who adheres to the path of Truth is constantly represented as awakening to vision, perception and right movement.[28] The Anigirasa Rishis, also known as the seven sages, or *sapta vipraḥ* of the Puranic tradition, are humanity's fathers who are enthroned in the constellation of the Great Bear in Indian astronomy. This gives us a glimpse of the simultaneously co-existing multi-layered reality that informed the Vedic worldview.

Part Two[29] is a more technical analysis of selected hymns to Indra, Agni, Surya, Usha, Bhaga Savitri, Vayu, Brihaspati, the Ashwins, the Ribhus, the Vedic Vishnu and Soma. Sri Aurobindo takes the interested reader deeper into the cryptic content of the Vedas to help them appreciate the psycho-spiritual nuances of the personalities of these godheads.

At the start of Part Three , Sri Aurobindo restates the gist of his approach to the Vedas, which seeks to uncover the hidden symbolism of the ancient mystics couched in terms of elemental figures of nature such as fire, rivers, mountains, the oceans and wind. We cannot understand the Vedas until we *become* the Vedas:[30]

> The soul of man is a world full of beings, a kingdom in which armies clash to help or hinder a supreme conquest, a house where the gods are our guests and which the demons strive to possess; the fullness of its energies and wideness of its being make a seat of sacrifice spread, arranged and purified for a celestial session… So understood the Rig Veda ceases to be an obscure, confused and barbarous hymnal; it becomes the high-aspiring Song of Humanity; its chants are episodes of the lyrical epic of the soul in its immortal ascension.

He also describes the entire symbolism of its essential content in the foreword and in the chapter 'The Doctrine of the Mystics' respectively. Free of technical terminologies, these two chapters provide readers with a clear and systematic understanding of the core aspects of Vedic symbolism. Sri Aurobindo then lays exclusive focus on unveiling the inner sense of Agni, the principal deity of the Vedas, by translating and commenting on the twenty-eight hymns of the Atris,one of the rishis, invoking the luminous godhead.

This is followed by an explanation of the Guardians of the Light, namely, Surya, the Light and the Seer, The Divine Dawn, Pushan the Increaser, Savitri the Creator, and the Four Kings—Varuna and Mitra, who have been discussed earlier, and Aryaman and Bhaga. The closing section consists of eleven Sanskrit hymns invoking the pair Mitra-Varuna, followed by two hymns to the Dawn and a final one to Savitri. Each hymn is translated with a commentary on its overall intent.

On a similar note, Part Four is dedicated to other hymns to individual and combined gods like the Thought-Gods and the Mystic Wine, Soma, as well as specific hymns by Rishi Parashara invoking Agni.

The appendix deals with Sri Aurobindo's 26 August 1914 letter, published in response to a critique on the opening chapter of *The Secret of the Veda* in *The Hindu*. Admitting that while his was not the first to attempt to give an *adhyatmic* or spiritual interpretation of the Veda, Sri Aurobindo wrote that he hoped that his philological reconstruction of the deeper sense of Vedic words would pave the way for a true science of language, which he proposed to develop in a later work.[31]

As one turns the last page of this volume, it is important to remember Sri Aurobindo's closing words to the foreword of Part Three:[32]

> The Rishis sought to conceal their knowledge from the unfit, believing perhaps that the corruption of the best might lead to the worst and fearing to give the potent wine of the Soma to the child and the weakling… Small is the chance that in an age which blinds our eyes with the transient glories of the outward life and deafens our ears with the victorious trumpets of a material and mechanical knowledge many shall cast more than the eye of an intellectual and imaginative curiosity on the passwords of their ancient discipline or seek to penetrate into the heart of their radiant mysteries. The Secret of the Veda, even when it has been unveiled, remains still a secret.

* * *

13

Hymns to the Mystic Fire

Reading by Pranjal Garg

Among all the writings compiled in the *Complete Works of Sri Aurobindo*, two subjects have been raised to an exceptionally distinguished level, so much so that an entire volume has been devoted to each of them. One is the Isha Upanishad[1] (See Chapter 14), which contains merely eighteen mantras, and the other is Agni, the mystic fire of sacrifice in the Vedas. This volume deals with the latter.

Agni, or fire, is a unique element, present in different forms in creation. The Vedas—physically, psychologically, philosophically, metaphysically and occultly—ordain it as the connecting force between the creator and the creation through *yajna*, the sacrifice. The importance attested to the multiplicity of powers and virtues manifested by the mystic fire is reflected in Sri Aurobindo's acknowledgement:[2]

> Agni in the Veda is always presented in the double aspect of force and light. He is the divine power that builds up the worlds, a power which acts always with a perfect knowledge, for it is *jatavedas*, knower of all births, visvani vayunani vidvan,—it knows all manifestations or phenomena or it possesses all forms

> and activities of the divine wisdom. Moreover it is repeatedly said that the gods have established Agni as the immortal in mortals, the divine power in man, the energy of fulfilment through which they do their work in him. It is this work which is symbolised by the sacrifice.

After his arrival in Pondicherry, Sri Aurobindo studied the Vedas and wrote on various aspects of the scripture. Of these, is his commentary on the hymns to Agni, and his theory of Vedic interpretation with reference to these hymns. The principal subject of his studies in *Hymns to the Mystic Fire*[3] are the hymns to the Vedic god Agni, whom he considered 'the most important, the most universal of the Vedic gods'.[4] First published in 1946, it appears in *The Complete Works* as part of a larger volume.

This volume is divided into three parts, of which the first, 'Hymns to the Mystic Fire', consists of selected hymns to Agni with a foreword, and extracts from the essay 'The Doctrine of the Mystics',[5] which prepares and initiates the seeker-reader in a formal yet novel manner to help build mental lucidity and an insight finally leading to the inner understanding of the hymns.

The second part has translations of hymns to Agni that were not included in the initial edition of *Hymns to the Mystic Fire*. An appendix to this part contains Sri Aurobindo's complete translation of the first hymn of the Rig Veda, and demonstrates the rigorous discursiveness his hermeneutic approach to translating the Veda gained over the years. Sri Aurobindo returned frequently to this hymn (Mandala One, Sukta 1)—which he translated into English in its entirety on at least fourteen occasions—in his study of the Vedas, a reflection of its importance, depth and vastness.[6]

The last part compiles translations of hymns to Agni from Sri Aurobindo's manuscripts with more extensive annotation than the occasional footnotes he provided for many of the translations in the first two sections, along with a large body of previously unpublished material.[7]

It is important to highlight the painstaking efforts made by Sri Aurobindo to bring to light the secret knowledge withheld in the Vedic scriptures, a knowledge esoteric and symbolic in nature. 'The Rishis saw the truth, the true law of things, directly by an inner vision,'[8] yet for many in the materialistic age of reason, the kernel of the Vedic hymns was 'barbaric sacrificial liturgy'[9] or, for the uninitiated, too codified. Sri Aurobindo's translations and interpretations are an aid to the yogic process for those who aspire and seek inner truth.

He was aware of the limitations impeding him from translating and expounding on the deeper sense of a series of visions and yogic experiences that were too distant and unintelligible to present civilization:[10]

> The turn of phrase and the syntax of English and Vedic Sanskrit are poles asunder; to achieve some sense of style and natural writing one has constantly to turn the concentrated speech of the Veda into a looser, more diluted English form. Another stumbling-block for the translator is the ubiquitous double entendre marking in one word the symbol and the thing symbolized.

The approach he took was to highlight the psychological dimension of the Vedic verses, and include contrasting translations according to Sayana's interpretation and his own, along with a discursive explanation of each verse.[11] His interpretations are inclusive and comprehensive; they do not establish a rival theory to refute previous work, but bring to fruition and rectify where necessary what has already been re-discovered in the Vedas through the centuries. He builds upon past knowledge and imbues a greater depth through his writings. His syllogistic, inferential and coherent writings reflect various aspects of his approach to understanding the Veda—'philological, psychological and mystical'.[12]

> Yaska [ancient Indian lexicographer] himself declares that there is a triple knowledge and therefore a triple meaning of the Vedic hymns, a sacrificial or ritualistic knowledge, a knowledge of the gods and finally a spiritual knowledge; but the last is the true sense and when one gets it the others drop or are cut away. It is this spiritual sense that saves and the rest is outward and subordinate.[13]

Just as he expounds upon in *The Secret of the Veda* (See Chapter 12), here too he argues that the Vedic gods 'must not be mistaken for mere imagery'. The gods were, to the Vedic seers, 'not simply poetical personifications of abstract ideas or of psychological and physical functions of Nature, but living realities'.[14] As this volume indicates, among these gods, Sri Aurobindo attested an exceptional importance to Agni and devoted much of his writings to interpreting and expounding the hymns dedicated to him.

This finds its justification in the tradition observed in the established text of the Vedas, where the 'hymns to Agni are placed before those to other gods in each book or each section of a book.'[15] Agni is the first word of the Vedas, Agni is the first and foremost god to be invoked, Agni is the priest, the *purohit*, the *ritwik* who stands before the gods. Amply significant are the titles adorned for Agni, right from the opening lines of the Rig Veda: 'A hymn of praise, welcome and prayer to Agni, Lord of Tejas, composed when the mind of the Yogin Madhuchchhanda was full of sattwic energy and illumination.'[16] Or, 'Agni I adore who stands before Yajna, the god that seeth right, the offerer of the oblation, chief disposer of delight.'[17] Or, 'The Fire I pray, the divine vicar of the sacrifice and ordinant of the rite, the Summoner (or, priest of the offering) who most founds the ecstasy.'[18]

The journey to the realization of Brahman needs 'sacrifice', and Agni must be called upon to accompany us, lead us: 'Our sacrifice is a journey, a pilgrimage and a battle—a travel towards the Gods and we also make that journey with Agni, the inner Flame, as our path-finder and leader.'[19] Sri Aurobindo marshalled imagery from the hymns to illustrate the different manifesting powers of the mystic fire god and his subsequent importance:[20]

> Agni first, for without him the sacrificial flame cannot burn on the altar of the soul. That flame of Agni is the seven-tongued power of the Will, a Force of God instinct with Knowledge. This conscious and forceful will is the immortal guest in our mortality, a pure priest and a divine worker, the mediator between earth and heaven. It carries what we offer to the higher Powers and brings back in return their force and light and joy into our humanity.

The indomitable and ever upward-rising flames of fire give an unfailing experience of rising, aspiring, tapas, purification and catharsis that cannot go unfelt regardless of one's cultural background. Fire is historically a crucial purifying factor in various walks of life, for a metal-smith or while cooking, in a chemical research lab, or in the legend of the phoenix. Symbolically, many religious rituals are connected with fire, for it is gleaned as a purifying agent, bringing new light, new birth and the right knowledge to the person concerned. And in its deeper sense, as the Rishi Medhatithi Kanwa implored, 'We choose Agni, the summoner, the all-knowing, the messenger, the will effective of this sacrifice.'[21]

These hymns to Agni were invoked by several rishis: Madhucchanda Vaishvamitra, Kanva, Parashara Shaktya, Gotama Rahugana, Dirghatama Auchathya, Kutsa Angirasa, Agastya Maitravaruni, Gritsamada Bhargava, Vishvamitra, Vamadeva, Atris, Bharadvaja and Vasishtha. All aspired to realize different aspects of the power and manifestations of the fire god.

As we read Sri Aurobindo's explanations and interpretations founded on a deep and methodical linguistic analysis, somewhere the perception of fire on the physical level and the inner meaning of Agni seems to supersede and dissolve dividing realities, and we begin to see the various layers of Agni, that the seven tongued, scintillating and luminous 'Agni is a seer-will, kavi-kratu, he is the "will in the heart", kratu hrdi.'[22] He is also, as the rishis in their hymns invoke, 'the godhead characterized by the supreme power of divine knowledge,'[23] the 'master of wisdom,'[24] who '... rulest over the wealth of inspired knowledge.'[25]

The in-depth linguistic and psychological analysis presented by Sri Aurobindo takes us deep into each word of the hymns, and the multiple psychological sense each letter and root word are filled with. We then start to see language, life and Vedas from a universal perspective. The inner meaning of the hymns, which are never disconnected from yogic aspiration, lead life and yoga to synchronously merge in order to culminate in an integration of Bhakti, Jnana and Karma.

* * *

14

Isha Upanishad

Reading by Debashish Banerji

Isha Upanishad[1] deals with all of Sri Aurobindo's translations of and commentaries on this Upanishad. It is interesting to see an entire volume dedicated to this single Upanishad, while his translations and commentaries of all the others constitute a single companion volume, *Kena and Other Upanishads*[2] (See Chapter 15). Further, while this volume on the Isha Upanishad is 597 pages long, the other Upanishads have been compressed into 449 pages. This is a sign of the importance of the Isha Upanishad for Sri Aurobindo. Indeed, this importance can be traced to the fact that the concise and enigmatic eighteen stanzas of this Upanishad provide confirmation for the central goal of Sri Aurobindo's yoga—identification with a principle of consciousness by whose power Brahman (Absolute Being), in its freedom, has become the cosmos, the ultimate reality capable of manifestation. The Isha refers to this principle as Vijnana; Sri Aurobindo named it Supermind.[3]

The volume is divided into two parts. Part One consists of his last and complete translation and commentary of the Isha Upanishad. This version was originally written for the monthly review in *Arya* and serialized in its pages from August

1914 to May 1915, published separately as a book in 1920–21 and lightly revised in 1924. Part Two comprises a collection of all his earlier commentarial attempts, chronologically arranged, none complete. Hence, those interested in 'the last word', should read Part One and need go no further. Those interested in supplementing their reading with further roughly contemporaneous elaborations by Sri Aurobindo can read the essay 'Ish and Jagat'[4] and the pieces following it in Part Two. And those interested in the development of Sri Aurobindo's views on the Isha should read the entire Part Two, preferably before reading Part One.

If considered chronologically, the volume's earliest essay is from around 1902, when Sri Aurobindo was vice principal of Baroda College (now Maharaja Sayajirao University of Baroda).[5] It is a short incomplete scrap but demonstrates the deep plunge he took into Indian philosophy in Baroda, to verse himself in Indian culture after his return from England. In the essay, Sri Aurobindo described the three major schools of Vedantic Nondualism, promoting Monism (*advaita*), Qualified Monism (*vishishtadvaita*) and Dualism (*dvaita*), and observed that the Upanishads as a whole held to all these views as 'soul stages'.[6] He identified the Isha as holding the view of 'a very slightly modified Monism'.[7] Though he was to nuance his view later, this was already the mark of an original interpretation, not subject to the dominant influence of Shankara's Advaita Vedanta or to any other exclusive Vedantic school.

The second essay—'The Ishavasyopanishad with a commentary in English'[8]—from around 1905, belongs to the beginning of Sri Aurobindo's active involvement in nationalist politics. The title page of this manuscript notated it as 'Materials for Bhavani Grantha-Mala I'. In his later talks and writings, Sri Aurobindo referred to a directive from the spirit of Sri Ramakrishna, the nineteenth-century Bengali saint, who was the guru of Swami Vivekananda, saying 'Mandir Gado' (build a temple).[9] He took this to mean the construction of a temple related to nationalistic activity and wrote a tract titled 'Bhavani Bharati', starting dramatically with the lines 'Om Namas Chandikayai. A temple is to be erected and consecrated to Bhawani, the mother, among the hills.'[10] As part of a *grantha-mala*, a garland of books, related to this 'temple', the essay on the Isha Upanishad was meant to be a text prescribed for revolutionaries in preparation.

In keeping with its Sanskritized name, ashram setting and nationalist intent, this commentary is structured as a conversation between a guru and a disciple, thus presenting a vivid dramatization of its ideas. The disciple raises the kinds of questions that the college-educated youth of Calcutta were likely to raise when confronted with traditional texts such as the Upanishads. The guru is familiar with these arguments but answers in the framework of the Upanishad itself, often using Sanskrit words to reinforce a distinction between 'mleccha' and 'arya', words coding for the foreign colonizer and the cultured native spiritual aspirant.[11] He ridicules *mleccha* commentators who see in the Upanishads only 'a mass of incoherent though often sublime speculations'.[12] He also takes to task Shankara, the eight century Indian philosopher who founded the school of Advaita Vedanta (Non-Dualism)which famously declares the illusory nature of the world, and who derided works (*karma*) as inferior to knowledge (*jnana*). In doing so, Sri Aurobindo sets the authority of the Gita against Shankara.[13] Many of these positions are repeated with further elaboration in later commentaries.

In the later commentaries, though the meanings of certain terms (*vasyam*[14] for instance) are changed, a much finer detail of concrete distinction brought to bear upon sequences (such as *Kavi, manishi, paribhu and swaymbhu*),[15] the role of the

Vedic deities brought into sharp relief,[16] and the category of *Vijnana* seen as pre-eminent,[17] the basics of Sri Aurobindo's philosophical understanding of the Isha are well on their way to their final formation. Even in these early commentaries of Sri Aurobindo, we see that the Isha teaches an understanding of reality as a single Being in its multiple Becoming, challenging the stark division made by Shankara between the ultimate reality and manifestation.

'The Karmayogin: A Commentary on the Isha Upanishad'[18] is a lengthy, unfinished commentary belonging roughly to the same period as 'The Ishavasyopanishad', and elaborates on its ideas, indeed even shares some passages with it. As the name suggests, it highlights the aspect of Karma Yoga succinctly stated in the second verse of the Isha Upanishad: 'Doing verily works in this world one should wish to live a hundred years. Thus it is in thee and not otherwise than this; action cleaves not to a man.'[19] On the basis of this verse, he draws a connection between this message of the Isha Upanishad and the Bhagavad Gita.[20]

The years between 1907 and 1909 were a watershed period in Sri Aurobindo's life and his understanding of the Isha Upanishad. In 1907, he had an unbidden Advaitic experience that made him realize the truth of a supracosmic Being and the unreality of the world. His incarceration in Alipore Jail between 1908 and 1909 became the occasion for other such experiences—the realization of the immanence of this Being in the cosmos and all its objects or entities. He also received internal guidance regarding cosmic mind planes that intervened between present mental experience and a link principle, vijnana or the Supermind, that was responsible for extending the supracosmic Being into the cosmic Becoming.

These realizations and experiences brought home for Sri Aurobindo the full significance of the Isha Upanishad—the division between Vidya and Avidya (Knowledge and Ignorance) or undifferentiated conscious Being and divided cosmic Becoming, the gradations of Consciousness expressed in/as cosmos, the immanence of Being as subject in cosmos and all its Becomings and the link principle, Vijnana, which could allow Vidya and Avidya to be known 'both in one'.[21] After his release in 1909 and his self-exile in Pondicherry in 1910, he further consolidated these experiences and began relating them to the recondite verses and beings of the Veda.

'Ish and Jagat' and the subsequent essays in the second part, as well as the final commentary of Part One, were all written between 1912 and 1914, following this leap in realization between 1907 and 1909. Particularly, the 'Chapters for a Work on the Isha Upanishad'[22] and the three drafts of 'The Life Divine: A Commentary on the Isha Upanishad'[23] occupies the same mind space as the final commentary and shares its ideas, building towards the final version. An interesting aspect of these essays is Sri Aurobindo's discussion of his principles of interpretation.

The question of interpretive method is important for all of Sri Aurobindo's translations and commentaries of Sanskrit texts, whether the Isha Upanishad, the Vedic hymns discussed in *The Secret of the Veda*[24] (See Chapter 12), the other Upanishads in *Kena and Other Upanishads*[25] (See Chapter 15) or The Bhagavad Gita in *Essays on the Gita*[26] (See Chapter 16). He was dissatisfied with the hasty, often incoherent philological speculations of Western commentators such as Max Mueller and the polemical, ideologically motivated projections of Indian ones, such as Shankara. In these essays, he presents a strong critique of both these tendencies and opposes them with his own method, ultimately resting on spiritual immanence—in other words, a knowledge by identity with the experience conveyed by the text.

Western systems of knowledge don't consider this to be possible, holding to an irremediable gulf between knower and known, established most powerfully in modern epistemology by Immanuel Kant in his *Critique of Pure Reason*. But just such a knowledge by identity is the desirable goal of epistemology in Sri Aurobindo's view.[27] This involves the development of an intuition, prepared methodically by following three practices: an awareness of the connotations of words based on historical philology; an awareness of the internal rhythmic arrangement of the words in lines amplifying a structure of ideas; and an awareness of the organic unity of the whole present in the relations of the parts.[28] A receptive openness of this kind can develop into communion with 'the soul of the thinker'[29] behind the words. This does not necessarily guarantee perfection of knowledge but an intimate approach to it in itself or as it reflects in the terms of his mind. Finally, Sri Aurobindo enjoined an offering of the result to 'the Master of All' to do with it his will and guide us towards clearer receptivity:[30]

> The text has to be studied with a great patience, a great passivity, waiting for experience, waiting for light & then waiting for still more light. Insufficient data, haste of conclusions, wilful ramming of one's own favourite opinions into the text, wilful grasping at an imperfect or unfinished experience, wilful reading of a single narrow truth as the sole meaning of this complex harmony of thought, experience & knowledge which we call the Veda,—these are fruitful sources of error. But if a man can make his mind like a blank slate, if he can enter into the condition of bottomless passivity proper to the state of the calm all-embracing Chaitanya Atma, not attempting to fix what the Truth shall be, but allowing Truth to manifest herself in his soul, then he will find that it is the nature of the Sruti to reveal perfectly its own message.....By entering into communion with the soul of the thinker which still broods behind the inspired language, we come to realise what he saw, and what he put into his words, what waits there to make itself known to us.

A good part of the three drafts of 'The Life Divine: A Commentary on the Isha Upanishad' is devoted to a discussion of method. In fact, Draft C, the last of the three, is almost entirely devoted to method and ends with a plea, with a reference to the example of Sri Ramakrishna of Dakshineshwar,[31] for subordinating archived or expert knowledge (*aptavakya*), inclusive of scripture (*shabda pramana*) and rational inference (*anumana*), to direct experience of knowledge by identity (*pratakshya*).[32] After writing Draft C, Sri Aurobindo began writing for *Arya*, and decided to reduce his commentary of the Isha Upanishad to the concise exposition of key ideas and their relations that we find in Part One. At the same time, he began elaborating these ideas in their wider metaphysical ramifications and detailed considerations in a separate series of articles under the title 'The Life Divine', which, when compiled, became the magnum opus of his own integral philosophy.

By Draft B of 'The Life Divine', written in 1913–14, Sri Aurobindo had arrived at an intuition of the relational structure of ideas in the Upanishad in terms of four movements, which he outlined in the first page of the draft as part of a chapter-wise breakdown of his commentary:[33]

> Part I. The Upanishad
> Part II The First Movement–God, Life & Nature
> Part III The Second Movement–Brahman Self Blissful and All-Blissful
>
> Part [IV] The Third Movement–God in World – Vidya & Avidya
> Part [V] The Fourth Movement–Surya & Agni
> Part [VI] The Divine Life

The final commentary (Part One) roughly reproduces these movements in its understanding of the Isha's structure, specifying the verses to each as follows:[34]

First Movement: Verses 1–3
Second Movement: Verses 4–7; elaboration of verse 2
Third Movement: Verses 8–14: elaboration of verse 3
Fourth Movement: Verses 15–18: elaboration of verse 4

As touched on earlier, this final commentary focuses on the reconciliation of radical dualities in the Isha—the One and the Many, Subject(s) and Object(s), Being and Becoming, stillness and movement, identity and difference, Knowledge and Ignorance, Existence and Non-existence. It does so through a consideration of relevant metaphysical categories such as Brahman, Self, Cosmos, the Order of the Worlds, Works, The Process of Manifestation, Knowledge and Ignorance, Rebirth and the Soul's Journey and Vedic Gods such as Matarishwan or Vayu, Agni and Surya, with the link principle of Vijnana as the key to the integration of dualities. It is this last category, Vijnana, which constitutes the central philosophical contribution of Sri Aurobindo. He saw it as an evolutionary necessity for earthly fulfilment and, calling it Supermind in his other works, he made it the goal or telos of his own yoga:[35]

> The principle of Maharloka is Vijnana, the Idea. But this Vijnana is intuitional or rather gnostic Idea, not intellectual conception. The difference is that intellectual conception not only tends towards form, but determines itself in the form of the idea and once determined distinguishes itself sharply from other conceptions. But pure intuitional or gnostic Idea sees itself in the Being as well as in the Becoming. It is one with the existence which throws out the form as a symbol of itself and it therefore carries with it always the knowledge of the Truth behind the form. It is in its nature self-conscience of the being and power of the One, aware always of its totality, starting therefore from the totality of all existence and perceiving directly its contents. Its

nature is *drishti*, seeing, not conceiving. It is the vision at once of the essence and the image. It is this intuition or gnosis which is the Vedic Truth, the self-vision and all-vision of Surya.

* * *

15

Kena and Other Upanishads

Reading by Anshul Sinha

Man's first and foremost preoccupation, ever since his thought awakened, has been an aspiration—'an impulse towards perfection'.[1] For India in particular, this impulse has perennially informed all facets of her civilization, influenced all phases of her long history and fields of experience. To our globalized minds today this impulse presents itself as 'spirituality'. The origin of this high and noble spirituality—the Vedas—are said to be the foundation upon which the entirety of Indian civilization is built, for the spirituality of the Vedas is nothing but a seeking after self-perfection.

The Upanishads, embedded within the Vedas, regarded 'as the crown & end of Veda' and hence also known as Vedanta, have in their turn served as 'the firm bedrock of Indian spirituality in later ages'.[2] The *Swetaswatara* Upanishad even suggests that the Upanishads contain the crux of Vedic thought: '[...] for the Upanishad is the secret of the Veda. This is that which Brahma knoweth for the Womb of the Eternal and the older Gods and the sages who knew This, became This & were immortal.'[3]

These scriptures are a record of the revelations and experiences of the rishis or seer-poets of ancient India, wherein the Truth was revealed or heard, thus described as *Sruti*. Often composed in condensed aphorisms or allegories or even dialogues, their expression is invariably symbolic and seeks to convey the deeper psychological and metaphysical truths of man and universe and God.

Kena and other Upanishads[4] is a compilation of Sri Aurobindo's translations, commentaries and thoughts on several important Upanishads and Vedanta philosophy in general, written over a span of twenty years from the early 1900s to the early 1920s. Some of this work appeared in the weekly review *Karmayogin*[5] (See Chapter 6) published in Bengal, and the monthly *Arya*, from Pondicherry, while others were left unpublished during his lifetime.

This volume comprises translations of the *Kena*, the *Katha*, the *Mundaka* and other important Upanishads. The Kena is explicitly mentioned in the title because, among the other Upanishads that are part of this volume, it is the one that received the most attention in terms of commentary. The volume also contains several general essays on the Upanishads—for instance, 'The Philosophy of the Upanishads',[6] though incomplete, is also valuable in helping us realize the spirit behind the letter.

Sri Aurobindo spent much of his time in the first two decades after his return to India immersing himself in the atmosphere of the Upanishads, and of the Sanskrit language, with the intent to reconnect with the ideals and spirit of his motherland. He gave so much importance to the Upanishads because he deemed them to be 'the basis of all Indian religion and morals and to a considerable extent of Hindu politics, legislation and society. Its practical importance to [our] race is therefore immense'.[7]

But the Sanskrit language in which these texts were written, even though native to this soil, had become alien in due course to its people and at best survived in the high altitudes of academia. Sri Aurobindo translated the Sanskrit verses into

English to rend this veil between modern circumstances and past revelations. For those who seek to understand Indian thought and spirituality, these translations and commentaries are priceless. While he admitted to the insufficiency of the English language to translate Sanskrit terms and warned us of its misleading tendencies, he elucidated that the purpose of his translation and commentaries was 'to draw aside this curtain, to translate the old Vedic language & figures into the form contemporary thought prefers to give to its ideas'.[8]

Sri Aurobindo's approach of penetrating into the soul of the language to decipher the mystic symbolism of the Upanishads, while at the same time eschewing his westernized temperament, remains pertinent even today. This approach allowed him to rediscover a truth that was perhaps lost for centuries but had never actually disappeared. He credited its survival to Shankaracharya's genius, and praised him for having preserved the truth of the Upanishads and safeguarded it from being misinterpreted to the extent of an irretrievable corruption of the original symbols:[9]

> ... [Shankara's] commentary has also done an incalculable service to our race by bridging the intellectual gulf between the sages of the Upanishads & ourselves. It has protected them from the practical oblivion in which our ignorance and inertia have allowed the Veda to rest for many centuries... It has kept these ancient grandeurs of thought, these high repositories of spirituality under the safe-guard of that temple of metaphysics, the Adwaita philosophy—a little in the background, a little too much veiled and shrouded, but nevertheless safe from the iconoclasm & the restless ingenuities of modern scholarship.

While Sri Aurobindo acknowledged Shankaracharya's immense contribution to the preservation of India's spirituality, he argued that it had also partially been the cause of India's ascetic tendency to seek only after the Brahman or Spirit to the exclusion of life and the material world in general. Shankaracharya's maxim 'the spirit alone is real, the world an illusion' set the tone for almost all the interpretations of the Upanishads that came after him. As a corollary, the conclusions reached by later medieval and modern interpretations had been a world-negating escape into the Brahman.

Today, as the world earnestly seeks harmony and reconciliation to the Matter-Spirit dichotomy, rather than accept escape as a solution, a more revivifying interpretation is the need of the hour, something Sri Aurobindo reckoned more than a century ago. In his commentary on the Brihad Aranyaka Upanishad, alluding to Shankaracharya, he wrote:[10]

> ... But it seems to me that both the demands of truth & the spiritual need of mankind in this age call for a restoration of old Vedantic truth rather than for the prolonged dominion of that single side of it systematised by the mediaeval thinker.

However, the function and prerogative of tradition is that it safeguards the truth by enveloping it in a hollow shell for a future date to retrieve when the time is conducive and right for a rebirth. He was hopeful of such a future where mankind would be more receptive to novel ideas and interpretations:[11]

> The time is fast coming when the human intellect, aware of the mighty complexity of the universe, will be more ready to learn & less prone to dispute & dictate; we shall be willing then to read ancient documents of knowledge for what they contain instead of attempting to force into them our own truth or get them to serve our philosophic or scholastic purposes.

So, what do the Upanishads contain and can these texts be understood without our utilitarian and rational minds obfuscating the process? Owing to the nature of these verses, which are not a record of ideas but rather a record of experiences, Sri Aurobindo advises us not to restrict ourselves to the narrow purview of the analytical mind, but rather to trust and go forward where intuition leads us:[12]

> For we must remember that we are dealing with a book full of mystical imagery, which starts with & looks on psychological truths in the most material things and we shall miss its meaning altogether, if in our interpretation we are afraid of mysticism.

Despite being moulded by a British education, Sri Aurobindo was able to denude himself of all preconceived notions and adopt means that would have been radically different to his temperament. In the unseen providence of things perhaps this was always intended; years later, when a people informed by similar westernized education seek the truth, they could follow the example of one that was not so different from them. The method that he employed to discern the meaning of the Upanishads was based on the theory of the ancients themselves:[13]

> [...] to listen in soul to the old voices and allow the Sruti in the soul to respond, to vibrate first obscurely in answer to the Vedantic hymn of knowledge, to give the response, the echo and last to let that response gain in clarity, intensity and fullness. This is the principle of interpretation that I have followed—mystical perhaps but not necessarily more unsound than the insistence and equally personal standards of the logician and the scholar.

And, indeed, this method is most befitting of a study on the Upanishads for these are texts that cannot be solely grasped by the mind owing to their complex symbolism and mystical nature. The paucity of the human mind and instruments to comprehend the Brahman are ubiquitous in the sacred texts themselves, such as in the beginning of the third verse of the *Kena*: 'there sight travels not, nor speech, nor mind'.[14] The main theme and subject of the scriptures—the Knowledge of the Brahman, the Absolute—can only be grasped by a faculty higher than the rational mind, such as intuition, inspiration and revelation.

It is therefore by employing the same mystical processes as the rishis that Sri Aurobindo discovered the secrets of the Upanishads. When referring to the writers of the Upanishads as mystics, Sri Aurobindo clarifies that he does not mean 'vague and loose-thoughted visionaries, but in the sense of being intuitional symbolists—who regarded the world as a movement of consciousness and all material forms and energies as external symbols and shadows of deeper and ever deeper internal realities.'[15]

That the universe is the expression and a manifestation of an innermost Reality, is the kernel of all the Upanishads. While science holds matter to be the eternal reality, Vedanta posits the eternal reality to be Consciousness or Brahman 'of which Spirit-Matter are in phenomena the positive and negative aspects'.[16] To the mind, these two fundamental principles of existence have usually presented themselves as antithetical. But the Upanishads, being records of experiences that transcend the mental outlook, often dwell on the coexistence of contradictory attributes of the Absolute, for example, describing the Brahman as 'nirguno guni', with and without qualities.

To the medieval thinkers' predominantly mental outlook, similar contradictory statements begot different schools of Indian thought. And so, when one approaches these scriptures, one must always remember 'that Brahman is not a Being with fixed attributes, but absolute Being beyond attributes yet, being absolute, capable of all, and the world a phenomenal arrangement of attributes in Intelligent Being, arranged not logically & on a principle of mutual exclusion, but harmoniously on a principle of mutual balancing and reconciliation'.[17]

Sri Aurobindo's interpretation of the Upanishads evinced not a dichotomy between matter and spirit, but a harmonious symmetry. The essence of the Upanishads is best extracted through a mystical approach that does not need to coerce the meaning of the verses to suit one's philosophy as has been the case with most interpretations in the past. With regards to philosophy, the Upanishads 'have borne the weight of three millenniums of thought and may well suffice for an equal period of future speculation'.[18] For those who are already familiar with the traditional narrative of the Upanishads that has dominated the discourse in academia, this book might present a refreshingly integral and life-affirming outlook that has been wanting in the past. Sri Aurobindo's commentaries embrace both the world and God and place the various Upanishads within that harmonious framework:[19]

> The Upanishads are an orchestral movement of knowledge, each of them one strain in a great choral harmony. The knowledge of the Brahman, which is the Universality of our existence, and the knowledge of the world, which is the multiplicity of our existence, but the world interpreted not in the terms of its appearances as in Science, but in the terms of its reality, is the one grand and general subject of the Upanishads.

The lost knowledge of the Upanishads that has been retrieved in this book is for readers to explore and imbibe for themselves. But no knowledge is complete 'if it stops with this single conception and does not proceed to the practical consequences of the conception'.[20] The knowledge of the absolute Reality makes it incumbent upon us to seek after it in all its integrality.

Pragmatically, therefore, the goal set by these scriptures before mankind is 'to become one with God and lead individually the divine life, but also to help others to the divine realization and prepare, by any means, humanity for the kingdom of God on earth—satyadharma, satyayuga.'[21] Hopeful of the people of the future who will usher in a new dawn and continue the work of rediscovering the soul of Indian spirituality for all mankind, Sri Aurobindo wrote, more than a century ago in 1912:[22]

> The business of my commentary is to lay a foundation; it is for the thinker to build the superstructure.

* * *

16

Essays on the Gita

Reading by Monika Halan

Essays on the Gita[1] is Sri Aurobindo's commentary on the Bhagavad Gita, one of sixteen Gitas in the Mahabharata. It is not a verse-by-verse translation, but a deep dive into the integral message of the Gita that goes beyond and behind the words and the text. If the Bhagavad Gita is the subject of the painting, *Essays* is the canvas that throws into sharp focus the story, and gives the story behind the story. It gives context to the grand synthesis that the Gita aims to achieve through its core message of the synthesis of the yoga of works—Karma Yoga; yoga of knowledge—Jnana Yoga; and yoga of devotion—Bhakti Yoga; and of the seemingly disparate Indian philosophical traditions of Sankhya, Yoga, Vedanta, Vedavada and Brahmavada. The object of *Essays*, Sri Aurobindo wrote, '…is a scrutiny and positive affirmation of the substance of the Gita and a disengaging of its contribution to the abiding spiritual thought of humanity and its kernel of living practice…'[2]

Written as a set of two series in *Arya*, a monthly philosophical review published between the years 1915 and 1921, *Essays* was published for the first time as a book in 1949. The first series, which has twenty-four essays, covers the first six chapters of the Gita. The second series, which covers the remaining twelve chapters of the Gita, is in two parts. Part One, with twelve essays, is the synthesis of the three different yogic paths of works (*karma*), love (*bhakti*) and knowledge (*jnana*). Part Two, with another twelve essays, is about the supreme secret—the core meaning and message of the Gita.

The first few essays instruct the reader how to approach the Gita and what to look for in the text. In Sri Aurobindo's quintessential style, we learn what something is not, and eliminate all possible options to arrive at what is. For example, he asks—what should we look for in the Gita? He answers, and I paraphrase—not an absolute truth that is in conflict with any other truth. Not an intellectual enquiry into the text. Not a reading into aspects that are bound to the time it was written in and the contexts therefore. We read the Gita to find a living truth. A truth that, much like the divine spark in us, does not die. This truth is universal. It has been experienced and lived. We read the Gita to imbibe the spiritual truths that are living truths because they have been lived, experienced and verified. We read the Gita for its light and its living message, for our own (and of humanity's) perfection and highest spiritual welfare.[3]

In *Essays*, we meet the main protagonists in both their embodied and their representative forms. Krishna, for example, as the avatar, is the manifestation of the divine consciousness that is present in us, though veiled behind ignorance and ego. Sri Aurobindo writes that it would be a mistake to view Krishna as a purely historical figure (which he was) because he is much more than that. He is the eternal incarnation of the Divine and not only the historical teacher and leader of men (which, indeed, he also was). Krishna's role in the Mahabharata is similar to that of the spark of the divine consciousness in us—rarely in the forefront, but always a secret centre and a hidden guide. Just as the divine spark stands behind the drama of human life, so also Krishna is at the core of the story: guiding, teaching and directing.[4]

The human protagonist, the battleground and the crisis, as Sri Aurobindo shows us, is the setting of the stage. We understand that the importance of the battle is more than just as a physical fight; it represents the battlefield of our everyday lives. In Arjuna, we find a hero who is gutted by a gigantic crisis that calls into question everything he has stood for and believed in. The Yoga of the Dejection of Arjun, the first chapter of the Gita, is every person's story when the world just does not match up to their high standards. It is the story of every human being who is forced to see the spectacle of the universe as it really is, with the veil of the ethical illusion, the illusion of self-righteousness, torn from their eyes.

Readers of the Gita vary in their understanding of the text; the subtle core of almost every philosophy finds itself forgotten as coarser and more easily understood interpretations achieve popularity. *Essays* brings this deeper context as part of a larger story of synthesis in sharp focus. For example, in the first series,[5] Sri Aurobindo warns the reader to not fall into the trap of a selective reading of the Gita. He cautions the readers of the Gita against catching a part of its message and then convincing themselves that that partial view is indeed the entire message.

The Gita has been seen as a discipline for renunciation by some. Others see its message of devotion as the entire teaching. Many look at the Gita as a scripture of works, a guide to Karma Yoga, with great emphasis on one part of the message—not to be attached to the fruit of works. Condensing the message of the text into just a disinterested performance of duty as the highest and all-sufficient law limits the depth and breadth of the book. A narrow interpretation of following one's dharma would lead to a superficial morality rather than a rise to the deeper moral code of each person and its manifestation. Sri Aurobindo emphasized the danger of understanding the Gita too superficially with wry humour, 'I cannot think that the Gita would solve such an inner situation by sending Buddha back to his wife and father and the government of the Sakya State, or would direct a Ramakrishna to become a Pundit in a vernacular school and disinterestedly teach little boys their lessons…'[6]

Essays, in a line, is all about stitching together the subtle learning:[7]

> The message of the Gita is the gospel of the Divinity in man who by force of an increasing union unfolds himself out of the veil of the lower Nature reveals to the human soul his cosmic spirit, in all beings.

To read *Essays* is in itself a yoga. This is no light reading, and I doubt if any of Sri Aurobindo's works can ever come in the category of an easy onboarding. Readers may want to read a compilation of translated verses of the Gita which have been extracted from the *Essays* and put together in some editions.[8] But do note that Sri Aurobindo himself warned against taking these extracts from the *Essays* as *his* translation of the Gita.

There are three kinds of readers, and each could approach the book differently. For the casual reader, it is enough to open the book at any chapter and begin reading. While they will not get the entire story, the part that they will get is worth the effort. Though there is a running narrative, an expansive synthesis, within which are pods of insights and knowledge that the casual reader can benefit from. For example, in the first series' 'The Creed of the Aryan Fighter',[9] the casual reader could get the answer to a contemporary question—isn't God about love and peace? How then does Krishna ask Arjuna to choose war over peace? Or in the second series 'Deva and Asura',[10] the apparent contradiction between the liberated embodied soul being above the three gunas and yet performing works is resolved.

For the more serious reader, but one who is unfamiliar with the Gita or the Indian philosophical landscape, there is work to be done ahead of attempting to pick up *Essays*. It is a good idea to have a working knowledge of the Bhagavad Gita, some basics of Indian spirituality, philosophy and *itihaas* (Ramayana and Mahabharata) before you begin.

For the scholar who is in tune with the Gita and Indian philosophical traditions, this book will deepen and widen their understanding of the Gita, its context and the grand synthesis that Sri Aurobindo articulated, explained and painted over the forty-eight essays.

Whatever your own stage and state, the one message most readers will take away from the book is this:[11]

> Know then yourself; know your true self to be God and one with the self of all others; know your soul to be a portion of God. Live in what you know; live in the self, live in your supreme spiritual nature, be united with God and Godlike. Offer, first, all your actions as a sacrifice to the Highest and the One in you and to the Highest and the One in the world; deliver last all you are and do into his hands for the supreme and universal spirit to do through you his own will and works in the world. This is the solution that I present to you and in the end you will find that there is no other.

* * *

17

The Renaissance in India with a Defence of Indian Culture

Reading by Devdip Ganguli

The essays contained in this volume are of the greatest value to those who love India. They offer a comprehensive and deep understanding of Indian religion, spirituality, philosophy, culture, art and polity. Though written a century ago, these essays are increasingly relevant. Then, as now, the value of ancient Indian culture in the context of modernity was being actively debated. Then, as now, India stood at a crossroads with regards to its future direction, having to choose between a mindless aping of the West, a regression towards the religious and social conservatism of the past or an India ancient, yet modern, spiritual, yet life-embracing. In these pages, Sri Aurobindo reveals to us the ancient soul of India and indicates how her eternal message is central to the modern idea of India.

As the First World War drew to a close, the question of Indian independence rose once again to the fore. Indian revolutionaries demanded self-rule in return for the services of the hundreds of thousands of Indians who fought valiantly for Allied victory on battlefields in Europe, Africa and Asia. The British responded to these demands by dangling the carrot of limited reforms. At the same time, they argued that India was not ready for independence, that its people were politically, culturally, rationally, even spiritually, unprepared for freedom and nationhood, and that colonialism was necessary to 'civilize' India.

In this series of thirty-two brilliant and illuminating essays published in *Arya* between 1918 and 1921, Sri Aurobindo debunked this notion and revealed the full sweep and depth of Indian culture. He wrote these essays equally for English-educated Indians who, by virtue of their foreign upbringing, had almost as little knowledge of their heritage as their foreign counterparts. The work of reshaping the hearts and minds of modern Indian youth that began under the inspiration of Sri Ramakrishna and Swami Vivekananda continues with a wider import in the pages of this volume. The book is divided into four parts, in the order that they were published in *Arya:*[1] The Renaissance in India (1918),[2] Indian Culture and External Influence (1919),[3] Is India Civilised? (1918–19)[4] and A Defence of Indian Culture (1919–21).[5]

Even after Sri Aurobindo moved to Pondicherry in 1910, he remained deeply engaged with world events, as with the literary currents of his time. In fact, *The Future Poetry* (See Chapter 21) and this present volume were both written in response to a contemporary writer, the Irish critic James H. Cousins. The critic was associated with a small but remarkable group of persons such as Annie Besant, E.B. Havell, Abanindranath Tagore, O.C. Gangoly and others, who played a key role in igniting a movement of cultural renaissance in India in the first few decades of the twentieth century. A contemporary of W.B. Yeats and an important literary figure in Ireland, Cousins developed a keen interest in Indian spirituality and culture through the Theosophical movement. He moved to India in 1915, and continued writing and travelling, exploring connections between Celtic and Hindu mysticism. Towards the end of his life, he formally accepted the Hindu faith. Cousins met the Mother in Japan in 1919 a number of times,[6] and two years later, in 1921, met Sri Aurobindo in Pondicherry.[7] Sri Aurobindo had a high regard for his literary criticism. When the four essays constituting *The Renaissance in India* were first published separately as a book in 1920, the publisher's note stated, 'The subject matter of the book was written in a way of appreciation of Mr. James H. Cousins' book of the same name.'[8]

Sri Aurobindo believed in the inevitability of an Indian renaissance. As one of the primary architects of the freedom movement, he envisaged an India that would be at once rooted in its spiritual identity, and yet ready to embrace new forms of expression and living. He warned that the word 'renaissance' should not automatically tie India to a Western idea of scientific renewal and progress—not that these were undesirable, but that the Indian approach must be true to her own spirit. Nor was Sri Aurobindo sympathetic to revivalist movements of religious and social conservatism that upheld habits and traditions of the past as sacrosanct.

Sri Aurobindo's idea of an Indian renaissance was spiritual, the word spiritual understood in the widest, most integral sense, '...the attempt to know and live in the highest self, the divine, the all-embracing unity and to raise life in all its parts to the divinest possible values.'[9] His was not an ascetic call to cast away life for the sake of the 'abstract, the hidden and the intangible,'[10] but to make '...this higher view of life, this sense of deeper potentiality once more a creative, perhaps a dominant power in the world.'[11] And for this he posited that India had to once again '...get back entirely the native power of her spirit at its very deepest and turn all the needed strengths and aims of her present and future life into materials for that spirit to work upon and integrate and harmonise.'[12]

But the question remained—how should India assimilate modern and foreign influences without losing itself in the process of learning from the West? Sri Aurobindo answered this question in 'Indian Culture and External Influence'[13] by affirming that growth implies a movement of self-development from within, but equally the capacity to receive impact from the environment that becomes material for future growth:[14]

> [T]hose who live most powerfully in themselves, can also most largely use the world and all its material for the Self,—and, it must be added, most successfully help the world and enrich it out of their own being. The man who most finds and lives from the inner self, can most embrace the universal and become one with it; the Swarat, independent, self-possessed and self-ruler, can most be the Samrat, possessor and shaper of the world in which he lives, can most too grow one with all in the Atman... Therefore to live in one's self, determining one's self-expression from one's own centre of being in accordance with one's own law of being, swadharma, is the first necessity.

The next essay series in the volume, provocatively titled 'Is India Civilised?',[15] was written by Sri Aurobindo in response to a book of the same title[16] by Sir John Woodroffe, also known by his pseudonym Arthur Avalon, who published extensively on the Tantra and other Hindu traditions, and whose books can still be bought in Indian bookstores today. An ardent admirer and defender of Indian culture, Woodroffe's book was itself a response to a book[17] by an author of a very different breed, one William Archer, a Scottish writer and theatre critic who kept harping on the need for India to 'rationalise' itself as soon as possible, and whose understanding of Indian culture may be gleaned from the following passage: 'Barbarian, barbarism, barbarous—I am sorry to harp so much on these words. But they express the essence of the situation...the plain truth concerning the mass of the [Indian] population—and not the poorer classes alone—is that they are *not civilized people*.'[18] (Emphasis in the original.)

Sri Aurobindo countered Archer's hostile and ignorant assertions throughout the course of this volume, but ignored Archer's political motive and his other extreme statements, and took up this criticism of Indian culture as one representative perspective of the time, widening the issue to a universal question—does the future of India, and even humanity as a whole, lie in the direction of installing science and reason as the fundamental truth of existence, or does humanity have a spiritual destiny? And what do we understand by spirituality? Against the kind of criticism that Archer represented, Sri Aurobindo argued in favour of an 'aggressive defence', an active effort to not just assimilate whatever is useful from the West, but also to create new and powerful formations true to its own spirit:[19]

> If we are to live at all, we must resume India's great interrupted endeavour; we must take up boldly and execute thoroughly in the individual and in the society, in the spiritual and in the mundane life, in philosophy and religion, in art and literature, in thought, in political and economic and social formulation the full and unlimited sense of her highest spirit and knowledge.

The largest and, arguably, most important section of this volume is the final series—'A Defence of Indian Culture',[20] consisting of essays organized across five themes—culture, spirituality and life, art, literature and polity. It is important to reiterate that these essays are not just of historical interest. They speak equally to the modern reader, for though India has been an independent country for seventy-five years, many of us remain shackled in narrow perspectives, and our understanding of Indian culture and religion is, for the most part, still shallow.

These essays offer readers many useful tools and insights as they deepen their engagement with India.

One learns, for instance, how to study a culture from various standpoints: the sympathetic, the dispassionate and the hostile, each with their own utility.[21] We understand how the culture of a people may be roughly described as the expression of a consciousness of life which formulates itself in three aspects, the soul, mind and body of a culture.[22] We are presented with the outlines of what Sri Aurobindo calls the 'triple quartette', a system of social organization to bridge the outer realities of human existence to the spiritual truths central to Hinduism.[23] Ideas that are intensely debated and discussed even today are taken up, such as, secularism[24] in the Indian context, concepts such as dharma and adhikara,[25] or social constructs such as the chaturvarna system that later degraded into the caste system.[26] We learn how all great cultures pass through three stages—a loose formation, then a fixing of forms, and finally disintegration—but also how there is always the possibility of a renaissance if the culture is able to renew itself.[27] Time and again we learn from these pages that Hinduism has a profoundly spiritual aim that seeks to influence every aspect of life and appeal to every individual in the measure that they can respond to its call, and that everything in Indian society and culture, even its failures, must be seen and understood in the light of this bold conception.

In the five essays under 'Indian Spirituality and Life', Sri Aurobindo takes his readers to the very heart and soul of Hinduism, not understood as some narrow, limited faith, but as a universal creed that contains in its depths the basis for a spiritual awakening of the deepest and highest kind. But what is Hinduism for Sri Aurobindo? In essence, he says, Hinduism has three ideas that suffice to define it comprehensively:[28] the existence of one absolute reality, call it what you will, which it is the duty of the individual to realise; that there are multiple ways to approach this Eternal and Infinite, a thousand paths, a thousand forms; and that this Divinity may be found within us as well, for It resides in us. 'These three things put together are the whole of Hindu religion, its essential sense and, if any credo is needed, its credo.'[29] This apparently simple perspective is, in fact, revelatory, for in one sweep it casts aside doctrinal and traditional differences and unites the many strands of this ancient culture, linking every development of Indian spirituality from the Vedas onwards in a movement of continuous growth and many-sided expansion.

And indeed, in the very next chapter,[30] Sri Aurobindo provides a comprehensive overview of each of the major spiritual ages of India, starting from the Vedas, to the Upanishads, to the Puranas and Darshanas, Buddhism, the system of Tantra, the various philosophical schools, right down to the Bhakti movement. The treatment of these movements is not academic; instead, it takes the reader straight to the spiritual essence of the age. As such, this is a priceless text to help us understand the spiritual history of India from the perspective of consciousness.

Sri Aurobindo also argues forcefully that ancient India engaged with life powerfully and creatively, whether it was through the lives of its numerous rulers, rishis and saints, or its scientists and mathematicians, thus putting to rest the lie that ancient India did not succeed adequately in life. He reveals to readers the secrets of Indian art, on how to see and appreciate the most spiritually inspired creative works the world has ever seen, be it in the form of architecture,[31] sculpture,[32] or painting.[33] Similarly, he takes up literature and presents detailed literary commentaries on the Vedas,[34] the Upanishads,[35] the Mahabharata and Ramayana,[36] classical Sanskrit writers such as Kalidasa and Bhartirihari[37] and even later writers in the regional tongues such as Vidyapati and Chandidas (Bengali), Ramdas and Tukaram (Marathi), Tiruvalluvar and the Alwars (Tamil),[38] always bringing out the spiritual import and value of these texts, and their role in the story of India. Finally, in the polity of ancient India too, Sri Aurobindo traces the development of a culture that tried its best to manifest the highest truth and idealism in a still imperfect and unready humanity, highlighting the earliest expressions of democratic forms of governance in the subcontinent, emphasising the central role of dharma in both individual and collective life, while acknowledging at the same time the failures that affected Indian polity.[39]

But Sri Aurobindo's approach to Indian culture is not backward-looking. He does not present a perfect golden age, a past that we must revert to. On the contrary, while recognizing the tremendous value of past realizations, his eyes are clearly fixed towards the work ahead, to what we must manifest. In my view, the most valuable insight in this volume is Sri Aurobindo's linking of India's past knowledge, present work and future destiny, to his own life's work and mission—the full and complete transformation of human nature and society.

Looking at the three large stages that Indian culture must traverse, he writes that the first two are complete, '...while a third has taken its initial steps and is the destiny of her future.'[40] The first is the Vedic age; and the second, the Purano-Tantric, or much of what we understand by Hinduism today, a combination of external worship and a growing psychological nearness to the Divine. Then Sri Aurobindo continues:[41]

> There has been long in preparation a third stage which belongs to the future...This greatest movement of the Indian spiritual mind has a double impulse...a highest vision which sees the possibility not only of an ascent towards the Eternal but of a descent of the Divine Consciousness and a change of human

> into divine nature....Its index vision is pointed to a truth that exceeds the human mind and, if at all realised in his members, would turn human life into a divine superlife.

Thus, for Sri Aurobindo, the rise of India, her religion, her spirituality, her culture, her art, her polity, is important not just for herself, but intimately tied to the future of the human race as well. It is in this sense that the popular idea of the *vishwaguru*, or world-guru, may be rightly understood. A militarily powerful, economically prosperous India is not adequate; it is only when the truth of India's soul manifests in its fullness that Indian culture may be said to have fulfilled its eternal purpose, its Sanatana Dharma. Only then '...can Indian civilization be said to have discharged its mission, to have spoken its last word... crowned and complete in its office of mediation between the life of man and the spirit'.[42]

In a nation seeking its roots but still confused and pulled in many directions, the essays in this volume invite us to realize once again the glory of ancient India within ourselves and manifest it in forms and expressions suitable to our age.

* * *

18

The Life Divine

Reading by Matthijs Cornelissen

In his own eyes, Sri Aurobindo was not a philosopher, but he did write philosophy, and *The Life Divine*[1] is his main philosophical work. In it, he described what he saw as the basic structure of the world: how the world must have come into being and where it is going; how we can know about it; what our role is as individuals in this huge, seemingly impersonal universe; why there is so much ignorance, pain and incapacity; why we humans have hope in spite of everything, and, perhaps most encouragingly, why this hope is justified. Sri Aurobindo did not arrive at this conclusion lightly, but on the basis of a well worked-out and finely detailed 'theory of existence'.[2] It is a theory that he constructed over many years from what he considered the very best that Indian and European civilizations have developed: the Indian understanding of consciousness and the subjective pole of reality, and the European understanding of matter and the objective pole. The integration of both led him to the vision of an ongoing evolution of consciousness, which forms the central theme of *The Life Divine* and, in one way or another, of almost all his other writings.

The first chapter of *The Life Divine*, 'The Human Aspiration', is devoted to this hope, this aspiration, and this striving of humanity for a better future:[3]

> The earliest preoccupation of man … is also the highest which his thought can envisage. It manifests itself in … the impulse towards perfection, the search after pure Truth and unmixed Bliss, … God, Light, Freedom, Immortality.

Sri Aurobindo then argues that the very fact that these ideals persist and return after each period in which they are forgotten or clouded over, indicates that they are based on a deep inner sense that this absolute perfection must be there somewhere. And when we object that such a utopian future would need a rather unlikely miracle, he points out that nature is in the habit of delivering miracles. If all we knew were the huge and barren vastness of galaxies, stars and planets, could we have thought of flowers and fruit trees, their incredible complexity, their elegance, their aspiration towards the light, their generosity? And when all this gentle beauty of the plant world was there, could anyone have imagined that nature would produce animals with but a small part of their physical body that would enable them to think, plan actions and become co-creators of the world? And then, if we look at the scale, the ingenuity, the absolute marvel of what nature has managed till now, are we to conclude that the humanity we now have is the endpoint of this evolution? Are we a worthy outcome of such gigantic labour? That's hard to believe. At best, we can claim to be transitional beings, creatures on their way towards something more beautiful, something more in harmony with the genius that has manifested this incredible world.

And so, after having put the proud human race in its place, Sri Aurobindo looks in the next two chapters at why neither

Europe nor India has found a fully satisfactory solution to what he calls in *Savitri*[4] (See Chapter 29) the 'indignity of mortal life',[5] and highlights the bankruptcy of both life and spirit acting exclusively:[6]

> In Europe and in India, respectively, the negation of the materialist and the refusal of the ascetic have sought to assert themselves as the sole truth and to dominate the conception of Life. In India, if the result has been a great heaping up of the treasures of the Spirit, – or of some of them, – it has also been a great bankruptcy of Life; in Europe, the fullness of riches and the triumphant mastery of this world's powers and possessions have progressed towards an equal bankruptcy in the things of the Spirit.

Sri Aurobindo then works out what deserves to be respected and what can safely be discarded from these two knowledge systems and begins the exposition of his own more integral vision. The core of that vision is his concept of consciousness, which differs radically from that of mainstream science, and even from that of most Indian traditions.

Science provides no consensus about what consciousness is, but the dominant view takes it as the kind of sense-based awareness that ordinary humans have of their surroundings and of their intentions, thoughts, feelings and sensations. Since it takes physical reality as primary, it assumes that consciousness is dependent on a working nervous system.

Among the Indian knowledge traditions there is no consensus either, but most have a much wider understanding of what consciousness is. Almost all of them[7] take an absolute, transcendent consciousness as the primary reality and hold that this transcendent consciousness has manifested not only the physical world, but also a complex hierarchy of subtle worlds located between the superconscious Divine above and the subconscious physical world below. They also agree that yoga[8] can help us overcome the pain and suffering inherent in our human lives by leading us back to the silent Consciousness of our origin.

While the Western and Indian traditions are in many ways mirror images of each other, both have managed, at least to some extent, to prove their point: both work. Western science has given humanity an unprecedented mastery over the physical world. Indian knowledge systems have given humanity effective methods to reach the absolute bliss of the Transcendent. But still, something is missing in both. An obvious issue is that both sides tend to deny the relevance, if not the reality, of what the other side has worked out. But there is another, perhaps even more serious problem. Sri Aurobindo argues that both have focused too exclusively on the passive side of consciousness, on awareness. Science, because it considers physical reality to be a closed system, upon which something as immaterial as consciousness cannot have any influence. The Indian traditions, because developing it leads to various powers which can distract the seeker and make reaching the Divine more difficult and perilous.[9]

Technology has been used, from the very beginning, for weapons as well as for tools, and our technical solutions tend to destroy the innate harmony of nature. Yoga and meditation allow some individuals to escape, but don't solve the social and economic problems humanity faces. So, what is wrong with humanity? Science takes it that evolution is a product of necessity and chance, and so it has no way of predicting anything radically new. But why did the Indian tradition not find the harmony between spirit and matter?

Sri Aurobindo has an interesting explanation. He says that when the Vedic age gave way to the more intellectual later traditions, the integrality of the older understanding was

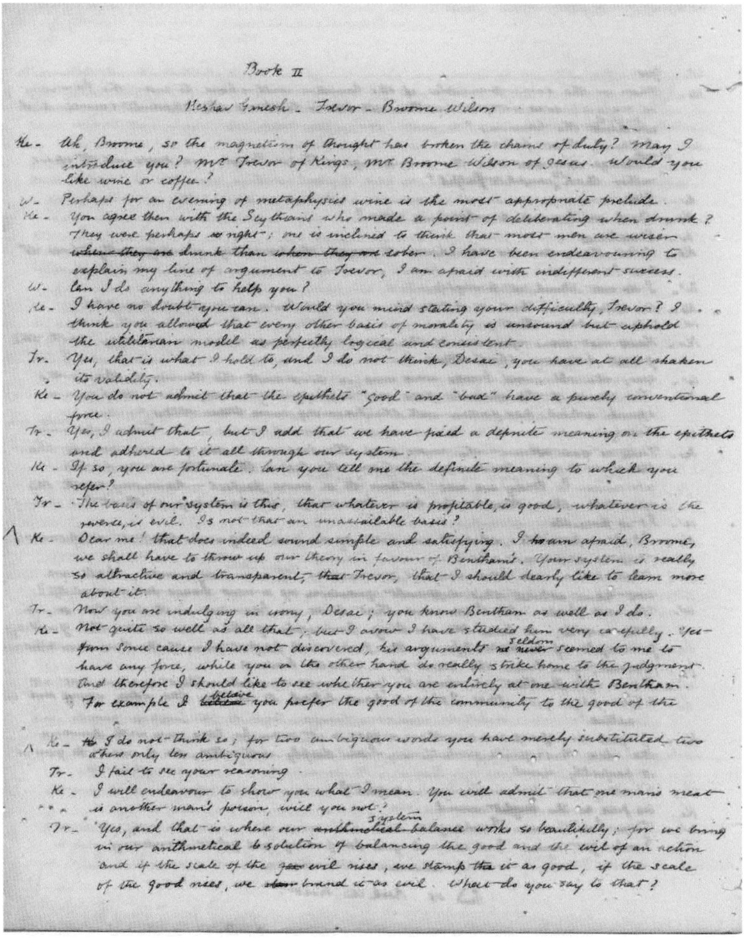
Book II

Keshav Ganesh – Trevor – Broome Wilson

Ke – Ah, Broome, so the magnetism of thought has broken the chains of duty? May I introduce you? Mr Trevor of Kings, Mr Broome Wilson of Jesus. Would you like wine or coffee?

W – Perhaps for an evening of metaphysics wine is the most appropriate prelude.

Ke – You agree then with the Scythians who made a point of deliberating when drunk? They were perhaps ~~so~~ right; one is inclined to think that most men are wiser ~~when they are~~ drunk than ~~when they are~~ sober. I have been endeavouring to explain my line of argument to Trevor, I am afraid with indifferent success.

W – Can I do anything to help you?

Ke – I have no doubt you can. Would you mind stating your difficulty, Trevor? I think you allowed that every other basis of morality is unsound but uphold the utilitarian model as perfectly logical and consistent.

Tr. Yes, that is what I hold to, and I do not think, Desai, you have at all shaken its validity.

Ke – You do not admit that the epithets "good" and "bad" have a purely conventional force.

Tr – Yes, I admit that, but I add that we have fixed a definite meaning on the epithets and adhered to it all through our system.

Ke – If so, you are fortunate. Can you tell me the definite meaning to which you refer?

Tr – The basis of our system is this, that whatever is profitable, is good, whatever is the reverse, is evil. Is not that an unassailable basis?

Ke – Dear me! that does indeed sound simple and satisfying. I ~~h~~ am afraid, Broome, we shall have to throw up our theory in favour of Bentham's. Your system is really so attractive and transparent, ~~that~~ Trevor, that I should dearly like to learn more about it.

Tr – Now you are indulging in irony, Desai; you know Bentham as well as I do.

Ke – Not quite so well as all that, but I avow I have studied him very carefully. Yet from some cause I have not discovered, his arguments ~~ne~~ ~~never~~ seldom seemed to me to have any force, while you on the other hand do really strike home to the judgment. And therefore I should like to see whether you are entirely at one with Bentham. For example I ~~believe~~ believe you prefer the good of the community to the good of the

Ke – ~~He~~ I do not think so; for two ambiguous words you have merely substituted two others only less ambiguous.

Tr – I fail to see your reasoning.

Ke – I will endeavour to show you what I mean. You will admit that one man's meat is another man's poison, will you not?

Tr – Yes, and that is where our ~~arithmetical balance~~ system works so beautifully; for we bring in our arithmetical solution of balancing the good and the evil of an action and if the scale of the ~~goo~~ evil rises, we stamp ~~tha~~ it as good, if the scale of the good rises, we ~~stam~~ brand it as evil. What do you say to that?

A page of 'The Harmony of Virtue' (*Volume 1, The Complete Works of Sri Aurobindo*)

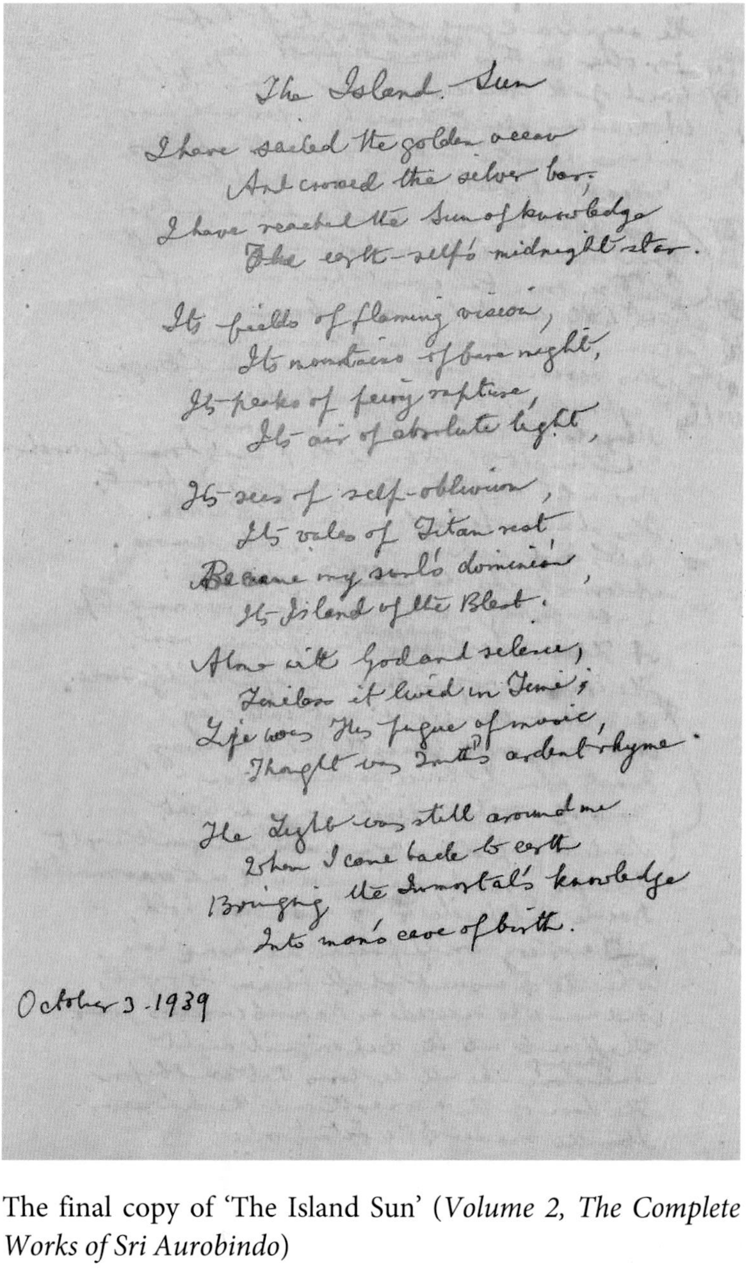

The final copy of 'The Island Sun' (*Volume 2, The Complete Works of Sri Aurobindo*)

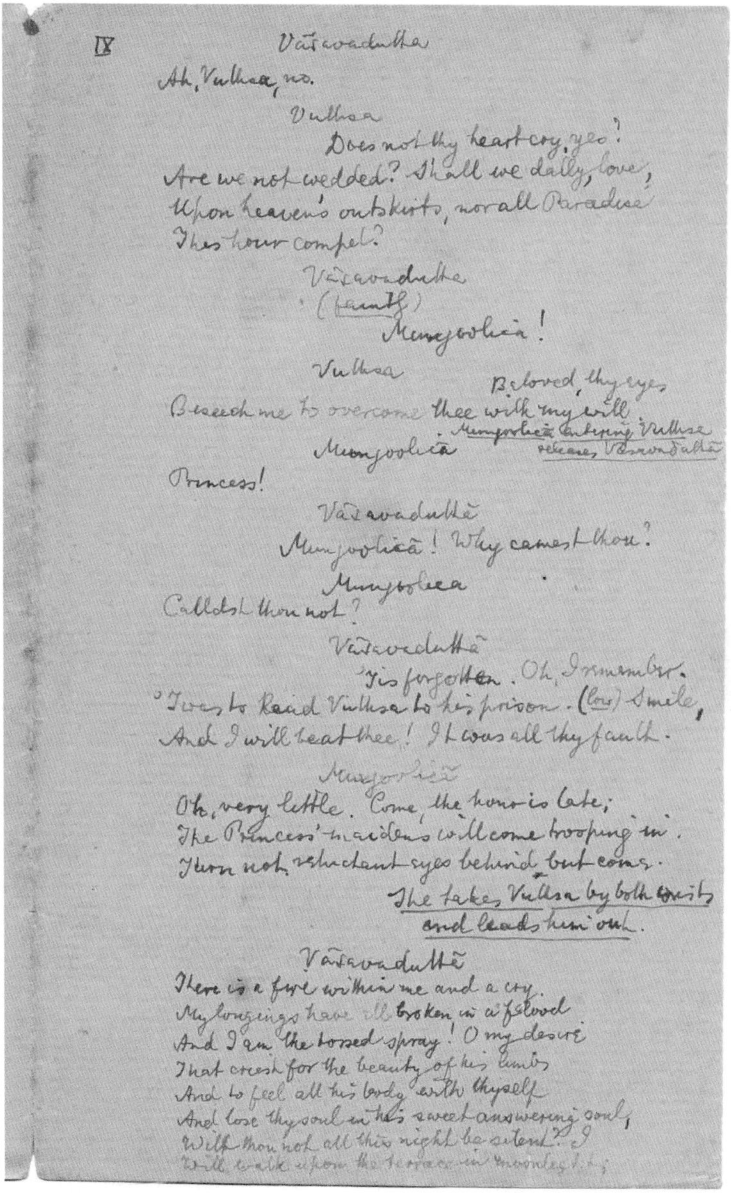
IX Vasavadutta
Ah, Vuthsa, no.
Vuthsa
Does not thy heart cry, yes?
Are we not wedded? Shall we dally, love,
Upon heaven's outskirts, nor all Paradise
This hour compel?
Vasavadutta
(faintly)
Mungoolica!
Vuthsa
Beloved, thy eyes
Beseech me to overcome thee with my will.
Mungoolica entering. Vuthsa releases Vasavadutta
Mungoolica
Princess!
Vasavadutta
Mungoolica! Why camest thou?
Mungoolica
Calldst thou not?
Vasavadutta
'Tis forgotten. Oh, I remember.
'Twas to lead Vuthsa to his prison. (low) Smile,
And I will beat thee! It was all thy fault.
Mungoolica
Oh, very little. Come, the hour is late;
The Princess' maidens will come trooping in.
Turn not reluctant eyes behind, but come.
She takes Vuthsa by both wrists and leads him out.
Vasavadutta
There is a fire within me and a cry.
My longings have all broken in a flood
And I am the tossed spray! O my desire
That criest for the beauty of his limbs
And to feel all his body with thyself
And lose thy soul in his sweet answering soul,
Wilt thou not all this night be silent? I
Will walk upon the terrace in moonlight;

A page of 'Vasavadutta' (*Volume 4, The Complete Works of Sri Aurobindo*)

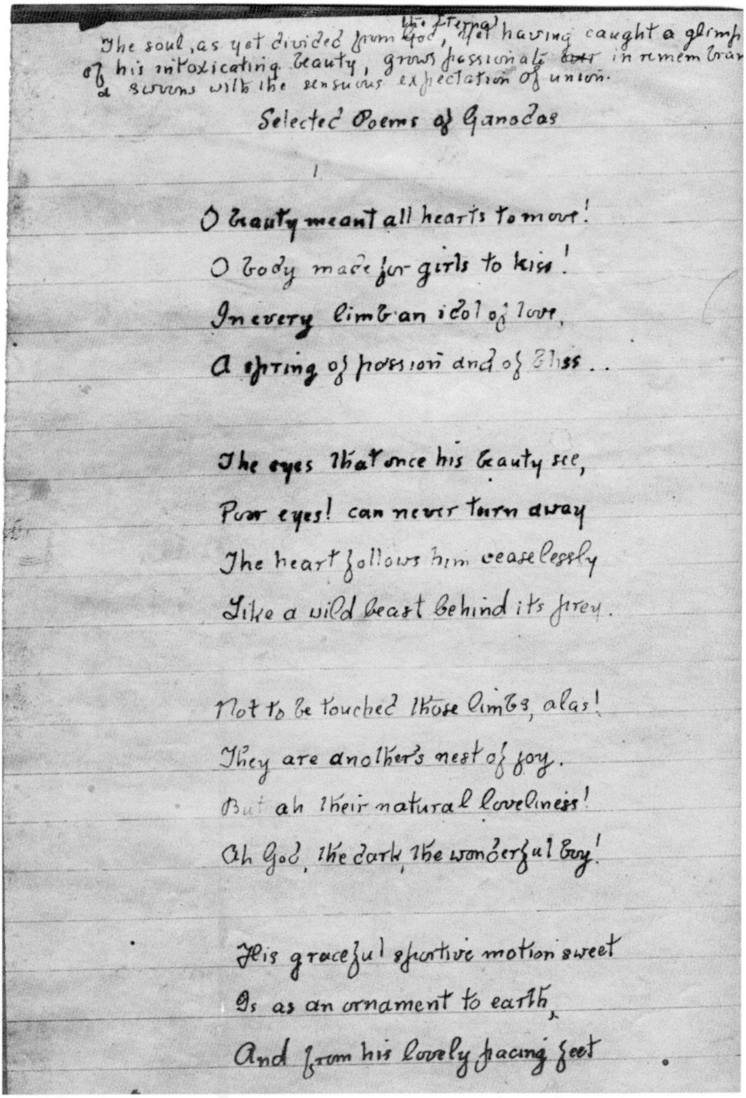

The soul, as yet divided from the Eternal, yet having caught a glimpse of his intoxicating beauty, grows passionate in remembrance & sorrows with the sensuous expectation of union.

Selected Poems of Ganodas

1

O beauty meant all hearts to move!
O body made for girls to kiss!
In every limb an idol of love,
A spring of passion and of bliss..

The eyes that once his beauty see,
Poor eyes! can never turn away
The heart follows him ceaselessly
Like a wild beast behind its prey.

Not to be touched those limbs, alas!
They are another's nest of joy.
But ah their natural loveliness!
Ah God, the dark, the wonderful boy!

His graceful sportive motion sweet
Is as an ornament to earth,
And from his lovely pacing feet

A page of 'Selected Poems of Ganodas' (*Volume 5, The Complete Works of Sri Aurobindo*)

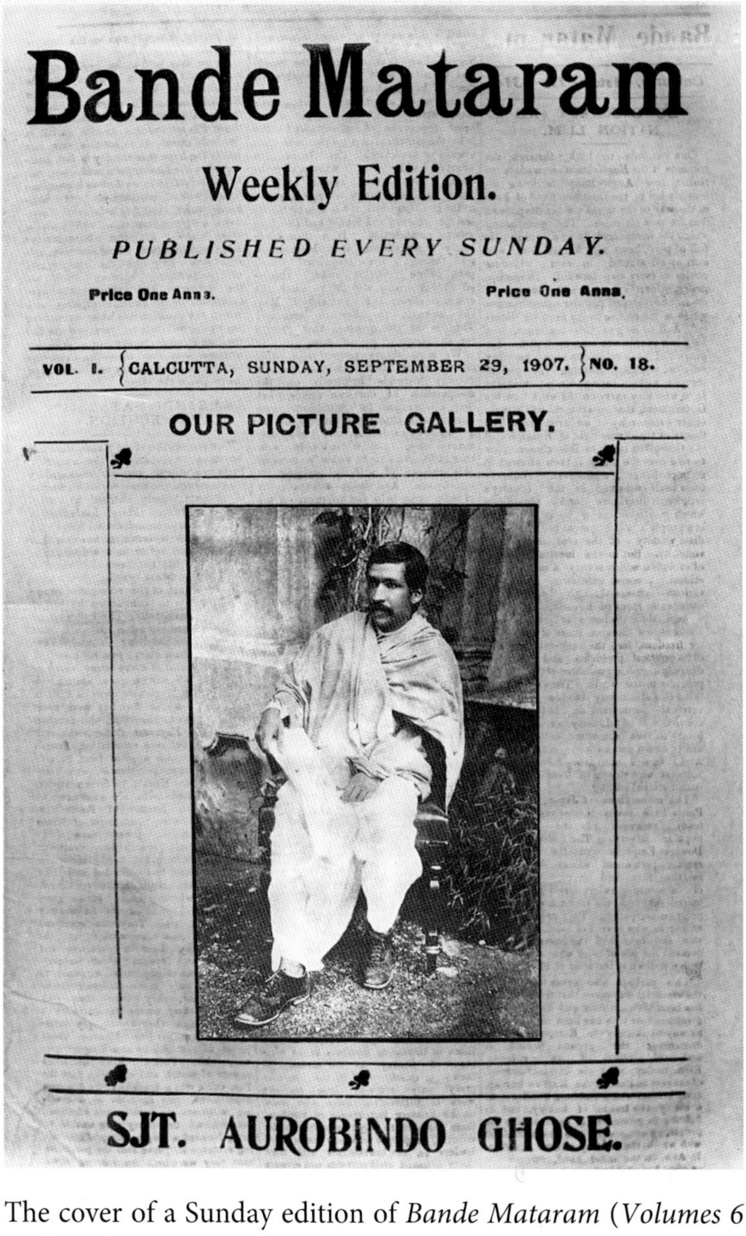

Bande Mataram

Weekly Edition.

PUBLISHED EVERY SUNDAY.

Price One Anna. **Price One Anna.**

VOL. I. CALCUTTA, SUNDAY, SEPTEMBER 29, 1907. **NO. 18.**

OUR PICTURE GALLERY.

SJT. AUROBINDO GHOSE.

The cover of a Sunday edition of *Bande Mataram* (*Volumes 6 and 7, The Complete Works of Sri Aurobindo*)

REGISTEREDNO. C532.

SUBSCRIPTION RUPEES 5.

SINGLE COPY ANNAS 2.

A WEEKLY REVIEW

OF

National Religion, Literature, Science, Philosophy, &c.,

Vol. I. | SATURDAY 7th AUGUST 1909. | No. 7.

Contributors :—SJ.. Aurobindo Ghose and others

OFFICE :—14 SHAM BAZAR STREET,
CALCUTTA.

The cover of an issue of *Karmayogin* (*Volume 8, The Complete Works of Sri Aurobindo*)

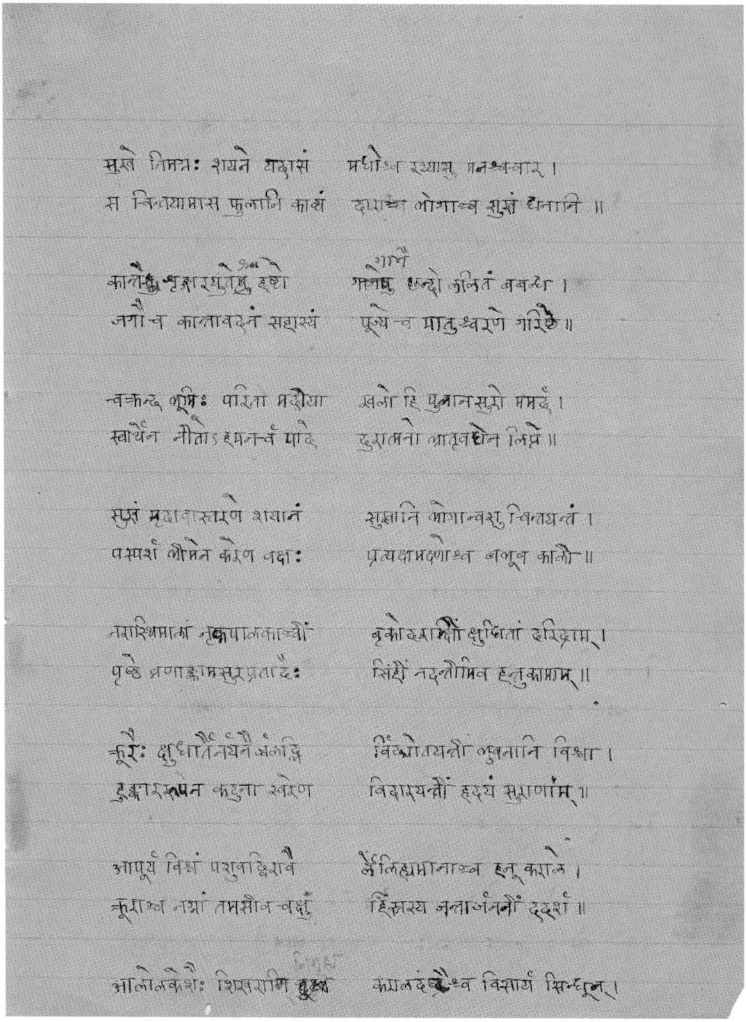

The first page of 'Bhavani Bharati' (*Volume 9, The Complete Works of Sri Aurobindo*)

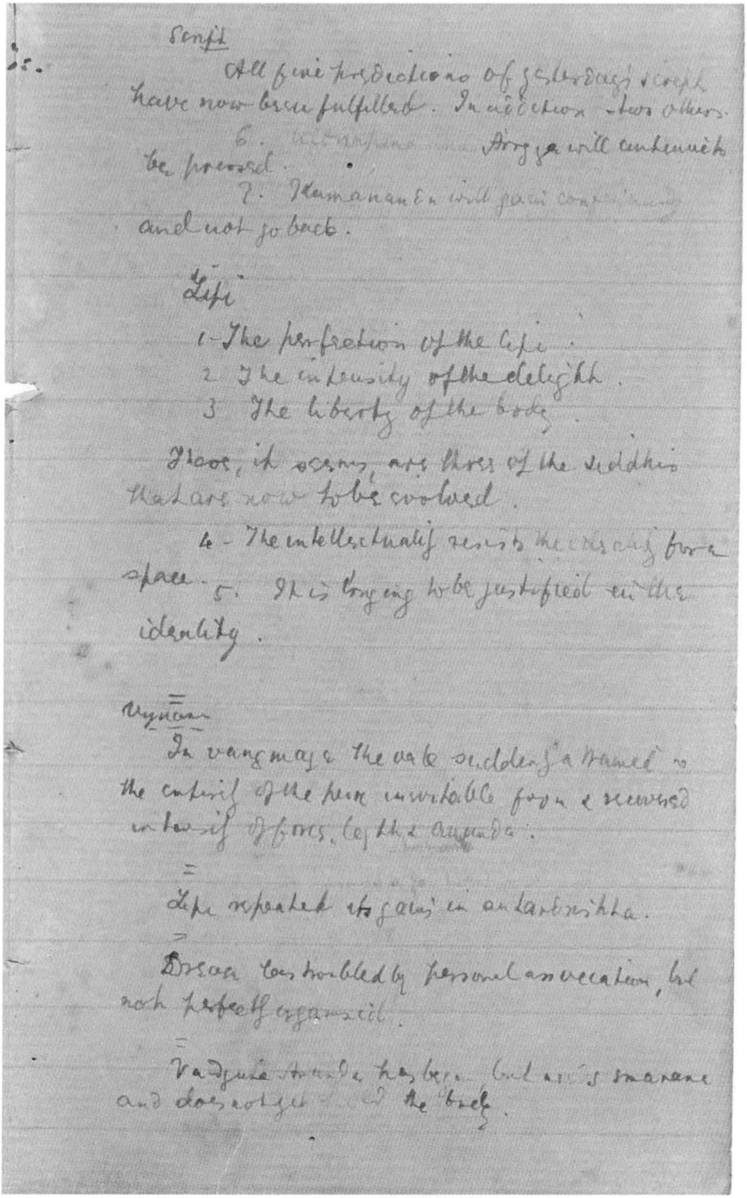
Script

All five predictions of yesterday's script have now been fulfilled. In addition two others.

6. [illegible] Arogya will continue to be pressed.

7. Ramananda will pass [illegible] and not go back.

Life

1. The perfection of the life.
2. The intensity of the delight.
3. The liberty of the body.

These, it seems, are three of the siddhis that are now to be evolved.

4. The intellectuality resists the [illegible] from space. 5. It is trying to be justified in the identity.

Vijnana

In vangmaya the vak suddenly attained to the entire [illegible] inevitable from a renewed intensity of force, [illegible].

Lipi repeated its gains in antariksha.

Drsya controlled by personal concentration, but not perfectly organised.

[illegible] has been, but [illegible] and does not [illegible] the body.

The entry of 3 December 1914 in the *Record of Yoga* (*Volume 10, The Complete Works of Sri Aurobindo*)

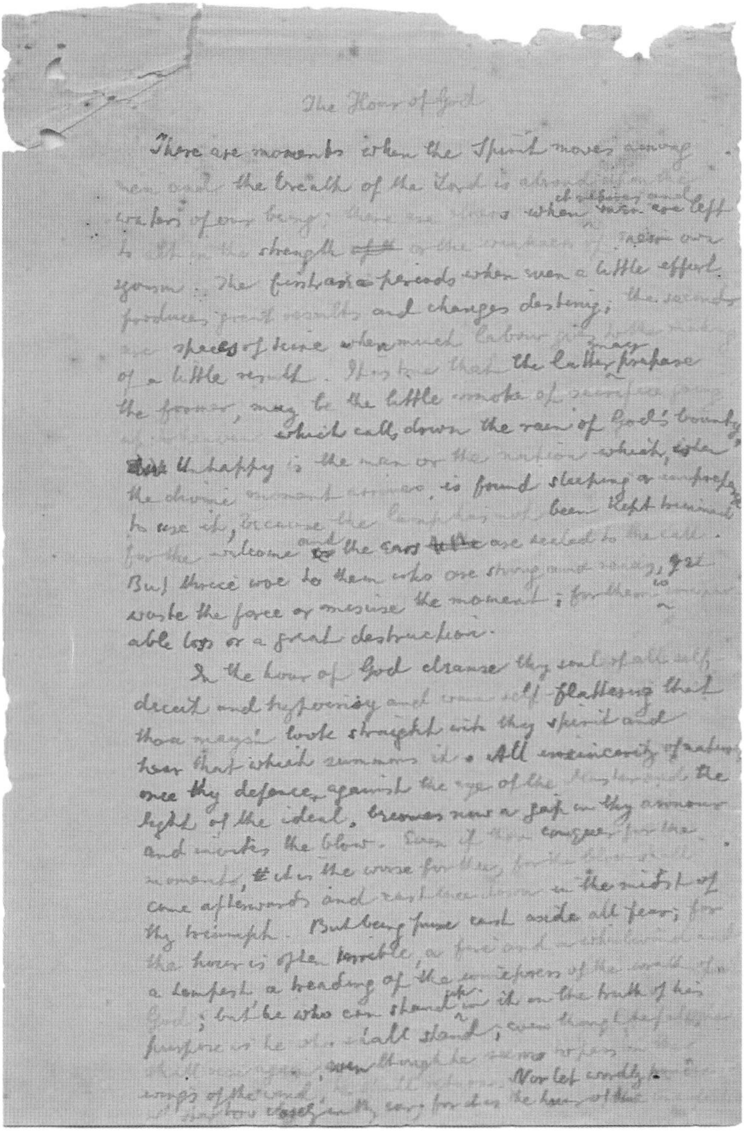

The first page of 'The Hour of God' (*Volume 12, The Complete Works of Sri Aurobindo*)

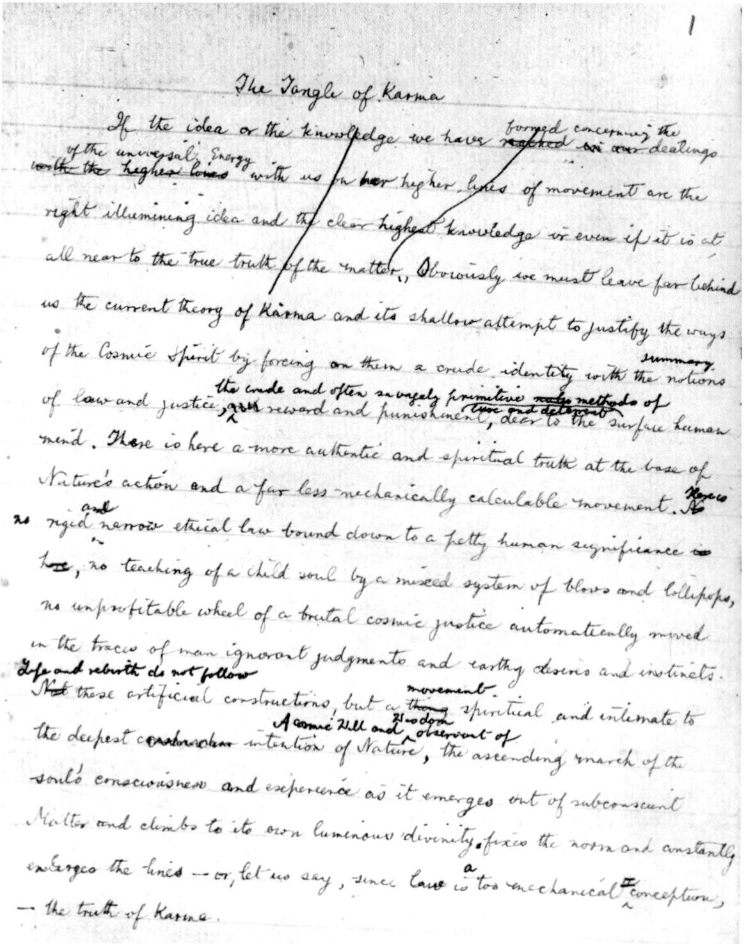
The Tangle of Karma

If the idea or the knowledge we have formed concerning the dealings of the universal Energy with us on higher lines of movement are the right illumining idea and the clear highest knowledge or even if it is at all near to the true truth of the matter, Obviously we must leave far behind us the current theory of Karma and its shallow attempt to justify the ways of the Cosmic Spirit by forcing on them a crude identity with the summary notions of law and justice, the crude and often savagely primitive methods of reward and punishment, lure and deterrent, dear to the surface human mind. There is here a more authentic and spiritual truth at the base of Nature's action and a far less mechanically calculable movement. Here is no rigid and narrow ethical law bound down to a petty human significance, no teaching of a child soul by a mixed system of blows and lollipops, no unprofitable wheel of a brutal cosmic justice automatically moved in the traces of man ignorant judgments and earthly desires and instincts. Life and rebirth do not follow these artificial constructions, but a movement spiritual and intimate to the deepest intention of Nature, A cosmic Will and Wisdom observant of the ascending march of the soul's consciousness and experience as it emerges out of subconscient Matter and climbs to its own luminous divinity, fixes the norm and constantly enlarges the lines — or, let us say, since law is a too mechanical conception, — the truth of Karma.

A page of 'The Tangle of Karma' (*Volume 13, The Complete Works of Sri Aurobindo*)

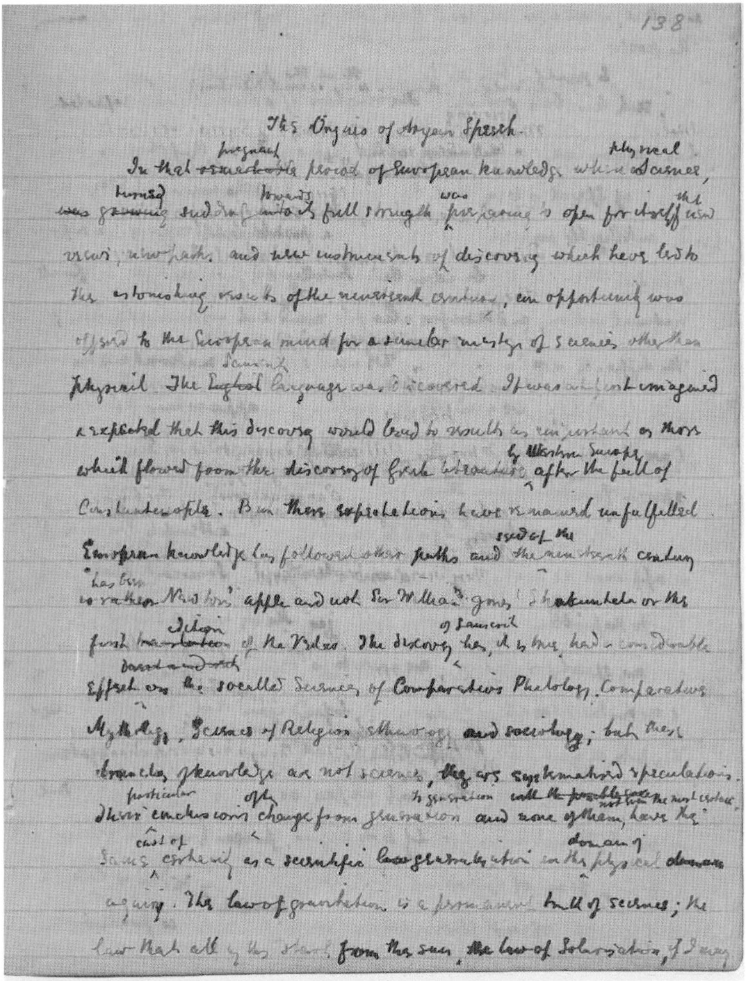

The first page of 'The Origins of Aryan Speech' (*Volume 14, The Complete Works of Sri Aurobindo*)

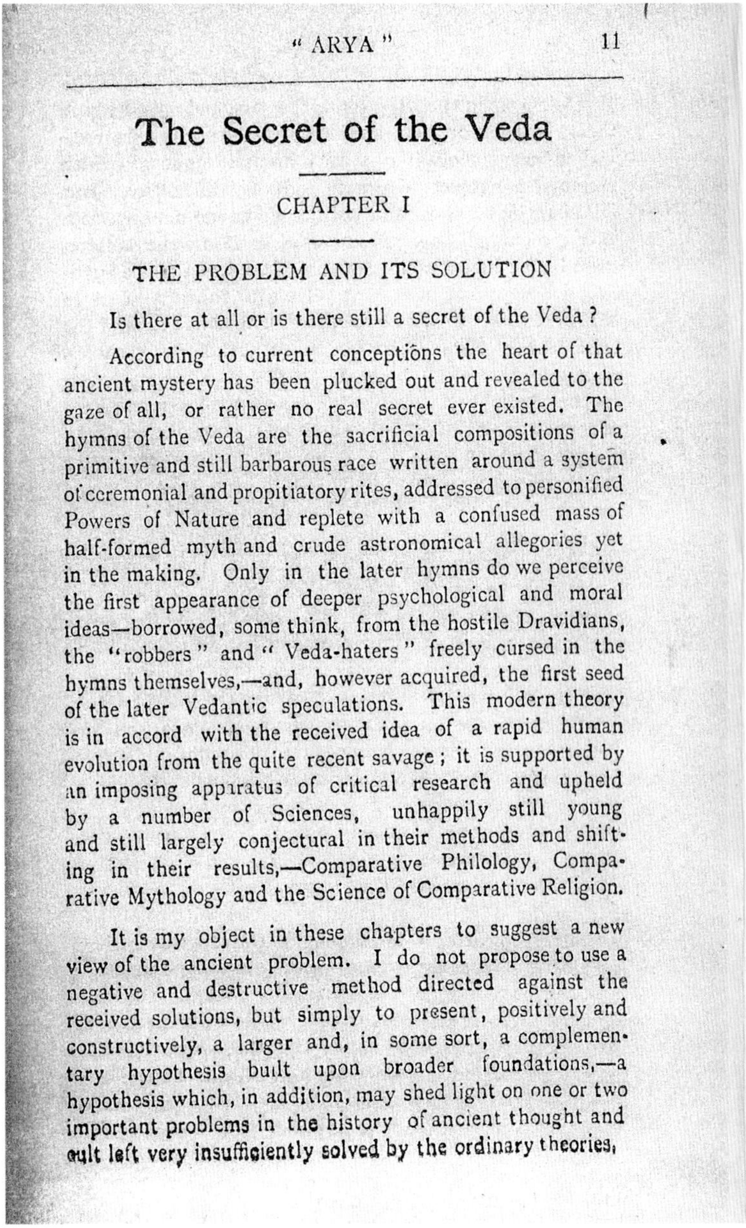

“ARYA” 11

The Secret of the Veda

CHAPTER I

THE PROBLEM AND ITS SOLUTION

Is there at all or is there still a secret of the Veda ?

According to current conceptions the heart of that ancient mystery has been plucked out and revealed to the gaze of all, or rather no real secret ever existed. The hymns of the Veda are the sacrificial compositions of a primitive and still barbarous race written around a system of ceremonial and propitiatory rites, addressed to personified Powers of Nature and replete with a confused mass of half-formed myth and crude astronomical allegories yet in the making. Only in the later hymns do we perceive the first appearance of deeper psychological and moral ideas—borrowed, some think, from the hostile Dravidians, the “robbers” and “Veda-haters” freely cursed in the hymns themselves,—and, however acquired, the first seed of the later Vedantic speculations. This modern theory is in accord with the received idea of a rapid human evolution from the quite recent savage ; it is supported by an imposing apparatus of critical research and upheld by a number of Sciences, unhappily still young and still largely conjectural in their methods and shifting in their results,—Comparative Philology, Comparative Mythology and the Science of Comparative Religion.

It is my object in these chapters to suggest a new view of the ancient problem. I do not propose to use a negative and destructive method directed against the received solutions, but simply to present, positively and constructively, a larger and, in some sort, a complementary hypothesis built upon broader foundations,—a hypothesis which, in addition, may shed light on one or two important problems in the history of ancient thought and cult left very insufficiently solved by the ordinary theories,

A page of *The Secret of the Veda* in the *Arya* (*Volume 8, The Complete Works of Sri Aurobindo*)

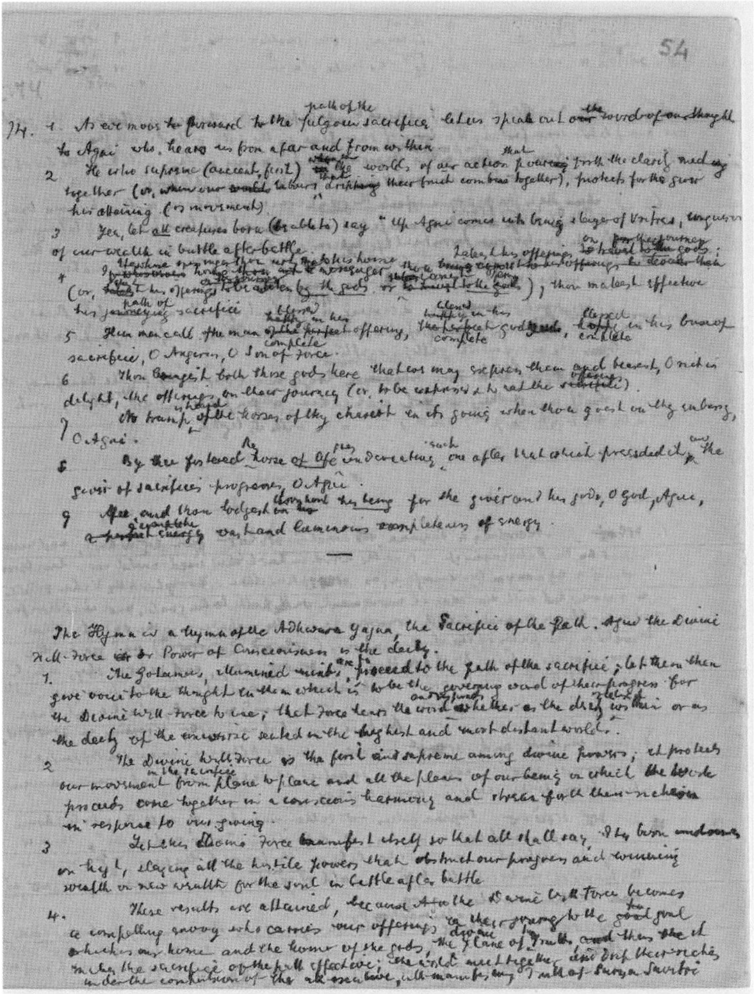

A page of Sri Aurobindo's translation of Rig Veda Mandala I, Sukta 74 (*Volume 16, The Complete Works of Sri Aurobindo*)

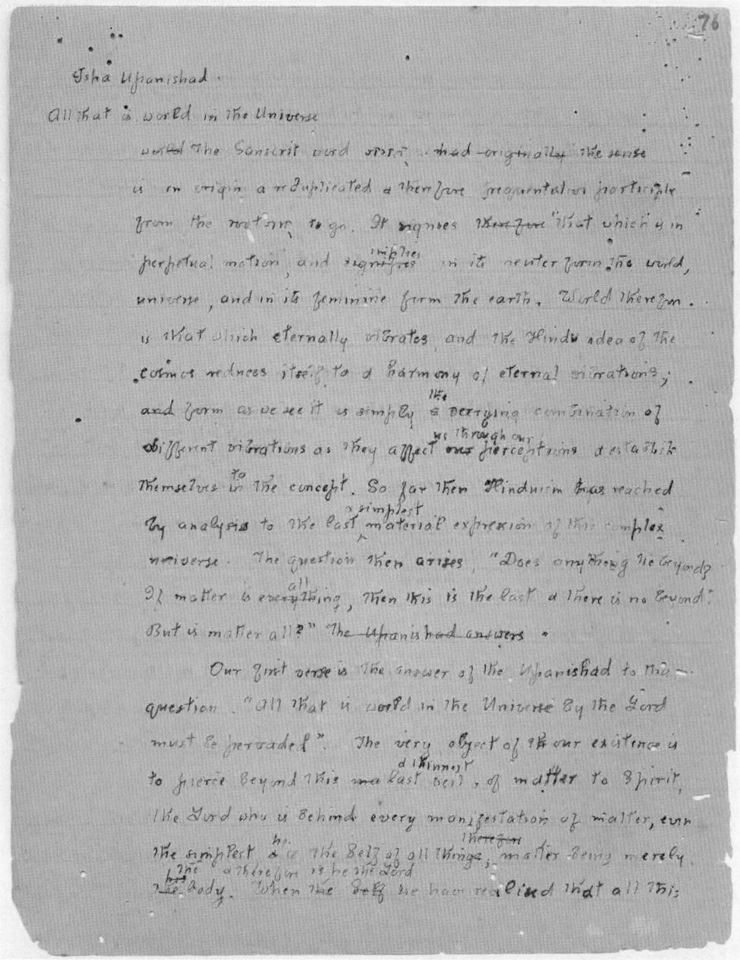
76

Isha Upanishad.

All that is world in the Universe

~~world~~ The Sanscrit word जगत् ~~had originally the sense~~ is in origin a reduplicated & therefore frequentative participle from the root गम् to go. It signifies ~~therefore~~ "that which is in perpetual motion", and ~~signifies~~ implies in its neuter form the world, universe, and in its feminine form the earth. World therefore is that which eternally vibrates, and the Hindu idea of the cosmos reduces itself to a harmony of eternal vibrations; and form as we see it is simply ~~a~~ the varying combination of different vibrations as they affect ~~our~~ us through our perceptions & establish themselves ~~in~~ to the concept. So far then Hinduism has reached by analysis to the last simplest material expression of this complex universe. The question then arises, "Does anything lie beyond? If matter is ~~everything~~ all, then this is the last & there is no Beyond. But is matter all?" The ~~Upanishad answers~~.

Our first verse is the answer of the Upanishad to this question. "All that is world in the Universe by the Lord must be pervaded". The very object of ~~th~~ our existence is to pierce beyond this ~~ma~~ last, thinnest veil, of matter to Spirit, the Lord who is behind every manifestation of matter, even the simplest & is the Self of all things, matter being therefore merely ~~his~~ the body & therefore is the Lord. When the Self we have realised that all this

The first page of an incomplete commentary on the *Isha Upanishad* (*Volume 17, The Complete Works of Sri Aurobindo*)

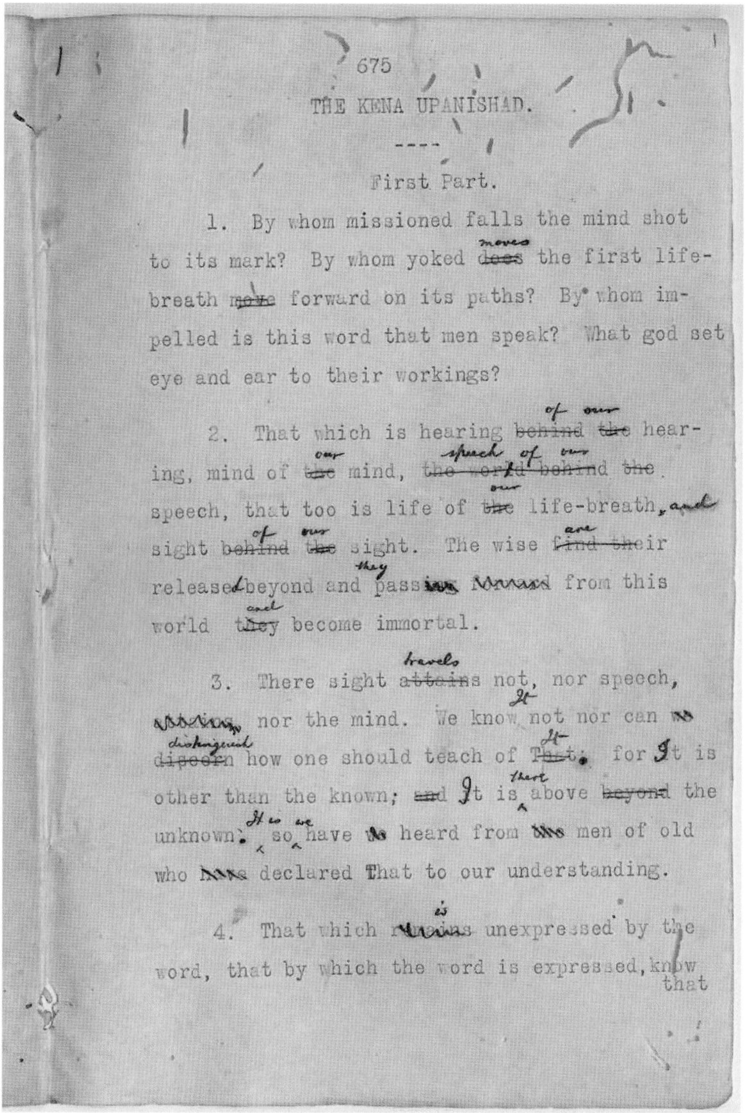

675

THE KENA UPANISHAD.

First Part.

1. By whom missioned falls the mind shot to its mark? By whom yoked does the first life-breath move forward on its paths? By whom impelled is this word that men speak? What god set eye and ear to their workings?

2. That which is hearing behind the hearing, mind of the mind, the word behind the speech, that too is life of the life-breath, sight behind the sight. The wise find their release beyond and pass onward from this world they become immortal.

3. There sight attains not, nor speech, nor the mind. We know not nor can we discern how one should teach of That; for It is other than the known; and It is beyond the unknown; so have we heard from the men of old who have declared That to our understanding.

4. That which remains unexpressed by the word, that by which the word is expressed, know that

A typescript of Sri Aurobindo's translation of the *Kena Upanishad*, with his revisions (*Volume 18, The Complete Works of Sri Aurobindo*)

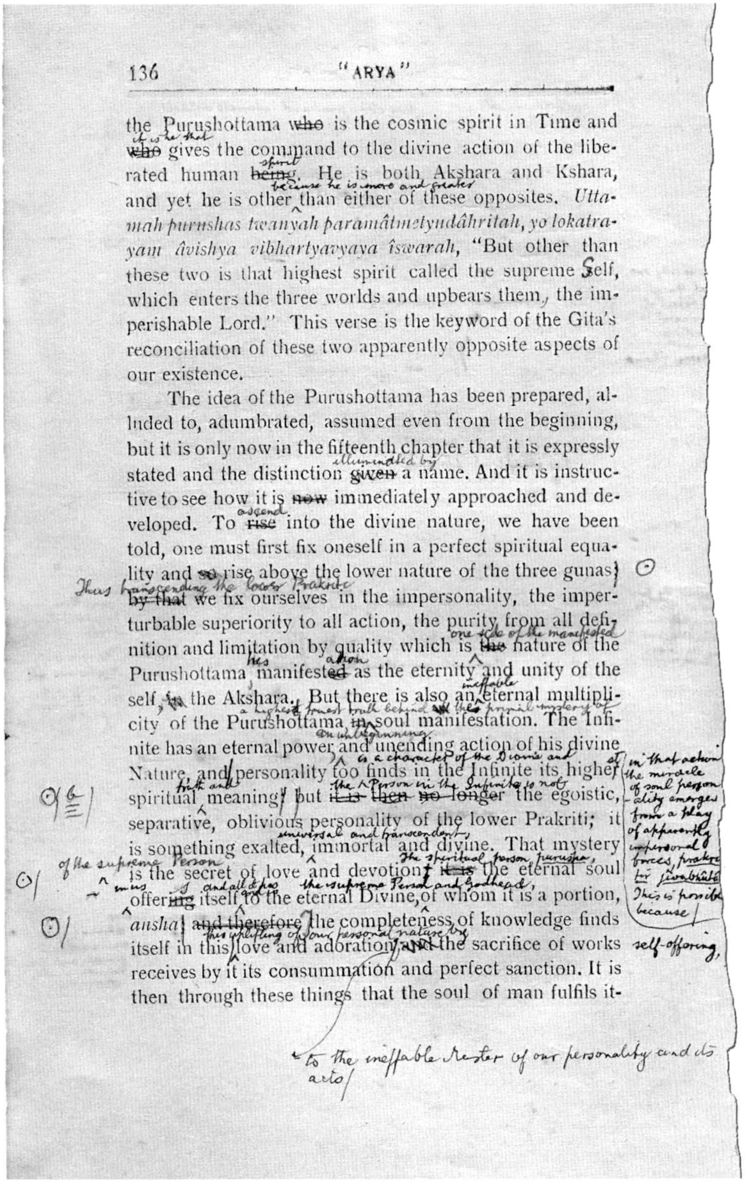

136 "ARYA"

the Purushottama who is the cosmic spirit in Time and who gives the command to the divine action of the liberated human being. He is both Akshara and Kshara, and yet he is other than either of these opposites. *Uttamah purushas twanyah paramâtmetyudâhritah, yo lokatrayam âvishya vibhartyavyaya îswarah,* "But other than these two is that highest spirit called the supreme Self, which enters the three worlds and upbears them, the imperishable Lord." This verse is the keyword of the Gita's reconciliation of these two apparently opposite aspects of our existence.

The idea of the Purushottama has been prepared, alluded to, adumbrated, assumed even from the beginning, but it is only now in the fifteenth chapter that it is expressly stated and the distinction given a name. And it is instructive to see how it is now immediately approached and developed. To rise into the divine nature, we have been told, one must first fix oneself in a perfect spiritual equality and so rise above the lower nature of the three gunas; by that we fix ourselves in the impersonality, the imperturbable superiority to all action, the purity from all definition and limitation by quality which is the nature of the Purushottama manifested as the eternity and unity of the self, in the Akshara. But there is also an eternal multiplicity of the Purushottama in soul manifestation. The Infinite has an eternal power and unending action of his divine Nature, and personality too finds in the Infinite its higher spiritual meaning; but it is then no longer the egoistic, separative, oblivious personality of the lower Prakriti; it is something exalted, immortal and divine. That mystery is the secret of love and devotion; it is the eternal soul offering itself to the eternal Divine, of whom it is a portion, *ansha*; and therefore the completeness of knowledge finds itself in this love and adoration, and the sacrifice of works receives by it its consummation and perfect sanction. It is then through these things that the soul of man fulfils it-

A page of *Essays on the Gita* in the *Arya* as revised by Sri Aurobindo (*Volume 19, The Complete Works of Sri Aurobindo*)

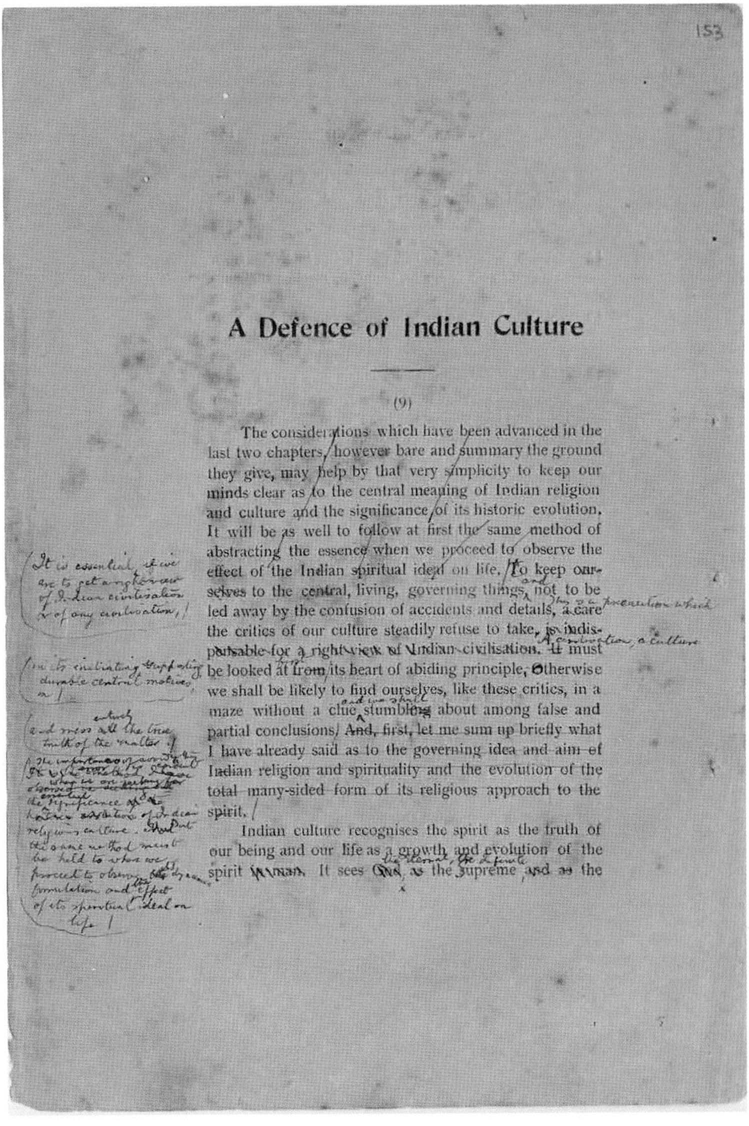

A Defence of Indian Culture

(9)

The considerations which have been advanced in the last two chapters, however bare and summary the ground they give, may help by that very simplicity to keep our minds clear as to the central meaning of Indian religion and culture and the significance of its historic evolution. It will be as well to follow at first the same method of abstracting the essence when we proceed to observe the effect of the Indian spiritual ideal on life. To keep ourselves to the central, living, governing things, not to be led away by the confusion of accidents and details, a care the critics of our culture steadily refuse to take, is indispensable for a right view of Indian civilisation. It must be looked at from its heart of abiding principle, otherwise we shall be likely to find ourselves, like these critics, in a maze without a clue, stumbling about among false and partial conclusions. And, first, let me sum up briefly what I have already said as to the governing idea and aim of Indian religion and spirituality and the evolution of the total many-sided form of its religious approach to the spirit.

Indian culture recognises the spirit as the truth of our being and our life as a growth and evolution of the spirit in man. It sees God as the supreme and as the

A page of *A Defence of Indian Culture* in the *Arya* as revised by Sri Aurobindo (*Volume 20, The Complete Works of Sri Aurobindo*)

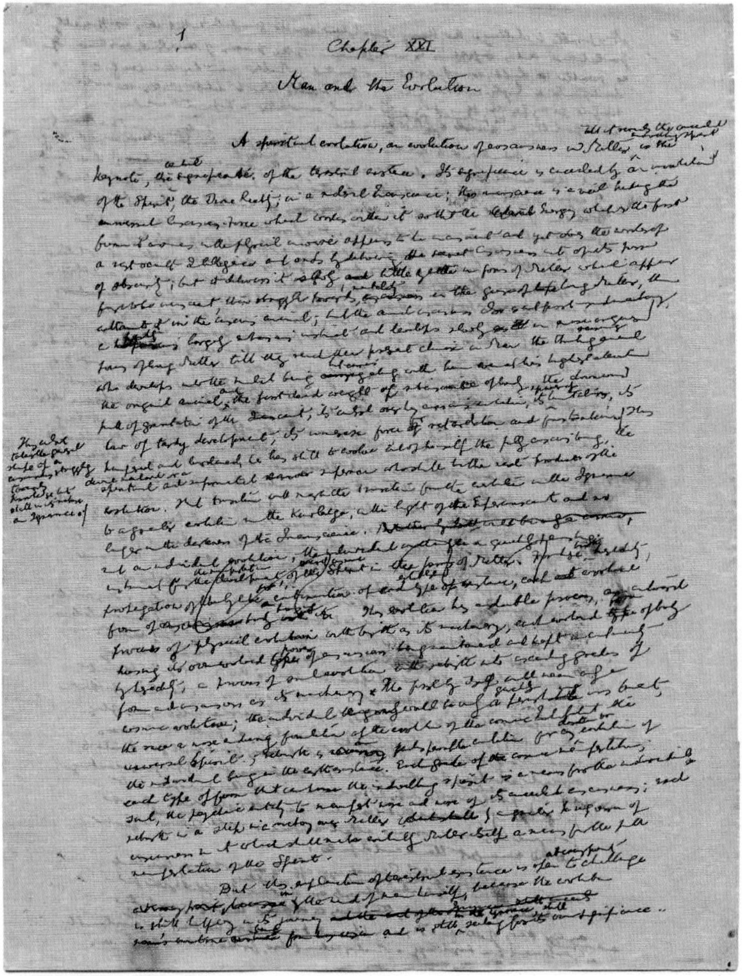
1

Chapter XXI

Man and the Evolution

A spiritual evolution, an evolution of consciousness in Matter …

A draft of the opening of one of the last chapters of *The Life Divine* (*Volume 22, The Complete Works of Sri Aurobindo*)

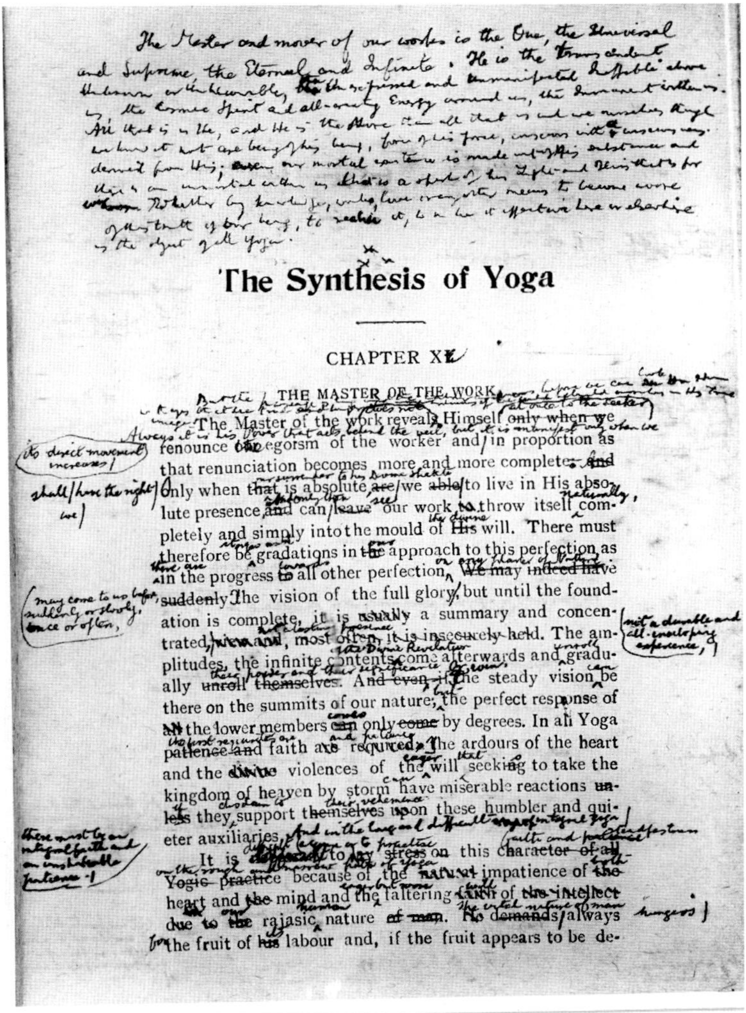
The Synthesis of Yoga

CHAPTER XI

THE MASTER OF THE WORK

The Master of the work reveals Himself only when we renounce the egoism of the worker and in proportion as that renunciation becomes more and more complete. And only when that is absolute, are we able to live in His absolute presence and can leave our work to throw itself completely and simply into the mould of His will. There must therefore be gradations in the approach to this perfection as in the progress to all other perfection. We may indeed have suddenly the vision of the full glory, but until the foundation is complete, it is usually a summary and concentrated, vivid and, most often, it is insecurely held. The amplitudes, the infinite contents come afterwards and gradually unroll themselves. And even if the steady vision be there on the summits of our nature, the perfect response of all the lower members can only come by degrees. In all Yoga patience and faith are required. The ardours of the heart and the divine violences of the will seeking to take the kingdom of heaven by storm have miserable reactions unless they support themselves upon these humbler and quieter auxiliaries.

It is difficult to lay stress on this character of all Yogic practice because of the natural impatience of the heart and the mind and the faltering faith of the intellect due to the rajasic nature of man. He demands always the fruit of his labour and, if the fruit appears to be de-

A page of *The Synthesis of Yoga* from the *Arya* as revised by Sri Aurobindo (*Volume 23, The Complete Works of Sri Aurobindo*)

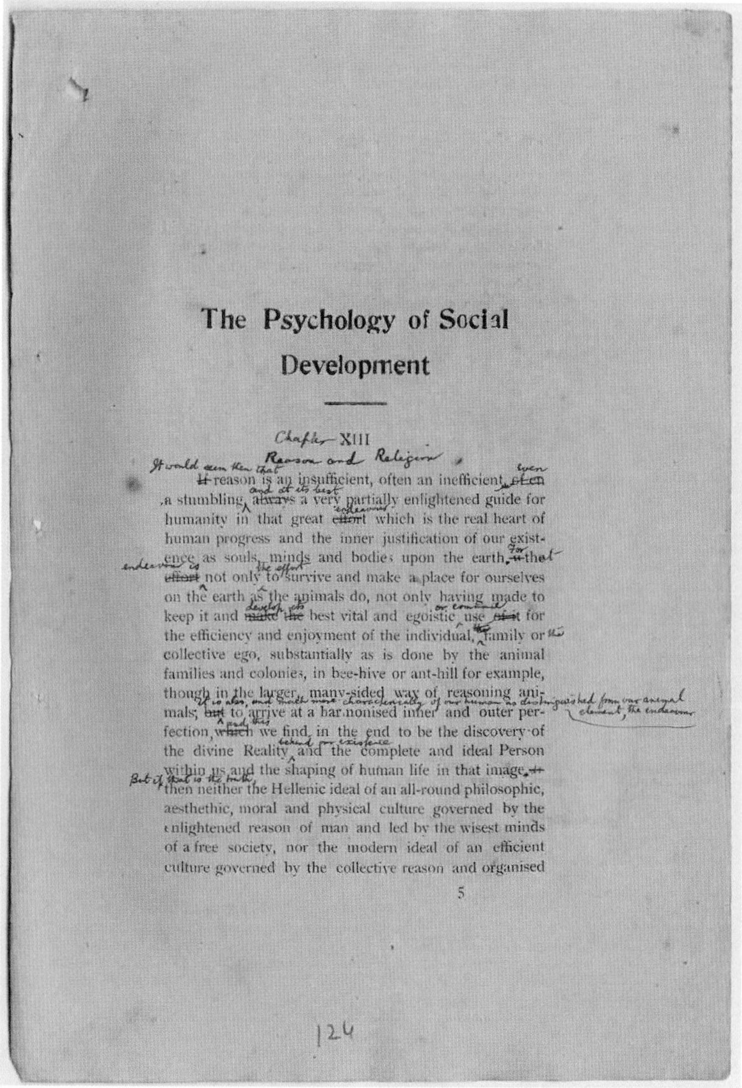

The Psychology of Social Development

XIII

If reason is an insufficient, often an inefficient, often a stumbling, always a very partially enlightened guide for humanity in that great effort which is the real heart of human progress and the inner justification of our existence as souls, minds and bodies upon the earth, — that effort not only to survive and make a place for ourselves on the earth as the animals do, not only having made to keep it and make the best vital and egoistic use of it for the efficiency and enjoyment of the individual, family or collective ego, substantially as is done by the animal families and colonies, in bee-hive or ant-hill for example, though in the larger, many-sided way of reasoning animals; but to arrive at a harmonised inner and outer perfection, which we find in the end to be the discovery of the divine Reality and the complete and ideal Person within us and the shaping of human life in that image, — then neither the Hellenic ideal of an all-round philosophic, aesthethic, moral and physical culture governed by the enlightened reason of man and led by the wisest minds of a free society, nor the modern ideal of an efficient culture governed by the collective reason and organised

5

124

A page of *The Human Cycle* from the *Arya* as revised by Sri Aurobindo (*Volume 25, The Complete Works of Sri Aurobindo*)

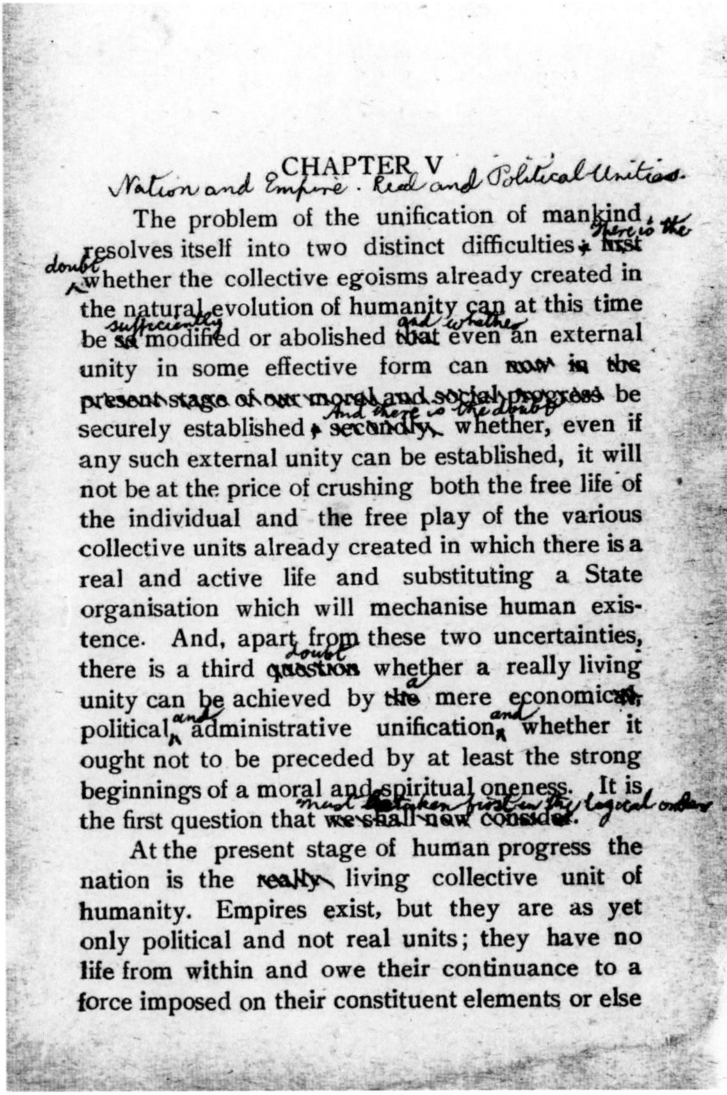

CHAPTER V

Nation and Empire. Real and Political Unities.

The problem of the unification of mankind resolves itself into two distinct difficulties; first whether the collective egoisms already created in the natural evolution of humanity can at this time be so modified or abolished that even an external unity in some effective form can now in the present stage of our moral and social progress be securely established; secondly, whether, even if any such external unity can be established, it will not be at the price of crushing both the free life of the individual and the free play of the various collective units already created in which there is a real and active life and substituting a State organisation which will mechanise human existence. And, apart from these two uncertainties, there is a third question whether a really living unity can be achieved by the mere economical, political, administrative unification, whether it ought not to be preceded by at least the strong beginnings of a moral and spiritual oneness. It is the first question that we shall now consider.

At the present stage of human progress the nation is the really living collective unit of humanity. Empires exist, but they are as yet only political and not real units; they have no life from within and owe their continuance to a force imposed on their constituent elements or else

A page of *The Ideal of Human Unity* from the *Arya* as revised by Sri Aurobindo (*Volume 25, The Complete Works of Sri Aurobindo*)

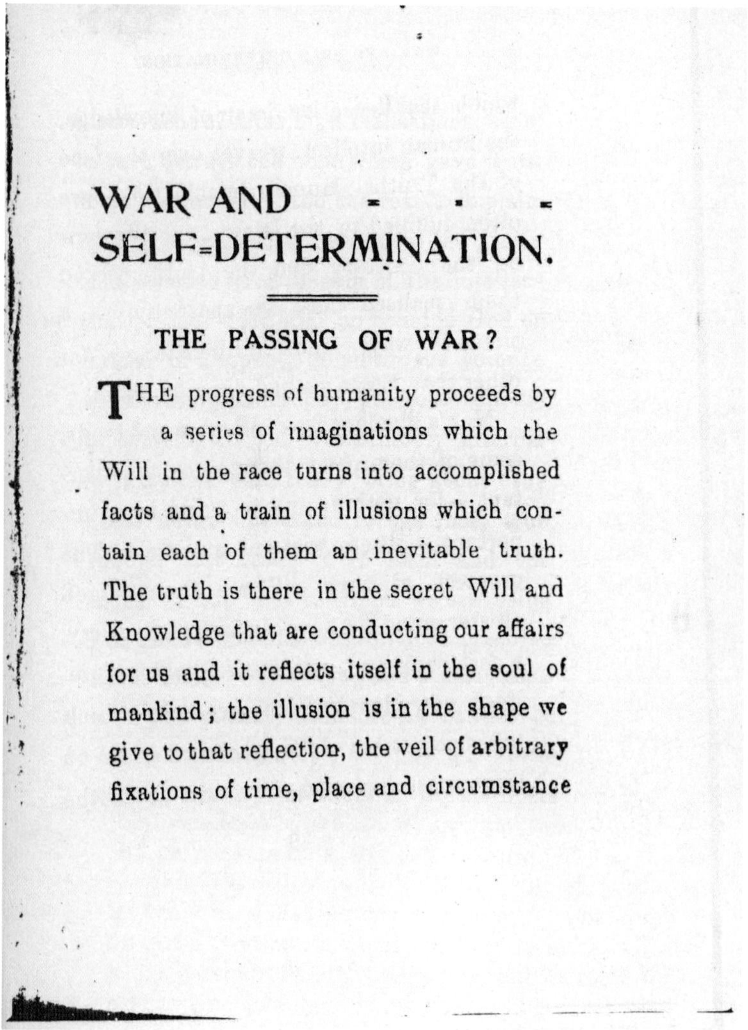

WAR AND SELF-DETERMINATION.

THE PASSING OF WAR?

THE progress of humanity proceeds by a series of imaginations which the Will in the race turns into accomplished facts and a train of illusions which contain each of them an inevitable truth. The truth is there in the secret Will and Knowledge that are conducting our affairs for us and it reflects itself in the soul of mankind; the illusion is in the shape we give to that reflection, the veil of arbitrary fixations of time, place and circumstance

A page of *War and Self-Determination* from the *Arya* as revised by Sri Aurobindo (*Volume 25, The Complete Works of Sri Aurobindo*)

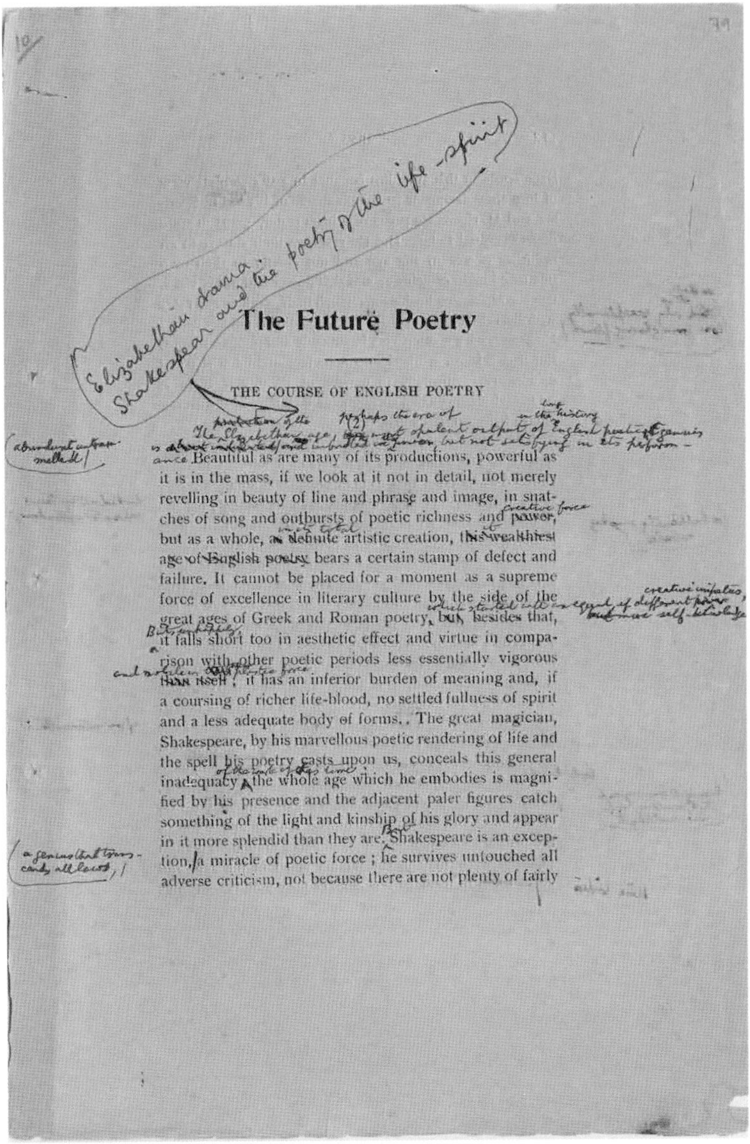

Elizabethan drama: Shakespear and the poetry of the life-spirit

The Future Poetry

THE COURSE OF ENGLISH POETRY

(2)

Beautiful as are many of its productions, powerful as it is in the mass, if we look at it not in detail, not merely revelling in beauty of line and phrase and image, in snatches of song and outbursts of poetic richness and power, but as a whole, as definite artistic creation, this wealthiest age of English poetry bears a certain stamp of defect and failure. It cannot be placed for a moment as a supreme force of excellence in literary culture by the side of the great ages of Greek and Roman poetry, but, besides that, it falls short too in aesthetic effect and virtue in comparison with other poetic periods less essentially vigorous than itself; it has an inferior burden of meaning and, if a coursing of richer life-blood, no settled fullness of spirit and a less adequate body of forms. The great magician, Shakespeare, by his marvellous poetic rendering of life and the spell his poetry casts upon us, conceals this general inadequacy; the whole age which he embodies is magnified by his presence and the adjacent paler figures catch something of the light and kinship of his glory and appear in it more splendid than they are. Shakespeare is an exception, a miracle of poetic force; he survives untouched all adverse criticism, not because there are not plenty of fairly

A page of *The Future Poetry* from the *Arya* as revised by Sri Aurobindo (*Volume 26, The Complete Works of Sri Aurobindo*)

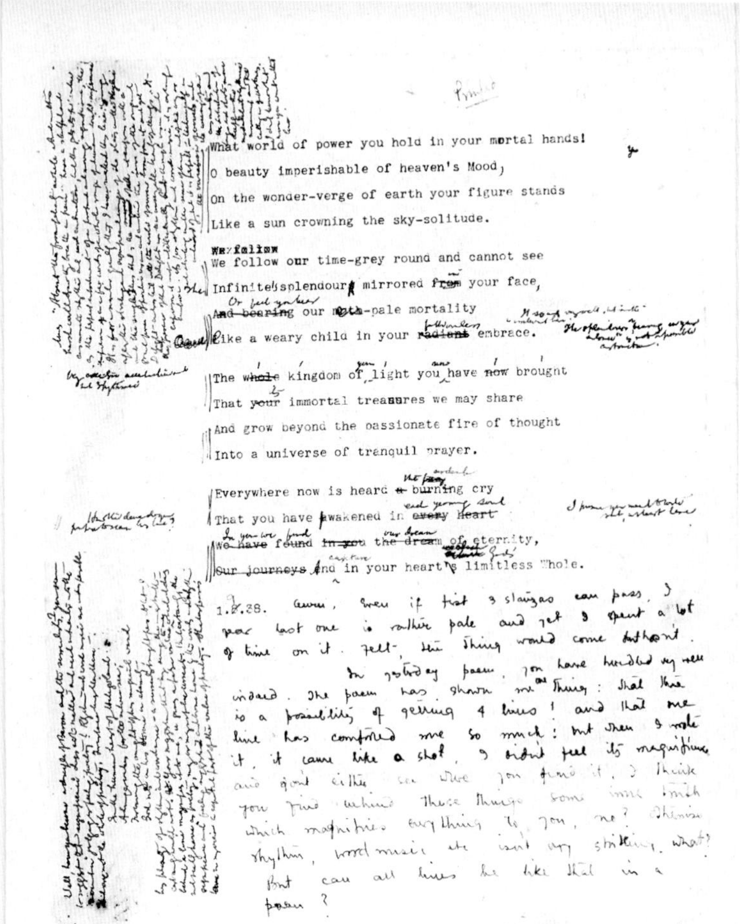

What world of power you hold in your mortal hands!
O beauty imperishable of heaven's Mood,
On the wonder-verge of earth your figure stands
Like a sun crowning the sky-solitude.

We follow our time-grey round and cannot see
Infinite splendour mirrored on your face,
And bearing our moth-pale mortality
Like a weary child in your radiant embrace.

The whole kingdom of light you have now brought
That your immortal treasures we may share
And grow beyond the passionate fire of thought
Into a universe of tranquil prayer.

Everywhere now is heard a burning cry
That you have awakened in every Heart
We have found in you the dream of eternity,
Our journeys end in your heart's limitless Whole.

1.[illegible].38. Guru, even if first 3 stanzas can pass, I fear last one is rather pale and yet I spent a lot of time on it. Felt, the thing would come out.

In yesterday poem, you have handled very well indeed. The poem has shown me one thing: that there is a possibility of getting 4 lines! and that one line has comforted me so much: but when I wrote it, it came like a shot, I didn't feel its magnificence and don't either see where you find it. I think you find where these things some inner truth which magnifies everything to you, no? Otherwise rhythm, word music etc isn't very striking, what? But can all lines be like that in a poem?

Sri Aurobindo's revisions of a poem, with comments (*Volume 27, The Complete Works of Sri Aurobindo*)

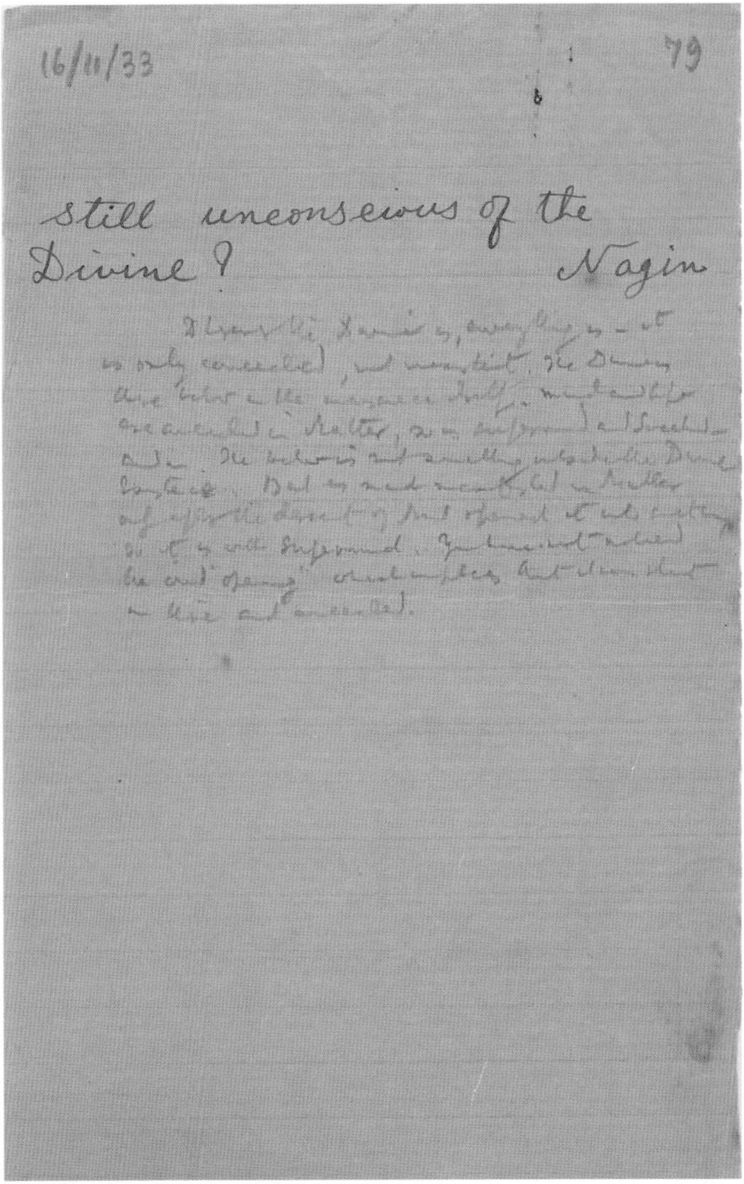

16/11/33

79

still unconscious of the Divine? Nagin

A letter to a disciple (*Volumes 28-31, The Complete Works of Sri Aurobindo*)

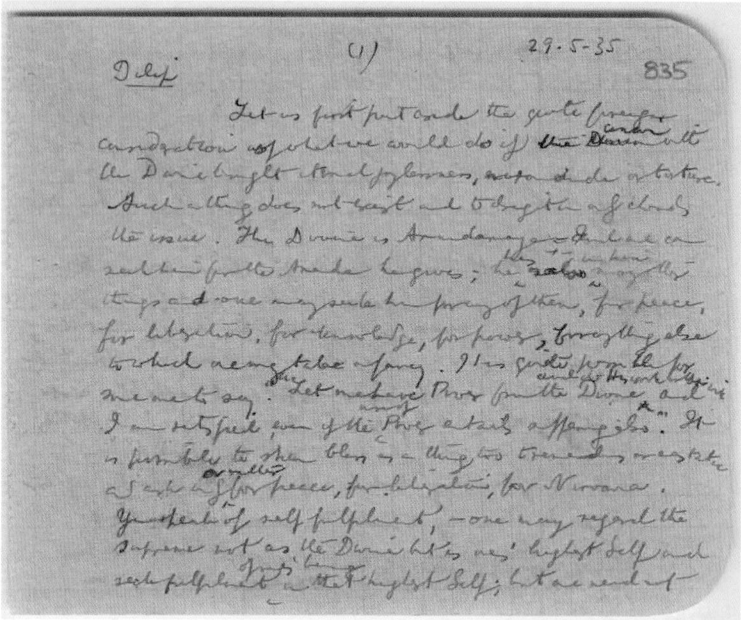

(1) 29.5-35

835

A letter to a disciple (*Volumes 28-31, The Complete Works of Sri Aurobindo*)

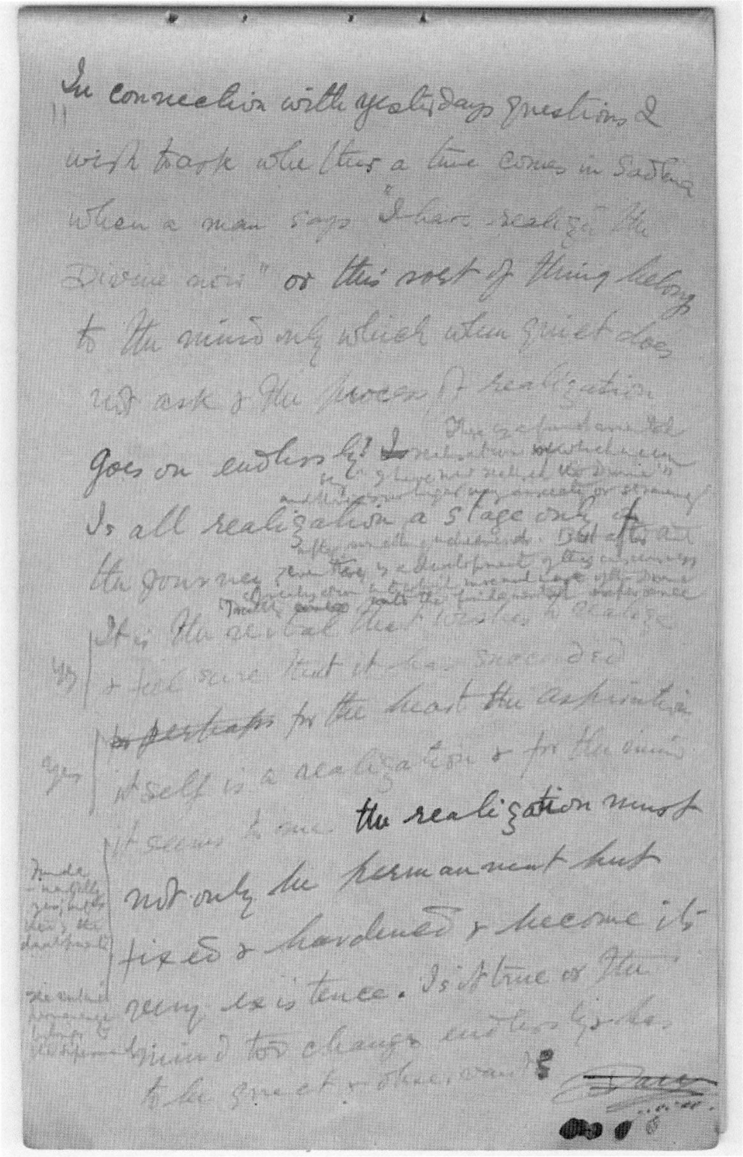
In connection with yesterday's question I wish to ask whether a time comes in Sadhana when a man says "I have realised the Divine now" or this sort of thing belongs to the mind only which when quiet does not ask & the process of realisation goes on endlessly? Is all realisation a stage only of the journey? It is the vital that wishes to realise & feel sure that it has succeeded, for the heart the aspiration itself is a realisation & for the mind it seems to me the realisation must not only be permanent but fixed & hardened & become its very existence. Is it true or the mind too changes endlessly

A letter to a disciple (*Volumes 28-31, The Complete Works of Sri Aurobindo*)

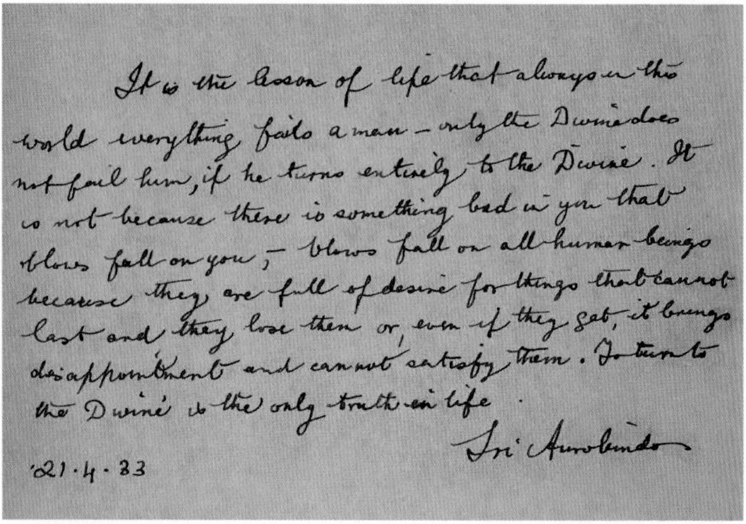

It is the lesson of life that always in this world everything fails a man – only the Divine does not fail him, if he turns entirely to the Divine. It is not because there is something bad in you that blows fall on you; – blows fall on all human beings because they are full of desire for things that cannot last and they lose them or, even if they get, it brings disappointment and cannot satisfy them. To turn to the Divine is the only truth in life.

Sri Aurobindo

21.4.33

A letter to a disciple (*Volumes 28-31, The Complete Works of Sri Aurobindo*)

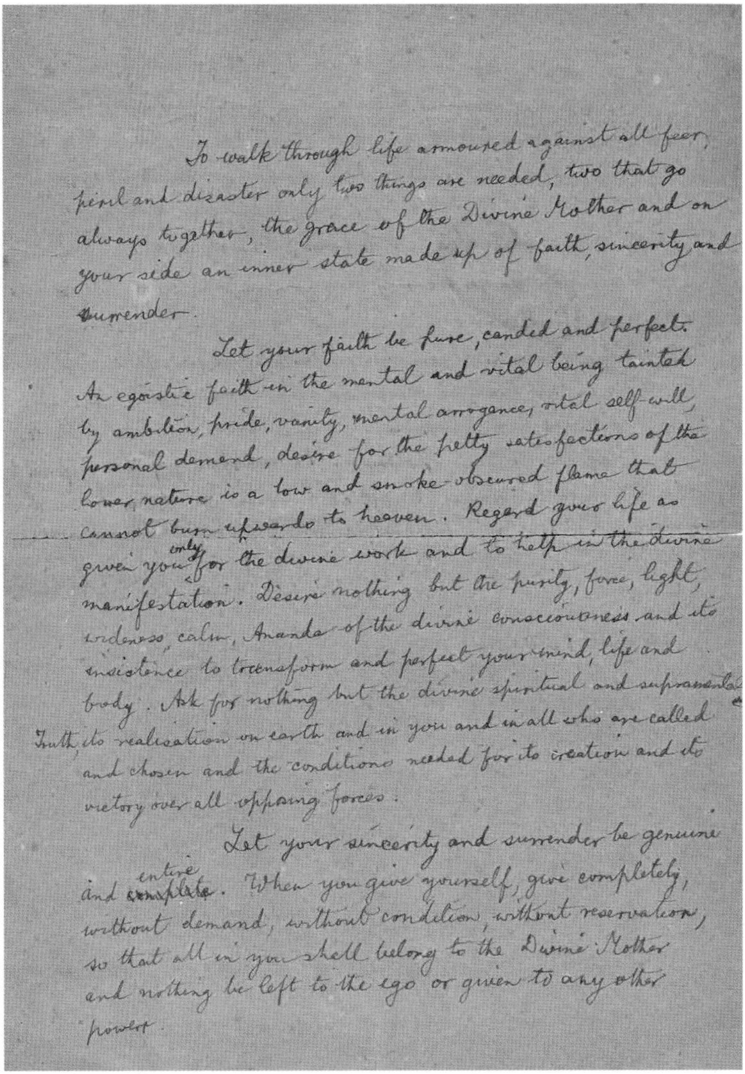

To walk through life armoured against all fear, peril and disaster only two things are needed, two that go always together, the grace of the Divine Mother and on your side an inner state made up of faith, sincerity and surrender.

Let your faith be pure, candid and perfect. An egoistic faith in the mental and vital being tainted by ambition, pride, vanity, mental arrogance, vital self-will, personal demand, desire for the petty satisfactions of the lower nature is a low and smoke-obscured flame that cannot burn upwards to heaven. Regard your life as given you only for the divine work and to help in the divine manifestation. Desire nothing but the purity, force, light, wideness, calm, Ananda of the divine consciousness and its insistence to transform and perfect your mind, life and body. Ask for nothing but the divine spiritual and supramental Truth, its realisation on earth and in you and in all who are called and chosen and the conditions needed for its creation and its victory over all opposing forces.

Let your sincerity and surrender be genuine and ~~complete~~ entire. When you give yourself, give completely, without demand, without condition, without reservation, so that all in you shall belong to the Divine Mother and nothing be left to the ego or given to any other power.

The first page of Chapter III of *The Mother* (*Volume 32, The Complete Works of Sri Aurobindo*)

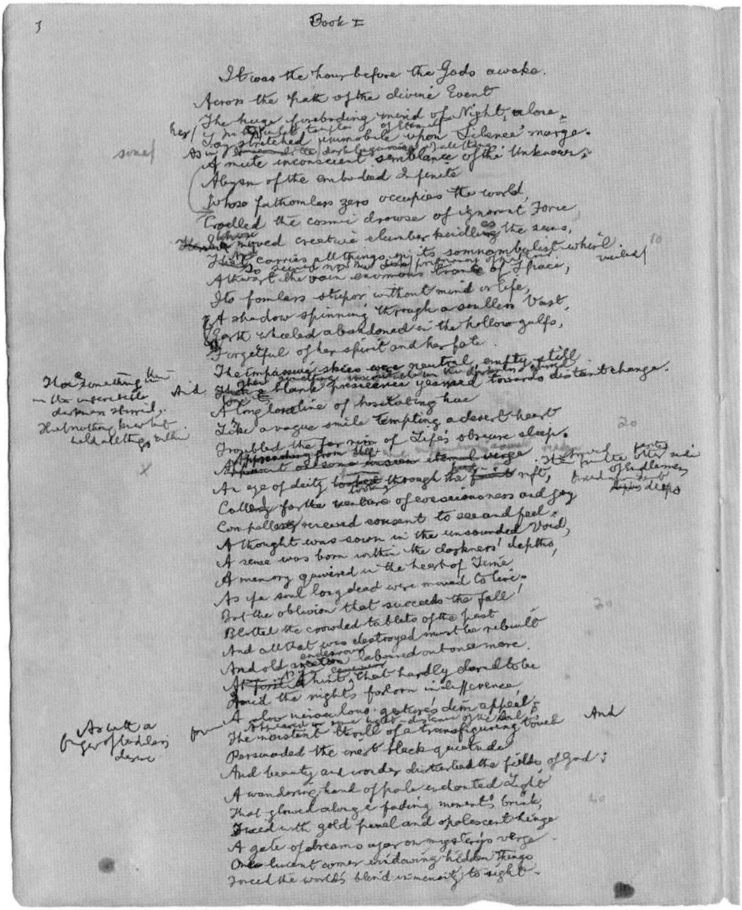

A draft of the opening lines of *Savitri* (*Volume 33, The Complete Works of Sri Aurobindo*)

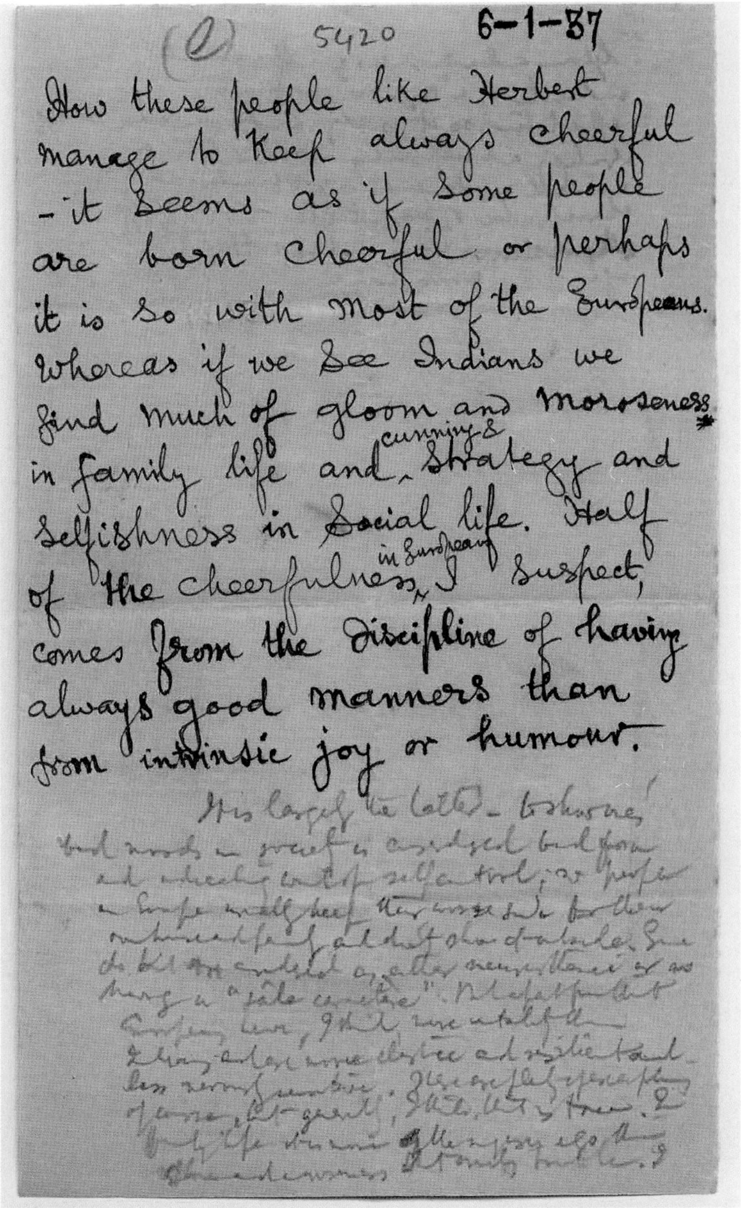

(l) 5420 6-1-37

How these people like Herbert manage to keep always cheerful – it seems as if some people are born cheerful or perhaps it is so with most of the Europeans. Whereas if we see Indians we find much of gloom and moroseness in family life and cunning & strategy and selfishness in social life. Half of the cheerfulness in Europeans, I suspect, comes from the discipline of having always good manners than from intrinsic joy or humour.

It is largely the latter – to show one's bad moods in society is considered bad form and indicating want of self-control; so people in Europe usually keep their worse side for their [illegible]

A letter to a disciple (*Volume 35, The Complete Works of Sri Aurobindo*)

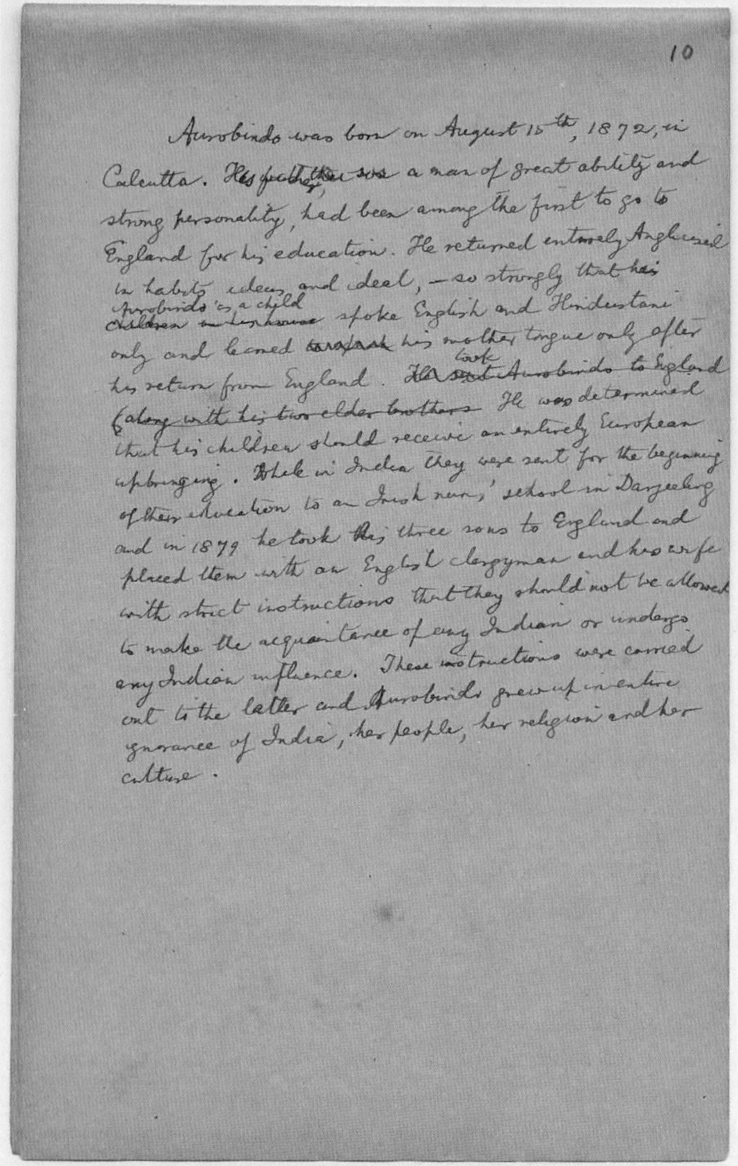

10

Aurobindo was born on August 15th, 1872, in Calcutta. His father, a man of great ability and strong personality, had been among the first to go to England for his education. He returned entirely Anglicised in habits, ideas and ideal, — so strongly that Aurobindo as a child ~~children in his house~~ spoke English and Hindustani only and learned his mother tongue only after his return from England. ~~He sent Aurobindo to England along with his two elder brothers~~ He was determined that his children should receive an entirely European upbringing. While in India they were sent for the beginning of their education to an Irish nuns' school in Darjeeling and in 1879 he took his three sons to England and placed them with an English clergyman and his wife with strict instructions that they should not be allowed to make the acquaintance of any Indian or undergo any Indian influence. These instructions were carried out to the letter and Aurobindo grew up in entire ignorance of India, her people, her religion and her culture.

Opening of a fragmentary life sketch (*Volume 36, The Complete Works of Sri Aurobindo*) lost. What came instead was a large number of powerful, but mutually exclusive spiritual traditions. The more knowledge-centred approaches, such as in Advaita Vedanta, realized that if one stills all mental activity and erases one's ego-sense, one's consciousness doesn't diminish: it actually grows and merges back into a conscious Infinity of bliss that exists eternally beyond the manifest reality. The more devotion-centred approaches in the various *bhakti* traditions found that if one focuses all one's love on one specific form of the Divine, one also finds an absolute bliss that goes beyond everything else.

The problem with these different approaches is not that they differ, or don't find the Divine; they do. But each school recognises only one aspect of the Divine, while the Divine is *anantaguna*, of infinite quality. What is more, they jump from the highest level of mind, straight to the ineffable Beyond, and this highest level of mind, which Sri Aurobindo later called Overmind, is still tainted with traces of duality and exclusivity. In other words, the highest level of the manifest world they know is still imperfect, and as a result there is a tendency to look down on life in the physical world.

In 1908, when Sri Aurobindo reached what he describes in *Letters on Himself and the Ashram*[10] (See Chapter 30) as 'an inexpressible Peace', 'above and without thought',[11] it initially gave him the same sense of the unreality of the world that many others in the Indian tradition had felt, but somehow, he was not swayed by that feeling. He patiently stayed with it till slowly, over many years, a new type of consciousness began to reveal itself to him. He called it 'supramental', as he saw it located between the highest ranges of mental consciousness and the transcendent Divine.

He then realized that some of the oldest Indian texts had hinted at the existence of this inner world, which they called *mahas* and knew as an inner world with an entirely non-dual, gnostic type of consciousness. They even described why it would later be missed; they wrote that it was protected by a golden lid, a light so bright it blinds. But Sri Aurobindo did not miss it, and he realized that it was radically different from anything else known to man—at the same time Divine *and* manifest, one *and* manifold, eternal *and* changing. He also realized that it must have been this almost forgotten type of consciousness that had created the world and that it would be this type of consciousness that will ultimately manifest in evolution.

We humans can receive in our mind glimpses, reflections and shadows of a higher, non-dual consciousness, but from within our mental consciousness we cannot know the supramental consciousness as it is in itself. Just as there is no way a monkey can imagine how it would be to write poetry, our human minds cannot fully understand the supramental. The only saving grace is that we have reached a stage where we can silence our mind, open ourselves up to what is beyond it and allow that higher consciousness to penetrate and transform us.

Sri Aurobindo explored the many layers of this new consciousness between the mind and the ineffable with a remarkable and unprecedented combination of determination, spiritual acumen and intellectual rectitude. *The Life Divine* is the magnificent rendering of the result of that labour in the language of philosophy. In its more than 1100 pages, Sri Aurobindo develops an ontological and epistemological framework that might well become the philosophical foundation for a new, more integral science. It is a framework that can not only support the hard sciences, but that works equally well for the social and human sciences.

Besides this, Sri Aurobindo offered, based on his own experience of the supramental consciousness, new and often surprisingly satisfactory answers to a whole range of age-old and seemingly intractable philosophical questions. He wrote about the future of the individual; the relation of the individual to others, the cosmos and the Divine; the hierarchy of different types of consciousness; the difference between ego, Soul and Self; the role of rebirth and karma; the origin of error and falsehood, pain and death, and why they exist and how they can be overcome. Of special interest to those with a background in Advaita Vedanta (or Plato's idealism), is his fascinating explanation of exclusive concentration as the mechanism behind Maya, the force that has created the world.

In the 1940 edition of *The Life Divine*,[12] Sri Aurobindo added several new chapters. In one of the first, he discussed why there was anything at all. In another, he described the different types of knowledge that could be used to develop a rigorous science of the subjective domain. The last six chapters of the book are all new and can be seen as the final version of ideas which he had explored earlier in other books. We find here two chapters on the social history of humanity, three on the stages and processes of transformation, and at the end, a chapter on what could be called the sociology of the transition from our present state to the future. In the concluding sentences of that last chapter, he summarises the reason we have for hope and for the courage to persevere:[13]

> Our evolution in the Ignorance with its chequered joy and pain of self-discovery and world-discovery, its half-fulfilments, its constant finding and missing, is only our first state. It must lead inevitably towards an evolution in the Knowledge, a self-finding and self-unfolding of the Spirit, a self-revelation of the Divinity in things...

* * *

19

The Synthesis of Yoga

Reading by Debashish Banerji

Sri Aurobindo is best known for *The Life Divine*[1] (See Chapter 18) and *The Synthesis of Yoga*.[2] These two books constitute, respectively, handbooks of *darshan* and yoga, philosophy and practice, for his teaching of spiritual transcendence and transformation, in keeping with the customary two-pronged description in Indian spiritual lineages. Sri Aurobindo's principal message is undoubtedly an urgent call to the human species for self-transcendence leading to the spiritual transformation of humanity and the divinization of matter, along with a vision and a practice for the same, which is what makes this work so central to his oeuvre.

As with most of his major works, *The Synthesis of Yoga* was first serialised as part of the monthly journal *Arya*, between 1914 and 1921. The articles were never published as a book in Sri Aurobindo's lifetime, though he revised portions with a view to publication in the 1930s and 1940s. The first complete book edition was published in 1955 and new editions were published in 1957, 1958, 1965 and 1970, prior to the present edition of 1999. The final version bears the structural organization of the original: four parts that discuss four forms of yoga—the yoga of divine works, the yoga of integral knowledge, the yoga of divine love and the yoga of self-perfection.

The term 'yoga' has gained universal currency in the English language but at the cost of a reduction in its meaning to a regimen of physical postures (asanas). Part of the multimillion-dollar 'new age' fitness industry, this understanding of yoga is based on a relatively minor form of Indian yoga, Hatha Yoga, and is not what Sri Aurobindo meant by the word yoga in this book, though he included it in passing.

The history of the reception of yoga in the modern West has gone through several waves, the first being its introduction to a popular audience at the turn of the nineteenth and twentieth centuries. A landmark figure in this transmission was Swami Vivekananda who, through his teachings and the Vedanta Centres he established, popularised the notion of yoga as a transcendental monism experienced in states of deep absorption (*samadhi*) arrived at through meditation. Around the 1960s, as a response to the countercultural revolution, a number of yogic lineages appeared in the West, pluralizing the understanding of yoga. What united these understandings was the general idea of yoga as an applied psychology leading to a goal of transcendental becoming. At present, these goals have reduced sectarian followings, while the hegemonic meaning of yoga has become that which is circulated by the popular yoga studio movement. In India, too, there are a variety of understandings of the word yoga, particularly a specialised path as one of six classic *darshans*, and a general sense of yoga as a 'yoking' or uniting of our normal consciousness with some aspect of a transcendental or divine consciousness.

It is in the last general sense that Sri Aurobindo uses the term in his book. Early in the text, he gives us a definition of yoga that supports this plural view, while also pointing to a more integral understanding:[3]

> For the contact of the human and individual consciousness with the divine is the very essence of Yoga. Yoga is the union of that which has become separated in the play of the universe with its own true self, origin and universality. The contact may take place at any point of the complex and intricately organised consciousness which we call our personality. It may be effected in the physical through the body; in the vital through the action of those functionings which determine the state and the experiences of our nervous being; through the mentality, whether by means of the emotional heart, the active will or the understanding mind, or more largely by a general conversion of the mental consciousness in all its activities. It may equally be accomplished through a direct awakening to the universal or transcendent Truth and Bliss by the conversion of the central ego in the mind. And according to the point of contact that we choose will be the type of the Yoga that we practise.

In the very first chapter, Sri Aurobindo pointed to the need and objective of his book. He brings our attention to our times as one of worldwide ferment marked by a forced co-existence of different traditional forms within various cultural contexts and histories and a pressure to submit to a universal drive for a future yoga.[4] The field of Indian yoga traditions is confronted with this co-existence and this pressure. To become meaningful to our times, he feels, its diverse approaches must engage with the plural energies of the world and, with them, aim for an integral life of the future. To do this, the various yogas must be seen as complementary to an integral image of the future human, must emerge from their secluded secrecy and become part of the mainstream of social life and must find one or more principle(s) of integration.[5] Thus, what is needed is a 'synthesis of yoga' towards this integral life.

The introductory section to *The Synthesis of Yoga* considers a variety of forms of yoga including Hatha Yoga, Raja Yoga and the Bhagavad Gita's triple path of works, knowledge and devotion, and shows how the latter is, in fact, a synthesis which, if properly followed, leads to a convergence of its three paths and the attainment of the Integral Yoga.[6] The next chapter, 'The Synthesis of the Systems', looks for a central key to the synthesis. In doing this, Sri Aurobindo considers Tantra as another bold and wide traditional synthesis which takes in the operations of the physical and vital life and aims at their divinisation in its purview.[7] With all these traditional attempts in front of him, Sri Aurobindo seeks a principle of synthesis that transcends traditional forms, though it may include any, all or none of them; that may be creatively individualised in all life circumstances; and that may lead to a full-scale transformed divine life of the future.[8]

For Sri Aurobindo, such a principle requires the discovery of a philosophical and metaphysical framework on which this synthesis rests. This metaphysical framework is more clearly articulated in *The Life Divine*. By the time of writing for *Arya*, he had realized this framework in experience and discovered it in his readings of the Veda (See Chapters 11, 12, and 13), the Upanishads, particularly the Isha Upanishad[9] (See Chapter 14), and the Bhagavad Gita[10] (See Chapter 16).

In the Upanishads, this metaphysical framework rests on the distinction between a 'higher hemisphere,' known as Vidya or Knowledge, and a 'lower hemisphere', known as Avidya or Ignorance.[11] The higher hemisphere is so-called because all things are known by identity, by realization, in this zone of existence. It is a knowledge of all differentiations by spontaneous and direct experience of oneness. On the other hand, the Ignorance of Avidya is so-called because in this reality, each experiencer is the centre of its own experience and knows all 'others' only indirectly, through external contact and inference on the basis of separateness.[12] This latter condition is the one in which we find ourselves. The bringing of the principle of Vidya into the Avidya to transform it was the metaphysical foundation for the synthesis Sri Aurobindo sought.

In Chapter Five, 'The Synthesis of the Systems', Sri Aurobindo explains this metaphysical framework in terms of two natures, a lower and higher one:[13]

> The lower Nature, that which we know and are and must remain so long as the faith in us is not changed, acts through limitation and division, is of the nature of Ignorance and culminates in the life of the ego; but the higher Nature, that to which we aspire, acts by unification and transcendence of limitation, is of the nature of Knowledge and culminates in the life divine. The passage from the lower to the higher is the aim of Yoga; and this passage may effect itself by the rejection of the lower and escape into the higher, — the ordinary view-point, — or by the transformation of the lower and its elevation to the higher Nature. It is this, rather, that must be the aim of an integral Yoga.

These two natures are spoken of in *Essays on the Gita* as *Para-prakriti* and *Apara-prakriti.*[14] *Apara-prakriti* is the nature of Avidya, and is made up of the triple principle of Matter (*annam*), Life (*pranah*) and Mind (*manah*). *Paraprakriti* is the nature of Vidya; in Vedantic terminology, it is made up of the four principles—*Sat*, *Chit*, *Ananda* and *Vijnana*. The first three are often referred to conjointly as Existence-Consciousness-Bliss. But, Sri Aurobindo says, if the goal of the Integral Yoga is to transform the lower Nature and elevate it to the higher Nature, this is possible only by the power of the fourth principle, Vijnana—the link principle between the higher and lower Natures:[15]

> [I]f Ananda is the creator and begetter of all becoming, its method is Tapas or force of the Purusha's consciousness dwelling upon its own infinite potentiality in existence and

> producing from it truths of conception or real Ideas, *vijnana*, which, proceeding from an omniscient and omnipotent Self-existence, have the surety of their own fulfilment and contain in themselves the nature and law of their own becoming in the terms of mind, life and matter. The eventual omnipotence of Tapas and the infallible fulfilment of the Idea are the very foundation of all Yoga. In man we render these terms by Will and Faith…

This gives us the foundation of the central method of synthesis. The method we have to pursue, then, is to put our whole conscious being into relation and contact with the Divine and to call Him in to transform our entire being into His. In effect, the pressure of the Tapas, the force of consciousness in us, dwelling in the Idea of the divine Nature upon that which we are in our entirety, produces its own realization. The divine and all-knowing and all-effecting descends upon the limited and obscure, progressively illumines and energises the whole lower nature and substitutes its own action for all the terms of the inferior human light and mortal activity.

In psychological fact, this method translates itself into the progressive surrender of the ego to the Beyond-ego with its vast and incalculable but always inevitable workings. It implies three stages—the attempt of the ego to enter into contact with the Divine, the wide, full and, therefore, laborious preparation of the whole lower Nature by the divine working to receive and become the higher Nature, and the eventual transformation.[16]

Along with the knowledge and action of Vijnana (which Sri Aurobindo translated into the neologism 'Supermind'), the metaphysical framework behind the Integral Yoga includes the fact that this method is really a coming into union with the process of the lower nature; in other words, that the principle of evolution in Nature follows this process. This foundation is the basis of the epigram on the title page of the book: 'All Life is Yoga.'[17]

> We see the divine method to be the same in the lower and in the higher working; only in the one it is pursued tardily and obscurely through the subconscious in Nature, in the other it becomes swift and self-conscious and the instrument confesses the hand of the Master. All life is a Yoga of Nature seeking to manifest God within itself. Yoga marks the stage at which this effort becomes capable of self-awareness and therefore of right completion in the individual. It is a gathering up and concentration of the movements dispersed and loosely combined in the lower evolution.[18]

Such a principle of yoga cannot but be conterminous with life and individually unique. This individual singularity is also what makes the synthesis of the Integral Yoga modern, because modernity is an age of the right to individual creative freedom:[19]

> [T]he perfection of the integral Yoga will come when each man is able to follow his own path of Yoga, pursuing the development of his own nature in its upsurging towards that which transcends the nature. For freedom is the final law and the last consummation.

This also makes it difficult from the viewpoint of tested mechanical formulae or routine practices. Sri Aurobindo himself followed a variety of methods, as dictated by his own inner guide. In the chapter 'The Four Aids', he pointed out that this guide, the guru of the Integral Yoga, was the inner Guide, the World-Teacher (*jagad-guru*) secret within us.[20] Similarly, the sacred text or scripture of the Integral Yoga 'is the eternal Veda secret in the heart of every thinking and living being'.[21] In his diaries, letters and talks, he referred to his 'teacher' sometimes as 'the Master of the Yoga'[22] and at other times identifies him as Sri Krishna.[23]

In the famous Uttarpara Speech,[24] (See Chapter 6) delivered shortly after his release from the Alipore Jail, Sri Aurobindo declared, 'Then He [Sri Krishna] placed the Gita in my hands. His strength entered into me and I was able to do the sadhana of the Gita. I was not only to understand intellectually but to realise what Sri Krishna demanded of Arjuna…'[25] We know from this and other writings of the importance of the Gita to his personal sadhana. Later, after his move to Pondicherry, he began maintaining a diary of his yoga practice, which has been published under the title with which he started it, *Record of Yoga*[26] (See Chapter 8). In the starting pages of this record, we find a programme of yoga divided into seven limbs, with four attainments or *siddhis* to each. Sri Aurobindo gave this programme the name 'Sapta Chatusthaya', or seven quartets.[27]

The Synthesis of Yoga presents approaches to the paths of Works, Knowledge and Divine Love taken from the Bhagavad Gita in its first three parts and four of the seven limbs of the programme followed in the *Record of Yoga*—the quartets of Yoga, Peace (*Shanti*), Power or Energy (Shakti), and Knowledge or Supermind (Vijnana)—in the fourth part. These parts, particularly the last one, remain incomplete, as a letter Sri Aurobindo wrote in 1936 indicates:[28]

> *The Synthesis of Yoga* was not meant to give a method for all to follow. Each side of the Yoga was dealt with separately with all its possibilities, and an indication [was given] as to how they meet so that one starting from knowledge could realise Karma and Bhakti also and so with each path. It was intended when the Self-Perfection was finished, to suggest a way in which all could be combined, but this was never written.

As a guru, Sri Aurobindo wrote extensively to his disciples on their yoga. A large number of these letters were published in four volumes as *Letters on Yoga*[29] (See Chapters 24, 25, 26 and 27) and form an important supplement to the study of *The Synthesis of Yoga*. *The Mother*[30] (See Chapter 28) elaborates a portion of Part IV of the *Synthesis*, the part related to the Shakti Chatusthaya or Quartet of Power/Energy of the *Record of Yoga*, and may be taken as another important line of approach that can integrate all the others in its movement. For a fruitful study and guidance of the practice of the Integral Yoga, all these sources need to be read together and correlated.

* * *

20

The Human Cycle

Reading by Anuradha Agrawal

On 15 August 1916, coinciding with his forty-fourth birthday, Sri Aurobindo published the first essay in a series titled 'The Psychology of Social Development' in *Arya*. The last of the essays, the twenty-fourth, was published on 15 July 1918, thus completing what was to become *The Human Cycle*.[1] These were the tumultuous years of the First World War. Momentous changes were afoot; social structures were crumbling. It was in this background that Sri Aurobindo put forth a theory of social development that examined the broad psychological principles lying at the core of large sometimes slow, at times rapid, social changes. Not only did he examine the past and decode it from the perspective of collective psychology, but he also projected the pattern into the future and previsioned the course of development the world might engage in.

The entire twenty-four-chapter series was first published as a book in 1949, after some revisions by Sri Aurobindo in the 1930s and in 1949.[2] By the time *The Human Cycle* was published, the world had seen yet another world war, and significant other changes:[3]

> At one time there suggested itself the necessity of bringing this part up to date, especially by some reference to later developments in Nazi Germany and the development of a totalitarian Communist regime in Russia. But afterwards it was felt that there was sufficient prevision and allusion to these events and more elaborate description or criticism of them was not essential; there was already without them an adequate working out and elucidation of this theory of the social cycle.

More than a century after it was first written, one is struck by the accuracy of Sri Aurobindo's predictions. His forecasts hold value even today, for the lines he traced then are still in the process of shaping up. They are not printed indelibly—in his characteristic style, Sri Aurobindo shows the inevitability of this progression yet, also presents us with an insight into our agency as active players in this process, who have the power to contribute to, and thus mould, the future:[4]

> …it is the natural work and should be the conscious hope of man… to know himself truly, to find the ideal law of his being and his development and, if he cannot even then follow it ideally owing to the difficulties of his egoistic nature, still to hold it before him and find out gradually the way by which it can become more and more the moulding principle of his individual and social existence.

This is why *The Human Cycle* is so exciting to read. It helps us understand the past of humanity and human societies, different civilizations, eras and cultures, from the inner perspective of psychology. It gives us the source code to decode our present, including aspects of society and the world that disturb us, fill us with foreboding or helplessness, or even frustration. It enables us to rise above the schisms created by right and wrong, and view the immediate objectively, in a wider context. It gives us the knowledge to determine our inner, as well as outer, response as a part of the collective, and empowers us to deal with our social reality.

In the first few chapters of the book, Sri Aurobindo traces the psychological forces that drive societies through cycles of change, highlighting five major stages societies go through and their underlying patterns. First, the symbolic age. This is when the structures and forms of society and religion serve as symbols of a deeper reality, mirroring what is perceived inwardly; the endeavour is to express that deeper reality in all activities and institutions. The various aspects and rhythms of life are seen through this sacred lens. Spiritual and religious ideas predominate, but with 'a large and vigorous freedom'.[5]

Second, the typal age. Here, psychological ideas and ethical ideals take the forefront. Everything else, even the spiritual and religious, recedes. Religion starts becoming other-worldly. In this age of Dharma 'the ethical motive and discipline', predominates and shapes the currents of society. The Symbolic idea of the direct expression of the divine Being or cosmic Principle manifesting in the forms of society recedes to the background and eventually disappears. [6] The typal is an age of great social ideals.

Third, the conventional age. The ideals of the typal age no longer 'spring naturally out of the inner life of the man',[7] but become conventions. The form, the outward expression, becomes more important than the ideal. Fixed systems, stereotypes, rigidities, binding traditions dominate; the spirit and inner meaning of the outer practices and structures lose their true sense.

Fourth, the individualistic age. The individual revolts against the stranglehold of the conventional age and questions the forms that are by now empty of any deeper truth. Reason and science gain predominance. The individual seeks some 'real and tangible Truth'[8] of himself and of society that can be perceived equally by all.

And finally, fifth, the subjective age. In this stage, reason no longer suffices; the human being is faced with the challenge of harmonising satisfactorily individual and collective progress, to discover their truth and law. A quest for true identity characterises the subjective age:[9]

> He finds that he can only know himself entirely by becoming actively self-conscious and not merely self-critical, by more and more living in his soul and acting out of it…; the rule of living according to the manifest laws of physical Nature is replaced by the effort towards living according to the veiled Law and Will and Power active in the life of the world and in the inner and outer life of humanity.

If we analyse our present society in the light of the evolutionary ages outlined above, we see aspects of all five stages present simultaneously, with individualism still holding sway, but at the same time being questioned from within, as the worst and the best in societies, regimes and nations come to the fore. We see signs of emerging subjectivism. We, it seems, are in a phase of transition. Sri Aurobindo provides us with the tools to step back and look at what is happening, understand it and decide how we can engage with ourselves and with life to be a part of this quest for truth and harmony.

In the next few chapters, Sri Aurobindo unveils the underlying psychological meaning of barbarism, civilization and culture, re-examining ancient and modern civilizations through the prism of consciousness. He further discusses the two dominating societal drivers, reason and religion,[10] bringing forth the contributions and limitations of both, and the need to go beyond both.

At the heart of the human quest lies a seeking for 'the true, the good and the beautiful'.[11] Both reason and religion fail to completely satisfy this quest. Liberty, equality, fraternity—these too are powerful ideals for society at present. For over two centuries humankind has experimented with various socio-economic-political structures to achieve these objectives of harmony. Despite some progress, the ultimate solution eludes human reason as well as religion. As the individual's quest deepens, he seeks a stage that looks beyond intellectuality and arrives at spirituality—not an other-worldly philosophy, but an integral mastery of life through the power of the spirit, an ultimate harmonizing of all opposites, a lasting and unclouded happiness, a dynamic and all-encompassing freedom.[12]

> A deeper, wider, greater, more spiritualized subjective understanding of the individual and communal self and its life and a growing reliance on the spiritual light and the spiritual means for the final solution of its problems are the only way to a true social perfection.

Further:[13]

> A spiritualized society can alone bring about a reign of individual harmony and communal happiness; or, in words which, though liable to abuse by the reason and the passions, are still the most expressive we can find, a new kind of theocracy, the kingdom of God upon earth, a theocracy which shall be the government of mankind by the Divine in the hearts and minds of men.

Sri Aurobindo devotes the last four chapters of the book to setting out the conditions for the coming of a spiritual age, its necessity for individual and social development, and the signs of its coming. He discusses present and emerging movements in art, literature, music, philosophy, education, science, politics, sociology, economics and ethics, to examine the turn they might take in a spiritual age. In all of these he stresses the importance of a free and progressive growth dictated by the need of an evolving humanity. For example, in science and research, new and unexpected departures can be expected which will thin the distinction between matter and spirit, attempts to understand in precise terms psychological and psychic realms will be made, and a realization that these planes too are subject to their own laws which are other than physical laws.[14]

He also cautions against the dangers and challenges that may accompany this evolution to a spiritual age and the avenues of distortion it may create as long as human nature is not purified. He forewarns against the tendency of a partial truth, a partial philosophy or religion to try and impose itself as the whole truth. Many such new spiritual waves may be the forerunners of a spiritual age: [15]

> …yet their claims must be subordinated in the general mind of the race and of its spiritual leaders to the recognition that all motives and disciplines are valid and yet none entirely valid since they are means and not the one thing to be done. The one thing essential must take precedence, the conversion of the whole life of the human being to the lead of the spirit. The ascent of man into heaven is not the key, but rather his ascent here into the spirit and the descent also of the spirit into his normal humanity and the transformation of this earthly nature."

Sri Aurobindo emphasizes that both the subjective age and its subsequent development into a spiritual age must necessarily start with the individual—or a few individuals—before it is taken up by the collective soul. Therefore, the freedom of the individual is a must. A society that lays greater importance on institutions at the cost of the individual is nothing but a machine and leads to atrophy:[16]

> …the coming of a spiritual age must be preceded by the appearance of an increasing number of individuals who are no longer satisfied with the normal intellectual, vital and physical existence of man, but perceive that a greater evolution is the real goal of humanity and attempt to effect it in themselves, to lead others to it and to make it the recognized goal of the race.

Focused on the psychology of social development, *The Human Cycle* is a celebration of human endeavour, individual freedom, collective progress and the promise of what Sri Aurobindo articulates as 'a greater dawn' in his epic, *Savitri*[17] (See Chapter 29). It is an invitation to collaborate consciously in personal and collective evolution. The revelations it makes have far-reaching consequences. And for those engaged in the fields of policy, governance, social change, education, culture or any form of work that deals with social systems, this book is as much an introspective journey as it is a guidebook that charts out a future destined.

* * *

21

The Ideal of Human Unity; and War and Self-Determination

Reading by Devdip Ganguli

Even while expounding upon the highest spiritual truths, Sri Aurobindo was never out of touch with reality; throughout his life, the Master remained acutely aware of the world events, the practical difficulties on the ground that stood in the way of change. In his writings, as much as in his life and inner work, he sought to bridge the gap between this imperfect human present and the supramental future he envisaged.

Volume 25 of *The Complete Works of Sri Aurobindo* includes three works, grouped together because they represent his social and political philosophy—*The Human Cycle*[1] (See Chapter 20); *The Ideal of Human Unity*,[2] and *War and Self-Determination*.[3] This volume takes up the collective aspect of human life, applying the evolutionary Integral Yoga lens to societies and humanity as a whole. It holds a special place, in that very few spiritual masters have sought to give their teaching a collective dimension; individual salvation has satisfied most. For Sri Aurobindo, the transformation he envisaged necessitated a collective change as well, and so his writings on social and political philosophy are ground-breaking among the spiritual literature of the world, for indeed, these are as much spiritual texts as any of his other works—the same integral consciousness and current runs through them.

Sri Aurobindo lived through some of the most seminal events of modern history, and his own life was intimately connected with them. He was born during the heyday of colonialism in Calcutta, the richest city of the British Empire, itself the richest colonial enterprise the world had ever known. He was educated in one of the most esteemed institutions of his day, at Cambridge. He returned to India to lead the first decisive freedom struggle, wielding ideas like sharp swords, inspiring bombs and revolution, and soon coming to be known as 'the most dangerous man'[4] in British circles. In Pondicherry, after 1910, he closely followed the developments of the First World War, wrote about the rise of totalitarian tendencies, and foresaw the coming of the Second World War. He publicly voiced support for the Allies and did everything in his power for their success against Nazism. He wrote about the League of Nations before it was formed, and foretold its failure before it failed. He was a little more optimistic about the United Nations, and predicted the rise of continental groupings as well, such as the European Union, decades before they manifested. India achieved independence on his seventy-fifth birthday, that is, on 15 August 1947. It is thus not surprising that Sri Aurobindo wrote extensively on socio-political issues and saw them as a crucial side of his work.

This volume features frequent references to past and contemporary world events to illustrate its points. Some of the key discussions in the book—such as the ideal relationship between the individual and the group, questions of what constitutes identity, the true business of the State, the role of law in controlling human societies, the steps in the formation of the nation—are placed in the context of historical and modern examples. Given that this book was being written during the First World War, a time of great international flux, Sri Aurobindo had a rich pool of contemporary examples.

It is true that some of the chapters are out of date in the light of later world events, but this was recognized by Sri Aurobindo himself when he issued the second edition in 1950. To a large extent, his footnotes help in bringing the text relatively up to date. But more important for students of Sri Aurobindo is to observe how he applies his integral perspective to world events, and to understand how the inner vision illuminates this external field. The ideas and principles of this book are universal and can be applied to many situations today. I would argue, for example, that those concerned with the future of the European Union may find the keys to many of the fundamental problems that plague it today, the nature of which are already foreseen and discussed in the pages of this book.

His perspective on these issues was profound. To truly understand what was happening, he felt it was essential to go beyond the events themselves and see the larger forces at play:[5]

> The surfaces of life are easy to understand…But they do not carry us very far. They suffice for an active superficial life from day to day, but they do not solve the great problems of existence. On the other hand, the knowledge of life's profundities, its potent secrets, its great, hidden, all-determining laws is exceedingly difficult to us…Yet it is these depths and their unseen forces that we ought to know if we would understand existence.

The Ideal of Human Unity was first published in the pages of *Arya* in thirty-five chapters, between 1915 and 1918. It was subsequently brought out as a book in 1919. Later, Sri Aurobindo was keen to rewrite parts of the book and make extensive alterations to bring the text up to date, but this was never done. Instead, for the second edition of the book, he made some minor changes, added many footnotes throughout the text, and incorporated a postscript. This edition was published by Sri Aurobindo Ashram in 1950.

The book begins with a paradox. The growth of larger and larger aggregates—from clans and tribes to kingdoms and empires, to nations and beyond—is inevitable and part of Nature's plan. At the same time, Sri Aurobindo observed, the most interesting periods of human life, when people have lived most richly, creatively and contributed most to the sum of human progress, have been periods when they were grouped into smaller centres engaging intensely with each other, but not fused into one big whole. Classical Greece, mediaeval Europe and the *mahajanapadas* of ancient India, are examples of these periods.

However, these smaller entities always suffered from a major defect. They did not last—they fought among each other, and they were disorganized and helpless in the face of invasions by larger organizations. And so, they eventually gave way to kingdoms and empires. But empires, by their very nature, even if more stable and secure, tend to suffer in richness, colour, and variety. The individual is less important in such large organizations, and eventually the aggregate stagnates, as happened with the Roman Empire. Such empires may be useful for consolidating the gains of ages past, but in the end, life and growth are arrested.

In light of this, the question of human unity takes on a more complex hue. Certainly, human unity is desirable. But of what use is unity if it ends up creating a large and autocratic superstructure in which the importance of the constituent groups and individuals progressively diminishes, and prosperity and safety are secured at the cost of richness and variety of life? Such an approach will inevitably lead to the decay and death of the organization itself, thus bringing us back to the question of what kind of unity we need and want.

Sri Aurobindo approached the question in a methodical manner, taking the world situation as it was in the early decades of the twentieth century, and moving forward from there. A few early chapters were dedicated to considering whether the form of the empire still had any role to play. After discussing the improbability of this, Sri Aurobindo proposed that the basis of human unity must be a grouping of free nations, something that he would see increasingly become a reality towards the end of his life. But given free nations, the question as to the nature of such a unity would still stand. Would such a grouping be organized along the lines of a world-union, or a world-state? Would it be a free grouping of countries, or a rigid organization stressing on uniformity of its constituent members?

In 1915, Sri Aurobindo wrote a letter to the Mother in which we find the answer to this question:[6]

> I have begun in the issue of the Arya which is just out a number of articles on the *Ideal of Human Unity*. I intend to proceed very cautiously and not go very deep at first, but as if I were leading the intelligence of the reader gradually towards the deeper meaning of unity — especially to discourage the idea that mistakes uniformity and mechanical association for unity.

Here, we have the central message of this book—that unity is not uniformity. The unity Sri Aurobindo envisaged was not an organizational monolith in which each constituent member subjugated itself for the sake of a large whole, an idea tempting to the rational mind because it is convenient to deal with the complexity of human life by simplifying it through a common rule. His idea of unity was that it could support an infinite diversity of being and living, a unity full of the richness of humanity:[7]

> To remove freedom in order to get rid of disorder, strife and waste, to remove diversity in order to get rid of separatism and

> jarring complexities is the impulse of order and regimentation by which the arbitrary rigidity of the intellectual reason seeks to substitute its straight line for the difficult curves of the process of Nature.
>
> But freedom is as necessary to life as law and regime; diversity is as necessary as unity to our true completeness. Existence is one only in its essence and totality, in its play it is necessarily multiform. Absolute uniformity would mean the cessation of life, while on the other hand the vigour of the pulse of life may be measured by the richness of the diversities which it creates.

As we approach the end of the text, we come closer to answering these core issues: How do we manifest diversity? How do we prevent diversity from leading to conflict and disunity? Sri Aurobindo points to a higher truth of unity that each individual carries within, and argues in favour of a 'religion of humanity'. A phrase without any specific religious connotation, it refers to a spiritual realization that will inevitably lead to a concrete and deep sense of inner unity, which would yet support a tremendous diversity of life: [8]

> ...the growing realization that there is a secret Spirit, a divine Reality, in which we are all one, that humanity is its highest present vehicle on earth, that the human race and the human being are the means by which it will progressively reveal itself here. It implies a growing attempt to live out this knowledge and bring about a kingdom of this divine Spirit upon earth.

Sri Aurobindo leads us always to central principles. The fundamental truths of Vedanta are presented in this text in the context of modern political philosophy, showing us the path to manifesting human unity on a spiritual basis. Referencing the three keywords of the French Revolution, he emphasises fraternity as the basis on which the other two principles of liberty and equality can be harmonised:[9]

> A society that pursues liberty as its ideal is unable to achieve equality; a society that aims at equality will be obliged to sacrifice liberty. For the ego to speak of fraternity is for it to speak of something contrary to its nature.
>
> Yet is brotherhood the real key to the triple gospel of the idea of humanity. The union of liberty and equality can only be achieved by the power of human brotherhood and it cannot be founded on anything else. But brotherhood exists only in the soul and by the soul; it can exist by nothing else. These three things are in fact the nature of the soul; for freedom, equality, unity are the eternal attributes of the Spirit.

Shifting focus from the ideal of human unity to the continuing necessity of war, the third book in *Volume 25, War and Self-Determination,* is a collection of six articles by Sri Aurobindo on current political events, written between 1916 and 1920. Of these, five were published in *Arya*, and the sixth was added when these essays were brought out in the form of a book in 1920 (along with a foreword that places these essays in context). Written during and just after the First World War, these articles are important for the light they shed on current events, and the direction Sri Aurobindo charts for the future.

A common thread ties these six chapters together, and links them to the central ideas of *The Human Cycle* and *The Ideal of Human Unity*:[10]

> ...they happen to be bound together by a common idea or at least look at four related subjects from a single general standpoint,—the obvious but practically quite forgotten truth that the destiny of the race in this age of crisis and revolution will depend much

> more on the spirit which we are than on the machinery we shall use.

As already seen earlier, Sri Aurobindo placed tremendous value on the modern political ideals of Europe, encapsulated in the keywords of the French Revolution—liberty, equality and fraternity. At the same time, he also emphasised the yogic perspective of a world shaped by universal forces, of human beings driven by Nature, prakriti, of large masses of people led by impulsions often beyond their understanding, leading to karmic consequences that play out on a global scale.

The central thesis of Sri Aurobindo's social and political philosophy remained consistent: until the inner workings are mastered, outer perfection cannot be accomplished; until the ego is overcome and unity with the Self is established, all attempts to arrive at a true liberty and equality are bound to be partial and inadequate; only a fundamental change of human nature can lead to the full and proper manifestation of the highest socio-political ideals known to us today, such as the passing of war, the quest for liberty and self-determination and the formation of an international alliance of nations to establish peace and global collaboration:[11]

> War is no longer, perhaps, a biological necessity, but it is still a psychological necessity; what is within us, must manifest itself outside.
>
> Only when man has developed not merely a fellow-feeling with all men, but a dominant sense of unity and commonalty, only when he is aware of them not merely as brothers,—that is a fragile bond,—but as parts of himself, only when he has learned to live not in his separate personal and communal ego-sense, but in a larger universal consciousness can the phenomenon

> of war, with whatever weapons, pass out of his life without the possibility of return.

Sri Aurobindo was unsparing in casting a searching light on the many hypocrisies that exist in political life, which hide behind big words and seemingly high ideals. He believed that intentions must be pure or else failure was inevitable, and success would wait patiently for a more sincere human hour. Writing towards the end of the First World War, Sri Aurobindo was already warning us of future conflagrations:[12]

> Two great words of the divine Truth have forced themselves insistently on our minds through the crash of the ruin and the breath of the tempest and are now the leading words of the hoped-for reconstruction,—freedom and unity. But everything depends, first, upon the truth of our vision of them, secondly, upon the sincerity with which we apply it, last and especially on the inwardness of our realization. Vain will be the mechanical construction of unity, if unity is not in the heart of the race and if it be made only a means for safeguarding and organising our interests; the result will then be only, as it was in the immediate past, a fiercer strife and new outbreaks of revolution and anarchy.

The genius of Sri Aurobindo was his clear perception and understanding of present realities even while he placed before us the highest ideals we must strive to manifest. Consider, for example, the closing lines of his essay 'A League of Nations':[13]

> The conditions of individual and social perfection are indeed the same, freedom and unity… But at present individuals and nations are equally remote from accepting any such inner mantra of unity and we can only hope at most that the best

> will increasingly turn their minds in that direction… Till then jarring leagues of nations and some mechanical dissoluble federation of the race must serve our turn for practice and for a far-off expectation. But only then can the dream of a golden age of a true communal living become feasible and be founded on a spiritual and therefore a real reign of freedom and unity when the race learns to turn its eyes inward and not any longer these things, but mankind, the people of God and a soul and body of the Divine, becomes the ideal of our perfection.

In a world of smoke and mirrors, grappling with idealisms and falsehoods of various hues, these essays remain as relevant as when they were written. With references to both contemporary events and ancient wisdom, they inspire us to contemplate the problems of our day and encourage us to interpret them in the light of the deeper perspectives these chapters present. Above all, these pages remind us of the imperative need to commit ourselves to a fundamental change of consciousness both individually and collectively if we wish to overcome the numerous challenges we face today and establish a world order that is harmonious, free, equitable and true.

* * *

22

The Future Poetry with On Quantitative Metre

Reading by Karen Ecke

The value of poetry in the life of people and nations rests at the centre of Sri Aurobindo's *The Future Poetry*.[1] It captures the idea he had explored in *The Life Divine*[2] (See Chapter 18), that in the past, poetry has played an essential part in man's aspiration, and in his search for 'God, Light, Freedom, Immortality'.[3] To express this aspiration for a higher truth in a new and greater light, to reveal the beauty and delight behind all existence, behind all that man has seen and has yet to see and feel, is the immense promise and destiny of the future poetry. It will be a deeper, more intuitive poetry that will have the power to push man's thought to accept a new way of seeing his life:[4]

> This poetry will speak of new things and of old things in a new way and with a new voice, not by any exclusion or diminution of its province, but by a great heightening above, a great intimacy within, a great enlargement and wideness around, a vision of inmost things and therefore a changed vision of the world and life and the untold potentialities of the soul's experience.

The thirty-two chapters of this book were originally published serially in *Arya* between December 1917 and July 1920. The book started out as a review of James H. Cousins's work, *New Ways in English Literature*. Cousins, an Irish writer, poet, playwright and critic, with a deep sympathy for Indian culture, wrote about new literary trends in the light of some contemporary writers: Tagore, Sri Aurobindo, W.B. Yeats, A.E., Stephen Phillips, Edward Carpenter, George Meredith, Alfred Austin, J.M. Synge and R.W. Emerson.

Sri Aurobindo quickly put aside the idea of a complete review, but he took the material in that book as a starting point to expound his own ideas on the nature of poetry and its evolution.[5] He sought to measure what the poetic mind and speech of the future poetry might have had in store for us; what new powers and psychological impulses would find new variations of rhythm, language and structure to express the character and beauty of the soul and its relation to the universe.[6] The aim of this evolution is a poetic speech that will be, as Sri Aurobindo wrote in the penultimate chapter, 'a direct and sovereign descent and pouring of some absolute sight and word of the spirit into the moulds of human language'.[7]

Although Sri Aurobindo revised the work during the late 1920s or early 1930s and again lightly in 1950, *The Future Poetry* was not published as a book in his lifetime. When asked in 1949 about the possibility of publication, Sri Aurobindo replied that he did not want to publish the book without a major rearrangement of its text, adding that a few chapters would have to be omitted or replaced by new ones. A lightly revised version of *Arya*'s text was eventually published in 1953; and in 1985, an edition incorporating all available revisions was brought out.[8] Despite Sri Aurobindo's professed reluctance to publish the work in an imperfect form, the reader can appreciate the development of his ideas on poetry past, present, and future—ideas that resonate with his thinking on the evolution of consciousness towards a spiritual society animated by soul-powers.

In Part One, Sri Aurobindo gives (what amounts to) a master class on the nature of poetry and its constituent elements. He repeatedly describes 'high poetry' to be a result of a 'spiritual excitement'[9] caused by a vision in the soul that pushes forward to express itself. Along with the soul's vision, such poetry requires the most intense forms of rhythmic movement and style.

The first chapter introduces the premise that poets must aim for a closer semblance to what Sri Aurobindo calls the 'mantra' in poetry, 'that rhythmic speech which, as the Veda puts it, rises at once from the heart of the seer and from the distant home of Truth.'[10] This, he says, will be the key to expressing the exaltation of the spirit. Poetic movement is always fundamentally important, but there must also be a soul-movement, a metrical form that lifts the rhythm toward the heavens.[11] The loftiest poetic style must go beyond the mere beauty of thought, emotion or image, and drench the listener with Ananda, a pure spiritual delight.[12] These early chapters are, in effect, lessons in how to understand what Sri Aurobindo means by the mantra in poetry, in how to raise all the elements of poetry to a new perfection.

In the chapter titled 'The National Evolution of Poetry'[13] Sri Aurobindo prepares us for chapters that follow by explaining that any assessment or appreciation of a poet's work must account for the spiritual, intellectual and aesthetic tradition of his nation and the age to which it belongs as well as be viewed from the wider stance of the evolution of the human spirit. But he reminds us, one must go beyond this limited approach straight to the poet and his poem for a pure response to the spirit of truth and beauty the poet seeks to express. With these considerations in mind, the next eighteen chapters take up first the character and course of modern English poetry, general movements in modern literature, the emergence of the English

Romantic poets heralding a spiritual impulse new to poetry, the Victorian poets, and finally contemporary English poetry of the time—the subject of Cousins's book.

These chapters are packed with insights, impressions and interpretations, all punctuated with specific references and almost a hundred lines and passages of poetry. As he leads us through nineteenth-century poetry, Sri Aurobindo observes two important trends—the change towards a direct subjective approach to Nature and the poet's concern with the larger and more conscious awakening of man to himself, 'to all that is meant by his present, his past and his future'.[14] He marks these changes as part of a movement from a literature of objective realism to one of conscious subjectivity, and traces how it unfolds through the English poetry of the period.

The last chapters in this section get to the core subject—the appearance of trends in English poetry that seem to promise a new possibility. In Sri Aurobindo's view, these poets were beginning to understand and to approach with greater or lesser success the mantric character and spirit of a future poetry. He singled out the British Edward Carpenter and the American Walt Whitman as pioneers in advancing a revolution in poetic method. Quoting some lines from Whitman…

> Out of the cradle endlessly rocking,
> Out of the mocking-bird's throat, the musical shuttle,
> Out of the Ninth-month midnight,

…and…

> Over the hoarse surging of the sea,
> Or flitting from brier to brier by day,
> I saw, I heard at intervals the remaining one, the he-bird,
> The solitary guest from Alabama,

...he comments, 'This then seems to be the natural high-water mark of free poetical rhythm; it is a use of the poetic principle of measure in its essence without the limitations of a set form.'[15]

In addition to the rhythmic change, he observes a subtle shift in poetry's language, which goes beyond the direct intuitive power we find in Shakespeare's work and, especially in the Irish poets, achieves an almost ethereal beauty of word and vision. It is a language capable of revealing the mystery of things as yet unknown, of things unseen or undreamed of in the age of Shakespeare.[16] The third change is of the substance, the turn of thought—the 'enlarging of the particular to meet and become one with the universal and infinite'.[17]

> Now increasingly the highest turn of the human mind indicates a large opening of its vision to the self as well as the person of man and the spirit of Nature, to supernature, to the cosmic, the universal and the eternal, but without any loosing of the hold on life and earth.[18]

In Part Two, Sri Aurobindo lays out his grand vision for the future poetry, the supreme harmony of what he called the five suns of poetry—Truth, Beauty, Delight, Life and the Spirit.[19] He sees these contemporary poets of his time attempting to satisfy an inner demand for synthesis—seeking for the truth and reality of the eternal self and spirit in man while insisting on life, on action in the world:[20]

> [T]he genius of the great poet will seize on some truth of being, some breath of life, some power of the spirit and bring it out with a certain supreme force for his and our delight and joy in its beauty. But nevertheless the poetry which can keep the amplitude of its breadth and nearness of its touch and yet see all things from a higher height...will more fully satisfy the whole

> of what we are and therefore the whole of what we demand from this most complete of all the arts and most subtle of all our means of aesthetic self-expression.[21]

The last six chapters revisit previous themes such as the rhythm and form of poetry in the context of Sri Aurobindo's expectations for the future. He sees the future poetry occupying a wider canvas, such as it did in ancient times:[22]

> One might almost say that ancient India was created by the Veda and Upanishads and that the visions of inspired seers made a people. The effect of the Homeric poems in Greece, the intimate connection of poetry and art with the public life of Athens spring from a similar but less steep height of poetic and artistic motive.

As the spirit of poetry changes so one expects its forms to change. The lyrical, dramatic, narrative and epic forms must undergo an essential transmutation—instead of form revealing the spirit, the spirit must create out of itself its own sure and certain form.[23] The epic form, for example, need not adhere only to a presentation of heroic action but can find its themes in the soul's journey. Sri Aurobindo started writing *Savitri*[24] (See Chapter 29) as a narrative poem retelling, in an original way, the tale of Savitri and Satyavan in the Mahabharata. In the 1930s, he began converting this narrative poem into an epic, adding a long description of Aswapati's yoga, before eventually revising and expanding it, adding a book on Savitri's yoga. The concluding words in this chapter on form and spirit are prescient of Sri Aurobindo's masterwork *Savitri*:[25]

> The epics of the soul most inwardly seen as they will be by an intuitive poetry, are his [the poet's] greatest possible subject,

> and it is this supreme kind that we shall expect from some profound and mighty voice of the future. His indeed may be the song of greatest flight that will reveal from the highest pinnacle and with the largest field of vision the destiny of the human spirit and the presence and ways and purpose of the Divinity in man and the universe.

Although Sri Aurobindo does not speak of his own poetry in the book, we find included in his essay *On Quantitative Metre*, written in 1942, fifteen of his poems in quantitative metres; one being the first 371 lines of the unfinished *Ilion*, his retelling of the fall of Troy, written in the classical hexameter. Most of us are familiar with English poetry written in accented or stressed metre, where the rhythm of the line is weighted by the heavy or light stress on its syllables. A quantitative metre, on the other hand, put very simply, depends for its rhythm on the time taken to pronounce the vowel on which the syllable rests. Sri Aurobindo examines why previous attempts at quantitative metre by English poets failed and specifically addressed the problem of adapting the hexameter, the metre of classical poetry in Greek and Latin, to the English language. This essay is not for the faint-hearted as it not only assumes a working familiarity with the mechanics of metre, but also brings home how Sri Aurobindo's feeling for poetry tackles its most demanding problems. For those interested, K.D. Sethna's *The Poetic Genius of Sri Aurobindo*[26] has a penetrating essay on the topic.

As man's external life expands its range and depth and variety, the modern poet must also find an authentic vision that seeks and finds the source of the universal delight and beauty of existence to shape a greater life for the human race.[27] This, in essence, is the message of *The Future Poetry.*

* * *

23

Letters on Poetry and Art

Reading by Patrick Beldio

This volume gathers letters that Sri Aurobindo wrote in response to about a dozen ashramites on the topics of poetry, literature, the visual and performing arts, the creative process, the development of taste, the nature and role of beauty and other related matters of aesthetics. The letters are written between 1929 and 1950, most between 1931 and 1937, when the ashram had about 200 members. They are unified by the yogic potential of their themes. Sri Aurobindo and his spiritual collaborator, the Mother, marshalled poetry and the arts, respectively, to convey their teachings and spiritual experiences. In terms of their own yoga, they used the iterative and transformative nature of the creative process to ascend the spiritual planes of consciousness and then to 'bring down' and unite those planes with physical matter for an integral transformation of the cosmos and transfiguration of the human species. The process of 'descent' could involve the direct collaboration of ashramites and the use of words, paint, musical instruments or other media, including the physical body. As such, this special collection of letters is a crucial window into the personal ways the Gurus used the arts in their own yoga, into the intimate ways they directed ashramites who were drawn to beauty and the creative process as part of their sadhana, and lastly, into the profound value of using poetry and art in service to beauty as instruments for spiritual growth.

This volume is divided into three parts that include: 1) significant features of the process of writing poetry; 2) commentaries on Sri Aurobindo's own poetry and creative methods as well as that of others; and 3) general statements about literature, poetry, the visual and performing arts and beauty in relation to yoga. These letters do not amount to an aesthetic theory, which can be found in *The Future Poetry with On Quantitative Metre*[1] (See Chapter 22); however, one finds tantalizing hints of one based on the mantra or 'word of power that comes from the Overmind inspiration'.[2]

The first part discusses the sources of poetry, the nature of poetry of the spirit, poetic techniques and the theory and practice of translation. In the first section, we learn that the three elements of poetry in service to spiritual growth and beauty are the originating sources of poetic inspiration, 'the vital force of creative beauty',[3] and the outer consciousness of the poet. Though inspiration might originate from any inner plane of higher consciousness, the poet's task, as Sri Aurobindo explains, is always the technical skill, will and mastery of the outer personality, such that it is well-trained yet surrendered, and conveys without modifying what it receives from within. One finds the contours of Sri Aurobindo's yogic psychology in these letters, which express how poetry can originate from the planes above the mind, the vital or desire nature and the body. He calls the poetry that emerges from graded levels he names the 'higher mind',[4] 'illumined mind',[5] 'intuitive mind',[6] and 'overmind'[7] and 'overhead poetry'.[8] These levels ultimately lead to the 'supermind', his translation of the Upanishadic term 'vijnana' that is the centrepiece and crown of his metaphysical thought and yogic praxis.

Poetry and art can be natural allies in this integral knowledge and experience, communicating it with polysemous symbols that if crafted with care, can bear the weight. Sri Aurobindo's overhead levels of consciousness might be thought of as increasingly talented inner musicians of the Divine Mother in her four powers of wisdom, strength, harmony and perfection—but especially harmony.[9] They strum the harp of one's outer being to play the celestial polyphonies of the unified, inmost core, the soul or 'psychic being'. Ultimately, the goal is for the psychic being to express itself with 'a perfect perfection', a perfection of its own kind in and as the body, life, and mind.[10] Innovative creative expression is one of the crucial ways Sri Aurobindo felt a supramental species would dawn but, just as the new species, this rarefied poetry and art had yet to be formed in his view. To bring this to pass, a 'new art of words written from a new consciousness demands a new technique'.[11]

A consummate teacher, Sri Aurobindo provides poetic examples of overhead altitudes throughout these letters to bring home the experience and knowledge of each and to train anyone to savour the complex overhead rasas. He even offers techniques to bring these levels into being while retaining a cosmic vision, a world-affirming embrace. In this part and throughout the volume, we read with him lines of classic voices like Virgil, Homer, Dante, Shakespeare, Milton, Shelley, Keats and Wordsworth, as well as Valmiki, Vyasa, Kalidasa, Rabindranath Tagore, Sarat Chandra Chattopadhyay, Bankim Chandra Chatterjee and many others, to experience the various poses of literary expression across time and culture that have prepared for the future poetry and art that is his standard. He also commented on original poems his disciples submitted, sometimes suggesting revisions that might push them into new octaves.

Sri Aurobindo explains how the same poem could be influenced by various planes of the mind. A passage may have a touch of say, the Overmind, in its substance, but the rhythm may be 'ordinary and the expression intellectual and imaginative'.[12] Other examples might arise from the intuition and still others that combine lower levels. It takes time to understand Sri Aurobindo's judgments, to see why he views one line as moving into a plane above and another below. As one does, one starts to get a sense for the differing levels of intensity in rhythm that he describes in *The Future Poetry* that accompany these examples, as well as the different intensities of form and vision. At the same time, one is invited to use inner faculties that may have been dormant, to discover what pleases and displeases one's own sensibilities.

At this period in his life (the 1930s), Sri Aurobindo himself was in the process of learning how to make these judgments, and so when a disciple challenged him on a certain categorization that he altered, he said, 'Yes, certainly, my ideas and reactions to some of the lines and passages about which you had asked me long ago, have developed and changed and could not but change. For at that time I was new to the overhead regions or at least to the highest of them—for the higher thought and the illumination were already old friends—and could not be sure or complete in my perception of many things concerning them.'[13]

Part Two turns the tables: Sri Aurobindo places his own work, which seeks to manifest the future poetry, under the critical gaze of his students and others. These conversations reveal some of the inner workings of his craft and, at the same time, help his students with theirs. Further, his responses to different critiques help his correspondents and the reader understand the inability of the lower mind to evaluate overhead poetry—poetry that by its very nature exists outside mental experience. This part of the volume also contains conversations on other poets and poetry and practical guidance for aspiring writers. He enunciates three rules for Indians writing English poetry, which can also serve as guides for poets today:[14]

1. Avoid rhetorical turns and artifices and the rhetorical tone generally…
2. Write modern English…
3. For poetic effect rely wholly on the power of your substance, the magic of rhythm and the sincerity of your expression — if you can add subtlety so much the better, but not at the cost of sincerity and straightforwardness. Do not construct your poetry with the brain-mind, the mere intellect — that is not the source of true inspiration; write always from the inner heart of emotion and vision.

Sri Aurobindo's epic poem *Savitri*[15] (See Chapter 29) is an especially salient topic of discussion in Part Two. He began this epic poem in sketch-form in 1916 and revised it until weeks before his passing in 1950. In the thirty-four-year discipline of creating Savitri one can detect what he called the 'triple labour of aspiration, rejection, and surrender'[16] through the creative process. One sees how his personal aim was a 'perfect perfection' in both poetry and yoga, calling *Savitri* 'a sort of symbolic epic of the aim of supramental Yoga'.[17] 'I used Savitri as a means of ascension,' he writes in a 1936 letter.[18] 'I began with it on a certain mental level, each time I could reach a higher level I rewrote from that level.' Attaining a higher level was the ascent-part of the dynamic; the descent part had to do with perfecting not only his consciousness, but the poetry itself, the physical words and the way they flowed together in the physical world of forms to manifest that higher consciousness in its fullness.

'Moreover I was particular—if part seemed to me to come from any lower level, I was not satisfied to leave it because it was good poetry,' he continued.[19] 'All had to be as far as possible of the same mint.' This is why, it would seem, his process took so long. It is herculean enough to still the mind in yoga and achieve mastery of the higher planes. Poetry that spontaneously comes from this experience will have a certain charm. More difficult still is the telos of 'perfect perfection',[20] to transform language itself so that it is able to hold the spirit in the world with the same intensity and light that it had in its own transcendent domain. 'In fact, Savitri has not been regarded by me as a poem to be written and finished, but as a field of experimentation to see how far poetry could be written from one's own Yogic consciousness and how that could be made creative.'[21]

The letters of Part Three explore yoga and the appreciation of poetry, the arts and beauty. They suggest a Vedantic perspective on art—that it is true to its nature when it is done in service to beauty, and that beauty along with love are materializations of the Divine Delight, or Ananda, that is the essence of all creation. There is practical advice about the use of the arts, that any endeavour in life can accompany one's sadhana if it is done as a sacrifice of the lower nature and an offering to the Mother. But, Sri Aurobindo points out, this takes time to accomplish: 'I myself never gave up poetry or other creative human activities out of tapasya [austerity]; they fell into a subordinate position because the inner life became stronger and stronger slowly.... But it took me years and years to get the ego out of them or the vital absorption.'[22] All through, Sri Aurobindo remains anchored in the spiritual pursuit and using every means as a yogic step to ascend the inner heights:[23]

> Literature, poetry, science and other studies can be a preparation of the consciousness for life. When one does Yoga they can become part of the sadhana only if done for the Divine or taken up by the Divine Force, but then one should not want to be a poet for the sake of being a poet only, or for fame, applause, etc.

This can be a lesson for our present collective growth. The pandemics of disease, ugliness and division that are in predominance today may fool us into devaluing the creative process, the development of taste and higher faculties that can savour and then manifest different levels of beauty in poetry and the arts. These take too long to train and what can they do anyway? However, if these aesthetic means are used as Sri Aurobindo demonstrates and explicitly advises in these letters, that is, in service to the Mother's power of harmony to yogically manifest beauty, love and Ananda, then we have a crucial resource. We hold a gift to transform any opposition into a perfect perfection that is 'superior not only in the essential character of the planes, but in all respects, in all parts and details, and consequently in all its creation'.[24]

* * *

An Introduction to Letters on Yoga

The Complete Works of Sri Aurobindo includes four volumes of *Letters on Yoga*—Volumes 28 (Part I), 29 (Part II), 30 (Part III), and 31 (Part IV), each containing letters pertaining to one of four broad categories:

Part I: Foundations of the Integral Yoga
Part II: Practice of the Integral Yoga
Part III: Experiences and Realizations in the Integral Yoga
Part IV: Transformation of Human Nature in the Integral Yoga

This edition includes approximately one-third more letters than the earlier *Sri Aurobindo Birth Centenary Library (SABCL)* collection, and is organized into more detailed categories for easier accessibility. The letters here have been selected from a larger body of letters written by Sri Aurobindo between 1927 and 1950 to hundreds of disciples and devotees. Most of them were written between 1931 and 1937 to a few dozen disciples who lived in his Ashram. The latter wrote to Sri Aurobindo on loose sheets or sent him notebooks which were diaries of their spiritual endeavours, and Sri Aurobindo usually replied on these same sheets or notebooks between the lines or in the margins, but occasionally on a separate sheet of paper. The letters are sometimes as short as a sentence, many are a paragraph or two, and some extend for several pages. Some of the letters were later revised by Sri Aurobindo for publication, but most were not. Readers may note that although they are of general interest, the letters were written to particular individuals to address their unique circumstances, and may not be equally applicable to everyone, something Sri Aurobindo himself cautioned his readers about.

* * *

24

Letters on Yoga I: Foundations of the Integral Yoga

Reading by Larry Seidlitz

Letters on Yoga–I,[1] as its subtitle indicates, provides a commentary on the foundations of the Integral Yoga. Arranged in five parts, this volume is a comprehensive and detailed view of Sri Aurobindo's overall system of spiritual philosophy and yogic psychology.

The first part focuses on some of this system's most important concepts, in particular, those relating to the nature of the Divine and its relation with the universe as a whole, and with the individual beings within the universe. Sri Aurobindo's conception of these issues, while based in part on earlier systems, such as those described in the Upanishads, the Puranas and Sankhya Yoga, is a unique synthesis that includes original concepts, as well as specific interpretations of older traditions' concepts. In addition to providing detailed definitions and explanations of concepts in his own system, a few letters include explanations of related concepts in other systems, for example, alternative conceptions of the Brahman, the Chinese Tao, the Buddhist Shunya and the Christian Trinity.

We get a good idea of Sri Aurobindo's conception of the Divine and its relation to the cosmos and the individual in this excerpt from a letter that identifies three aspects of the Divine:[2]

> 1. It is the Cosmic Self and Spirit that is in and behind all things and beings, from which and in which all is manifested in the universe — although it is now a manifestation in the Ignorance.
> 2. It is the Spirit and Master of our own being within us whom we have to serve and learn to express his will in all our movements so that we may grow out of the Ignorance into the Light.
> 3. The Divine is transcendent Being and Spirit, all bliss and light and divine knowledge and power, and towards that highest divine existence and its Light we have to rise and bring down the reality of it more and more into our consciousness and life.

This trinity of the transcendent, cosmic and individual aspects of the Divine is fundamental to Sri Aurobindo's philosophy, as it inextricably embeds our individual life into the life of the world and into the eternal existence of the Absolute. It provides a philosophical basis for our individual and collective spiritual growth and their opening into and unification with the transcendent Infinite. The transcendent Being is identified here with 'bliss and light and divine knowledge and power'—a reflection of the traditional concept of *sachchidananda*, that trinity of infinite existence, consciousness and bliss which is the nature of the cosmic spirit that underlies, supports, pervades and transcends all things, a concept discussed at length in this part of the book.

Part Two of the volume elucidates Sri Aurobindo's relatively complex system of the various aspects of our consciousness and being. We usually think of ourselves as unified beings with a certain uniqueness in character that sets us apart from others. But when we examine ourselves closely, we find that we are composed of a complex amalgam of different energies, tendencies and types of consciousness. For example, we can readily distinguish our thoughts and cognitive actions of judgment, reasoning and memory from our emotional reactions of fear, anger and sadness, our vital impulses of hunger, greed and sexual desire, and the disposition and condition of our physical body, such as a feeling of wellness or illness, strength or weakness, agility or sluggishness.

These differentiations are just the beginning, however. In Sri Aurobindo's system, they represent just the outer consciousness and being with which we are most familiar; there also exists within us an inner being that is vaster in its scope and abilities. Also within us is a higher consciousness with many ascending levels that reach towards the infinite divine consciousness, and equally, a lower subconscious and inconscient part of ourselves which anchors us to physical matter and its inertia and stability. We are normally unaware of these other parts of our being, but they nevertheless exert substantial influence on our outer, partial consciousness of ourselves.

Though we are unique in the particulars of how we express these conscious and subconscious energies, tendencies and abilities, the energies themselves are universal and pre-existent to our present individual life. These energies and levels of consciousness may be conceived as various levels, or planes, of a universal existence with which we, in our individual lives, are somehow connected. We might express these in our lives, but it is often the case that the energies express themselves through us as their semi-conscious instruments in the physical world, the physical plane that is the base of our complex existence.

All these various planes of existence and parts of our being are categorised and described in detail in this part of the book.

Part Three consists of letters explaining two primary and unique ideas in Sri Aurobindo's philosophy—the evolutionary process and the Supermind. 'The Riddle of This World', one of the longest letters in this volume, discusses the evolutionary process and presents a synopsis of Sri Aurobindo's philosophy that the earth is undergoing a spiritual evolution leading to a divine and supramental dénouement. It also elaborates the reason for pain, suffering and evil in the world and on their eventual dissolution. Sri Aurobindo explained that although the origin of the phenomena of darkness, sorrow and evil are beyond the intellect and are automatically justified in the Divine's cosmic vision and cognition, what could be said about it is that it was for some reason inevitable:[3]

> ...once manifestation began infinite possibility also began and among the infinite possibilities which it is the function of the universal manifestation to work out, the negation, the apparent effective negation — with all its consequences — of the Power, Light, Peace, Bliss was very evidently one. If it is asked why even if possible it should have been accepted, the answer nearest to the Cosmic Truth which the human intelligence can make is that in the relations or in the transition of the Divine in the Oneness to the Divine in the Many, this ominous possible became at a certain point an inevitable.

Sri Aurobindo further elaborated that the divine soul, while descending into manifestation, sees its own opposite as an irresistible unknown, a dichotomy which must be reconciled in an evolutionary ascent. Other letters on the theme of evolution relate spiritual evolution to human history, and some further clarify the higher levels of the evolution leading into the supramental consciousness.

Other letters in Part Three focus on the supramental denouement of the earth's evolution mentioned above. In Sri Aurobindo's conception, the supramental consciousness with its omnipotent force, existed prior to the evolution on earth and is its origin. A primary aim of his own yoga was to clear the way for its descent into the earth consciousness, establish it here as a higher principle above mind into which we could evolve and bring its enlightening and spiritually transforming effects into the earth's tardy evolutionary process to ease its difficulty and hasten its deliverance. It was this descent that the Mother announced had occurred on 29 February 1956.[4] This section of letters clarifies these processes, and discusses the eventual effects of the supramental descent, including the transformation of the physical body and the conquest of death.

The letters in Part Four discuss the relations and differences of various fields of knowledge and activity with yoga and spirituality. One section of letters focuses on the differences between intellectual understanding and discourse and spiritual experience and endeavour. It includes quite a number of longer letters that address intellectual arguments against the validity of spirituality, and that pointedly expose the limitations of intellectual and scientific knowledge:[5]

> Intellect has done many things for man; it has helped to raise him high above the animal; at its best it has opened a first view on all great fields of knowledge. But it cannot go beyond that; it cannot get at Truth itself, only at some reflections, forms, representations of it. I myself cannot remember to have ever arrived at anything in the spiritual field by the power of the intellect — I have used it only to help the expression of what I have known and experienced, but even there it is only certain forms that it provided, they were used by another Light and a larger Mind than the intellect.

In the same letter, Sri Aurobindo contrasts the uncertain, pale, reflective nature of the intellect with the vividness and overwhelming certitude that can come in spiritual experience:[6]

> When the peace of God descends on you, ...when you are driven like a leaf before the wind by the breath of the Divine Force, when Love flows out from you on all creation, when Divine Knowledge floods you with a Light which illumines and transforms in a moment all that was before dark, sorrowful and obscure, ...you feel at once by the spiritual contact, by the inner vision, by the illumined and seeing thought, by the vital sensation and even by the very physical sense, everywhere you see, hear, touch only the Divine.

A second section of letters in Part Four includes letters discussing the differences between religion, idealism, morality and yoga. Sri Aurobindo describes religion as a mixture of spirituality and the errors that come in when trying to ignorantly sublimate the lower nature of mankind. Religion, he feels, tends to degenerate into fixed dogmas and routine ceremonies. He suggests that idealism, particularly the striving for perfection in one or more aspects of life, has great value in the evolution towards spiritual realization, but that one cannot attain that perfection unless the endeavour is founded on an awakened spiritual consciousness. He indicates morality as an attempt to govern outer conduct by mental rules, and asserts that this control, however, was always partial and could be achieved only by spiritual transformation, which is the aim and object of Sri Aurobindo's Integral Yoga. Also included in this section are letters on the limitations of social duty, philanthropy, humanitarianism and political activism in delivering humanity out of its persistent suffering, for only a fundamental evolution of consciousness can resolve the inherent imperfections of nature.

Part Five covers particular issues in the large field of spiritual and occult knowledge. In Sri Aurobindo's cosmology there exist both gods and occult hostile beings, or asuras, which influence and assist or impede humanity's evolutionary ascent towards the Divine. One set of letters discusses their origin, nature, various types, as well as some of the specific deities that are recognized in the Indian tradition. A second section has letters discussing Avatars, the incarnations of the Supreme Divine Being in a physical body, which are said to occur in the world from time to time to spearhead its evolutionary unfolding, and Vibhutis, which are exceptional human beings that embody 'some power of the Divine and is enabled by it to act with great force in the world.'[7] A third section of letters discusses Sri Aurobindo's views of four important related topics in his philosophy: destiny, karma, death and rebirth. And finally, the fourth and last section contains letters discussing occultism in general, what it is and how it works, its place in yoga, as well as some of its familiar phenomena such as seances, ghosts, miracles, magic and use in healing.

For those who wish to have a thorough understanding of foundational philosophical concepts that have puzzled humankind since millennia, Sri Aurobindo in this volume shines a light of yogic clarity and illumines our understanding of ourselves and our place in the universe in a direct and accessible language.

* * *

25

Letters on Yoga II

Reading by Larry Seidlitz

Sri Aurobindo's correspondence on the Integral Yoga between the years 1927 and 1950 constitutes *Letters on Yoga II*.[1] This volume of letters on the practice of the Yoga is arranged in three parts—'The Path of the Integral Yoga',[2] 'The Synthetic Method of the Integral Yoga',[3] and 'The Integral Yoga and Other Spiritual Paths'.[4]

Part One lays out various preliminary considerations related to the practice of the Integral Yoga, such as its basic aims, principles and elements, its requisite conditions and its fundamental nature. These are followed by a discussion on the various psychological and spiritual qualities that are to be developed and fostered in the course of the yoga, including inner states and movements of the consciousness, such as sincerity, aspiration, patience and perseverance, vigilance, peace, equality or equanimity, quietness of mind, inner silence, rejection of wrong movements, surrender to the Divine, faith in the Divine, self-offering to the Divine and openness to the Divine. The development of these qualities is one important side of the practice of this yoga, one which is rather subtle and psychological in nature, and complements the more practical and behavioural aspects that are the focus of Part Two.

But there is another crucial side to the yoga discussed in Part One, and that is the role of the Divine Grace, the Divine Force and the Guru or Guide of the yoga. In most paths of yoga, but in this yoga especially, the Divine is viewed as the true bestower of all the gains that are made in the practice. Sri Aurobindo stresses on attitudes of humility, trust, devotion, obedience and a psychological openness to receive the Guru's influence and help. This emphasis on surrender to the Divine, and the Divine's response in the form of Grace, are illustrated in a letter:[5]

> All can be done by the Divine, the heart and nature purified, the inner consciousness awakened, the veils removed, if one gives oneself to the Divine with trust and confidence—and even if one cannot do so fully at once, yet the more one does so, the more the inner help and guidance comes and the contact and the experience of the Divine grows within. If the questioning mind becomes less active and humility and the will to surrender grow in you, this ought to be perfectly possible. No other strength and tapasya [austerities] are then needed, but this alone.

Part Two discusses four central processes of the sadhana, which also form the four main sections of *The Synthesis of Yoga*[6] (See Chapter 19)—the yogas of works, knowledge, devotion and self-perfection.[7] It starts by explaining in a general way what each of the four yogas entails, and emphasises that there is great flexibility in how these four processes develop in a person, depending on the individual's nature. Some people may emphasise one or two processes in their practice with the others coming in at a later stage: 'one may begin with knowledge or with works or with Bhakti [devotion] or with Tapasya of self-purification for perfection (change of nature) and develop the rest as a subsequent movement or one may combine all in one movement.'[8] At the same time, it gives special importance to the yoga of works, because it is primarily through dedicated action that the outer being can participate in the yoga and undergo the necessary change—the transformation of the nature into a divine life—that is the special focus of Sri Aurobindo's Integral Yoga.

The letters in this section focus on building the sadhana through works, concentration and meditation, and love and devotion. Again, given the importance of works in the Integral Yoga, as well as its complexity and the possibilities for confusion about its nature and role, about twice as many pages are devoted to it than to either of the other two yogas:[9]

> As for the work, it is a means of preparation, it can also be a means of growing into the inner consciousness. But then it must be done not as work only but as an offering to the Mother, without insisting on the ego, with an aspiration to feel her Force working in one, her Presence presiding over the work, seeking to give all to her, not claiming anything for oneself. That is the spirit of work offered as a sacrifice; done like that, work becomes a sadhana and a Yoga.

Other letters describe the internal processes that occur in the course of the yoga of works, while some provide advice on how to view outer obstacles that come up in work as opportunities to overcome weaknesses in one's nature or to gain greater mastery over interpersonal and other external challenges. There is practical advice about dealing with subordinates and superiors in work,[10] avoiding disturbances and anxiety in work[11] and engaging in creative activities[12] as a dedicated work for the Divine. The letters also impart useful guidance on how to work while centred within and concentrated on the Divine, for knowing the Divine's Will, and for receiving the Divine Power in work.

In his letters on concentration and meditation, Sri Aurobindo distinguishes between these two practices:[13]

> Concentration means fixing the consciousness in one place or on one object and in a single condition. Meditation can be diffusive, e.g. thinking about the Divine, receiving impressions and discriminating, watching what goes on in the nature and acting upon it etc.

For concentration, he suggests, 'The method of gathering of the mind is not an easy one. It is better to watch and separate oneself from the thoughts till one becomes aware of a quiet space within into which they come from outside.'[14] He delineated different ways of getting rid of thoughts, 'one is to reject them one by one before they can come in; another is to look at them with detachment till they fade away.'[15]

Concentration, writes Sri Aurobindo, is of different types. He expresses a preference for a concentration that is done in the heart rather than the head in some cases: 'It may be better to concentrate in the heart rather than in the mind, offer yourself from there and call the Mother into the heart leaving the thoughts to fall silent of themselves.'[16] This kind of concentration 'is what brings about the opening of the psychic', whereas the concentration at the top of the head 'is the right place for Yogic concentration in reading or thinking'.[17] While Sri Aurobindo sometimes exempted particular sadhaks from meditating or concentrating, he generally recommended setting aside a fixed period of time for it each day.

The volume also has valuable advice on various related details of concentration and meditation, such as on postures, length and regularity and difficulties encountered, as well as a dedicated section of letters on the use of mantra (repetition of a sacred word or phrase) and japa (repetition of a name of the Divine) in the practice.

The section on sadhana through love and devotion concentrates less on specific methods and more on distinguishing and clarifying different types of love and devotion—that is, divine love, psychic love and human love. He distinguishes between divine love and psychic love. saying that 'the Divine's love is that which comes from above poured down from the Divine Oneness and its Ananda on the being—psychic love is a form taken by divine love in the human being according to the needs and possibilities of the human consciousness.'[18] He further explains that 'psychic love is pure and full of self-giving without demand, but it is human and can err and suffer. The Divine Love is something much vaster and deeper and full of light and ananda.'[19]

In ordinary human love, 'there is usually a hope of return, of benefit or advantage of some kind, or of certain pleasures and satisfactions mental, vital or physical, that the person loved can give.'[20] When a person first turns to the Divine, Sri Aurobindo explains, this human egoistic element is usually mixed in and must be purified so that the love becomes essentially psychic and spiritual. Nevertheless, all the parts of the being—physical, vital (the life-nature) and mental included—can love the Divine in the true way, and when they do so, it brings in the fullest and most complete love. Sri Aurobindo also discusses the role of devotion and worship in the yoga. Bhakti, or devotion, in which the emotions are turned towards the Divine in love and self-giving, is 'the very basis of this Yoga',[21] and worship and prayer have a useful place when they are done with the true psychic attitude, that is, under the influence of the soul.

The final section is a collection of letters clarifying the characteristics of the Integral Yoga that set it apart from other spiritual paths, but also those it has in common with them. It discusses the path's relation with Jainism, Buddhism, Christianity, Sankhya, Patanjali's Yoga, Shankara's Mayavada, Tantra, Vaishnavism, Theosophy and the teachings of several recent Indian yogis. It includes a dedicated selection of letters on the distinctive nature of the transformation of life that is sought in the Integral Yoga.

On the whole, this volume lays out in an accessible language the essential methods of the Integral Yoga in detailed manner. Composed of letters tailored to each sadhaka's unique nature and temperament, it is a comprehensive manual of practice for sincere seekers and outlines the various pathways of the Integral Yoga, a yoga which does not prescribe a common method for all.

* * *

26

Letters on Yoga III: Experiences and Realizations in the Integral Yoga

Reading by Georg Stollenwerk

The third volume of Sri Aurobindo's *Letters on Yoga*[1] covers the wide field of experiences and realizations in the yoga—experiences understood as not yet settled, temporary happenings and movements in the yoga; and realizations understood as well-established psychic and spiritual truths in the consciousness of the seeker or Yogi. The collection consists of four parts:

1. The Place of Experiences in the Practice of Yoga[2]
2. The Opening of the Inner Senses[3]
3. Experiences of the Inner Consciousness and the Cosmic Consciousness[4]
4. The Fundamental Realizations of the Integral Yoga[5]

In Part One, we learn about the value of experiences as a promise of future realizations, the importance of small beginnings in the early period of the sadhana, the relation of inner experience to our outer life as well as the indispensable role of the psychic being for safety on the path of the Integral Yoga. For instance, we receive valuable advice on how to deal with experiences:[6]

> You have to watch and see how they [experiences] develop. For the most part they carry their own meaning and if you go on observing them with a silent and vigilant mind you will understand more than if you were in a constant turmoil of thought about them.

Sri Aurobindo encourages us not to be dispirited by temporary, inconsistencies in the working of the spiritual forces within us, temporary drops or falls of consciousness as well as natural phenomena like fatigue or inertia, as 'the system has to take rest so as to assimilate and renew its receptive power'.[7] Periods of emptiness and blankness, he says, are in most cases not only transitional, but helpful preparatory stages, if not basic conditions for further progress, increased receptivity to the higher consciousness and a coming realization.

Part Two plunges into the nature and symbolic meaning of a large variety of inner visions, sounds, smells and tastes. Sri Aurobindo teaches us that the opening of the inner, subtle senses (here related to visions) is 'very important for the Yoga and should not be rejected'.[8] Although an actual change of consciousness and not any power of occult seeing or hearing is the central aim and process of the sadhana, visions and other experiences in the inner senses can help to approach and finally enter into touch with the Divine. We are advised, however, not to get attached to these phenomena but to simply observe them and move on. This attitude avoids the danger of falling prey to wrong visions or voices that mislead the seeker by aggrandising the ego.

Visions can be of different natures and origins. Usually, they start with colours, and later one begins to see figures, scenes and people. They can occur on different planes of our inner consciousness—in the mental, vital or subtle physical sphere. It is not easy to decipher the symbolism of light and colours, as it varies with the field or play of forces. Yet, Sri Aurobindo offers us some very clear and precise indications. White light, for example, is the Mother's light, the light of the Force of the Divine Consciousness with its forces of purity and peace; the golden light, the light of the Divine Truth.

Likewise, the awareness of subtle sounds, smells and tastes is a sign of the opening and awakening of the subtle senses and the inner consciousness. One of the most prominent experiences in the field of sound might be the hearing of bells, which 'has always been considered a sign of a premonition of the opening of the inner being to spiritual experience.'[9]

The world of inner symbols when it comes to visions of figures, scenes and people is even more wide-ranging. Sri Aurobindo details the deeper meaning of various natural elements like the sun, moon, stars, fire, the sky, different weather phenomena, night and dawn, water and various bodies of water, the earth and mountains. He defines several visions of gods, goddesses and semi-divine beings (Krishna of the Gita, for instance, as a bringer of spiritual knowledge, will and bhakti), and explains some symbolisms of the human world (like children, parents and relatives), as well as of the plant and animal world. A view on certain buildings, such as temples or pyramids, and different objects (crowns or diamonds) closes this collection of Sri Aurobindo's letters on specific symbols we might meet in our dreams and visions. Sri Aurobindo stresses, however, that it is not the mental understanding and interpretation of a symbol that counts, but the concrete experience:[10]

> One puts an intellectual label on the "White Light" and the mind is satisfied and says "Now I know all about it; it is the pure Divine Consciousness light," and really it knows nothing. But if

one allows the Divine White Light to manifest and pour through the being, then one comes to know it and get all its results.

Part Three of this volume relates to experiences of the inner consciousness and the universal or cosmic consciousness, which can be met in the subtle body, the inner physical realm and more often and more intensely on the vital plane with its numerous forces and beings. Sri Aurobindo advises us to always keep a strict vigilance and a clear inner perception and will—and to rely on the Mother in any circumstance. His closing remarks on exteriorization and any going out of the body are important for those who have the tendency to enter other worlds by leaving their own vital sheath, especially during sleep.

An inward movement, to become aware of one's inner being, is an essential condition in the Integral Yoga, as 'To change the outer consciousness entirely without developing this inner consciousness would be too difficult.'[11] Sri Aurobindo maps out some general steps on this marvellous journey—detaching oneself from one's outer being, living within and from within, first from one's inner mind, vital and physical, then from the corresponding witness purushas or selves of the levels of the being, and finally in and from one's psychic being or inmost soul. His letters comment on a number of experiences and movements connected with these stages and their relation to the external being, as well as on inner experiences in the state of samadhi or trance.

The conscious awareness of the different planes and parts of his individual inner being puts the seeker in touch with the universal or cosmic consciousness standing behind the individualised personality—an opening to the universal self and forces:[12]

> When one has the cosmic consciousness, one can feel the cosmic self as one's own self, one can feel one with other beings

> in the cosmos, one can feel all the forces of Nature as moving in oneself, all selves as one's own self.

Sri Aurobindo's letters on this topic cover a number of aspects. These include the relation of the cosmic consciousness to other planes (like the Overmind, the transcendent, or the cosmic self), the different realms of cosmic ignorance and cosmic truth, universal harmony and discords, the cosmic will, the experiences of opening to the cosmic mind and life as well as the broad range of universal and cosmic forces. He explicitly warns of the dangers we might meet when delving into these inner and cosmic experiences. As long as the opening of a wider consciousness above, and the coming forward of the psychic being from behind is not yet a living reality, we might stumble into 'The Intermediate Zone',[13] a realm of transition between our ordinary consciousness and the true yogic knowledge, where we are not yet in direct touch with the Truth on its original levels, but receive only indirect impressions. There we can be 'subjected to all sorts of voices, suggestions, ideas, so-called inspirations which are not genuine'[14] and which might lead to a downfall if we pay heed to them. Thus, Sri Aurobindo advises us to look on all these things with a calm indifference, to observe them without lending them any credibility. Fortunately, however, not all seekers have to deal with these phenomena:[15]

> If one has purified oneself, if there is no abnormal vanity, egoism, ambition or other strong misleading element, or if one is vigilant and on one's guard, or if the psychic is in front, one can either pass rapidly and directly or with a minimum of trouble into the higher zones of consciousness where one is in direct contact with the Divine Truth.

After these preparatory stages, one enters the fundamental experiences of the Integral Yoga. In Part Four of this volume,

Sri Aurobindo elaborates on the foundations of his sadhana, the triple transformation—psychic, spiritual and supramental as well as the different processes and experiences connected with them.

The importance of the psychic change as a first stage cannot be overstressed. When the psychic being or soul being comes forward, it offers the seeker a desireless love and bhakti, the presence of the Mother within, an unerring guidance and a quieting of the outer being, the mind, the vital and the physical consciousness. It allows an opening up to the higher spiritual consciousness, thus preparing the seeker for the second stage in Sri Aurobindo's yoga, the spiritual transformation.

What are the means of bringing forward the psychic? Sri Aurobindo offers several answers according to the nature of the seeker: a constant and sincere aspiration, the will to surrender in the central being, the elimination of selfishness and demand, or a true will to get rid of the movements of the lower nature. In the end, he says, it will simply happen 'when [we] are sufficiently advanced'.[16] Sri Aurobindo then elaborates on different experiences related to the psychic plane—such as the psychic influence in our ordinary life, psychic joy and sorrow, the psychic flame as a first manifestation of the psychic being and the relation of Agni with the psychic fire—and he stresses the different movements of psychic and spiritual transformation:[17]

> Psychisation means the change of the lower nature, bringing right vision into the mind, right impulse and feeling into the vital, right movement and habit into the physical – all turned towards the Divine, all based on love, adoration, bhakti – finally the vision and sense of the Mother everywhere in all as well as in the heart, her Force working in the being etc., faith consecration, surrender.

In contrast, he describes spiritual transformation as an 'established descent of the spiritual peace, light, knowledge, power, bliss from above, the awareness of the self and the divine and of a higher cosmic consciousness and the change of the whole consciousness to that'.[18] The path to spiritual transformation leads the seeker through several experiences and realizations: temporary stages of peace, calm and silence; the discovery of the Self and its experience on various planes of consciousness; and experiences on the higher planes with its different layers—Higher Mind, Illumined Mind, Overmind. Not only to receive influences from these planes, but to actually live in them is, according to Sri Aurobindo, 'a definite stage in the movement towards transformation'.[19]

Finally, we learn about the two main and alternating movements leading to spiritual transformation—the ascent of the lower consciousness towards the higher, and the descent of the higher, of peace, force, light and Ananda, into the lower to transform it. These and the experiences connected with them end this remarkable journey from the first opening of the inner veil to the psychic and spiritual transformation of all the planes and parts of the being, opening the gate to the essence and crown of Sri Aurobindo's yoga: the supramental transformation.

* * *

27

Letters on Yoga IV: Transformation of Human Nature in the Integral Yoga

Reading by Payal Adhikari

The entire premise of Sri Aurobindo's Integral Yoga rests on a change of human nature. This process of transformation is long, arduous and complicated. The sadhaks who attempted this work wrote of all their major and minor problems to Sri Aurobindo, who provided guidance to each through letters. This volume is a compilation of answers to problems concerning transformation, and provides valuable insights into the psychological process involved. The letters in this volume deal directly with the fundamental challenges posed by human nature.

This book has four parts. The first three deal with problems that arise from the mind, vital (life-centre), physical and subconscient levels. The fourth part focuses on major difficulties in the sadhana, and the general aids and attitudes required to deal with them. Despite being addressed specifically to sadhaks of the Integral Yoga, the general nature of the problems enunciated make the letters useful to any seeker on the path of self-discovery and self-development.

Most of us identify with our manifested behaviour, traits and attitudes, and believe them to be an essential part of who we are. Effecting a change in these outer patterns is considered sufficient to bring about personality changes in the quest for self-development. However, the outer act or quality or attitude is often a result of movements and intermixtures of the different underlying parts of our being. Steady, substantial and consistent outward changes require an assiduous study and transformation of all the underlying processes. A yogic understanding of our psychology reveals to us various parts of the being.

The outer nature is made up of three parts, each with its own distinct type of consciousness. These three parts are the mind, vital and body. Mind is that component of our being that deals with thoughts, ideas, intellect and knowledge. The vital compromises of life-energies, emotions, sensations, desires and impulses. The body includes the physical structure along with organs and physiological systems. Most of us are aware of these three layers of our being and mistakenly identify them as our true personality.

This outer nature is fraught with many imperfections that prevent one from leading a harmonious and satisfied life. At the mental level, these can manifest in the form of obsessive thoughts, rigidity of ideas and lack of concentration. Difficulties of the vital include depression, jealousy, ego-centricity and other such problems. The vital also plays a central role in our relations and interactions with others. The difficulties of the physical are related to various bodily issues such as food, sleep, sex, and diseases and ailments of various kinds.

The Integral Yoga introduces the concept of the inner being, the field of the person within, which is veiled by the outer nature. Comprising of the inner mental, vital and physical being, this inner being connects the soul within, the psychic being, with the outer nature. Complete identification with one's inner nature brings progressive self-mastery, as it acts always under the guidance and influence of the inmost soul.

The psychic being is the evolving, individualised, and thus unique Divine element within us. Most often, it is covered by the outer being and thus cannot function uninhibitedly. It has inherent power and knowledge of the highest parts within us, and enables Divine qualities, such as self-giving, beauty, gratitude, peace and joy, to manifest in our personality.

Another plane, below the waking physical consciousness, is the subconscient, a storehouse of memories and habits of the mental, vital and physical parts, which are constantly and subtly influencing the individual. Unless it is illumined by a higher light and its ignorant habits and movements transformed, this influence is usually not positive.

Finally, the *Jivatman* is the universalized Divine centre that is untouched by the movements of nature. It supports the evolution of the being but is not involved with it.

Ordinarily, our outer nature acts under the influence of the habitual patterns of each of these parts of the being, environmental influences, attitudes picked up as children, ego and the unconscious. These influences affect us in diverse and sometimes contrary ways, and the result is often a discordant personality. Sri Aurobindo's Integral Yoga aims at a psychological transformation wherein the outer, flawed nature is transmuted into a Divine nature, which means bringing all the different parts of the being under the individualised Divine, the psychic being.

As the one central controlling agent, the psychic being is able to harmonise these different parts, and help each part to function perfectly in its true role. The inner nature, which is directly under the influence of the psychic being, then takes on the helm of affairs of the human personality; the outer nature exists as an instrument, as a means of expression. The key is to discern the true soul or psychic being, perceive its guidance and make the mind, vital and body manifest those intimations. In this way, our thoughts, feelings and sensations are freed from common human flaws, resulting in a more joyous and actualized life.

Sri Aurobindo also places emphasis on the role of invisible forces in the shaping of human personality. There are helpful forces that aid in the evolution of an individual, as also forces that retard forward movement. The aim of the Integral Yoga is to help seekers open themselves to the higher Shakti that has the ultimate transmuting power over the personality. As individuals, we can only prepare ourselves psychologically to receive the force; the decisive change, however, is brought about only by this Divine force.

As in other yogas, union with the Divine is the primary aim of this yoga as well. However, its ultimate thrust is the transformation of human nature that has mostly been seen as intractable in traditional paths of yoga, and the full manifestation of the Divine in life by the agency of higher powers of consciousness beyond the mind. As individuals progressively evolve into actualized harmonious beings, they can bring about a change in the larger environment and society that they live in.

The letters in the first three parts of the volume serve as a compendium of the types of practical problems and defects one can encounter in the outer nature explained above. Sri Aurobindo's guidance on these matters can help the seeker in multiple ways. The mind, for all its capacities, remains still an inadequate mediator between spirit and matter:[1]

> The mind is always building up ideas, some of which are wrong, some a mixture of truth and error, some true in their way, but true only in a certain field or in certain conditions

> or for some people, and it proceeds not only to make "pets" of them, but to try to impose them as universal and absolute truths or general standards which everybody must follow. The mind is a rigid instrument: it finds it difficult to adapt itself to the greater plasticity of the play of life or the freedom of the play of the Spirit. It wants to catch hold of either or both of these spontaneous powers and cut them into its own measures. It poses as the mediator and interpreter between life and the spirit; but it knows neither; it only knows itself and its own constructions out of life and its own deformations or half reflections of the truth of the Spirit. Only the supermind can be a true mediator and interpreter.

Sri Aurobindo brings forth the limitations of the mind, an instrument that is usually considered the epitome of human personality in the modern world. Because it is inherently flawed, it too must be modified to become a receptacle of the higher Spirit. If we extend this idea, it also brings home the point that today, life, business, politics, and the other activities of ordinary existence are laid on the lines of mental conceptions, and therefore will be inherently flawed. Transformation at a large scale is not possible unless individual minds are transformed to receive higher and wider truths from the world of the Spirit.

Sri Aurobindo also writes a series of letters on the subject of the vital, and advises disciples on how to negotiate this powerful but challenging aspect of ourselves:[2]

> Be careful to reject always movements (like vexation, discontent, etc.) that bring back confusion or depression. One cannot always help these movements coming, but one can reject them when they come; the more they are rejected, the more difficult it becomes for them to recur – or, if they recur, they hold only for a moment and then drop away. To entertain them means to give them a chance to cover the true consciousness once more.

Through these letters he provides the sadhaka various insights into how to become conscious of the problems of the vital being and how to deal with them. For instance, in today's context of loosening social and moral structures, modern men and women have a lot of freedom to allow full play to their feelings, impulses and sensations. As a result, they are plagued by many vital problems which take the form of depression, despondency, anxiety, phobias, restlessness, and over-sentimentality. Sri Aurobindo stresses on the psychological tool of 'rejection' to deal with wrong movement originating in the vital being: '...by constant rejection they are pushed out; you feel them no longer rising in you but coming from outside.'[3] This kind of inner work even leads to better interpersonal relations and harmonious functioning in the larger family, professional and community context. For instance, this is the practical advice Sri Aurobindo gives to a sadhaka troubled by the offenses of co-workers:[4]

> One must try to look calmly on others, not overstress either the virtues or defects, without ill-feeling or misunderstanding or injustice, with a calm mind and vision.

Part Three takes up the body and the physical consciousness, whose influence extend to the whole being in myriad ways. The ultimate change of nature that Sri Aurobindo envisaged encompassed not just a psychological change, but eventually, a physical transformation as well. Hence, the inner work of purifying and changing the physical consciousness is an essential and novel aspect in the Integral Yoga:[5]

> The greater difficulty [in freeing oneself from vital desire] is because the sadhana is now taking place directly on the physical plane, where the force of a habit or habitual movement once formed is very great. When the sadhana is taking place on the mental or vital plane, it is more easy to control or change,

> because the mind and vital are more plastic than the physical. But on the other hand if something is definitely gained on the physical plane, there is a more lasting and completer fulfilment than when it is on the mental or vital alone.

Sri Aurobindo's perspective on physical wellbeing is noteworthy too, as it is a holistic outlook that stresses that any illness requires a curative strategy at all levels of the being, an insight that can be applied to the manner in which we can approach the ongoing pandemic as well:[6]

> They [the forces of illness] first weaken or break through the nervous envelope, the aura. If that is strong and whole, a thousand million germs will not be able to do anything to you. The envelope pierced, they attack the subconscient mind in the body, sometimes also the vital mind or mind proper – prepare the illness by fear or thought of illness.

This brings us to the problem of the subconscient, another recurrent theme. Unregenerated instincts are the most difficult to handle because they often come with an impulsion that is beyond the control of the seeker:[7]

> If consciousness and light is not brought into the subconscient, then there can be no change. For it is in the subconscient that there are seeds of all the old lower vital instincts and movements and however much they may be cleared in the lower vital itself, they may sprout up again from below. Also the subconscient is the secret basis of the bodily consciousness. The subconscient must admit into itself the higher consciousness and the Truth light.

The true and lasting change sought for in the Integral Yoga can only occur when the unseen higher force is able to replace, correct or sublimate the instincts that are harmful for the seeker. Sri Aurobindo helps the sadhaka identify the nature of the higher force and enunciates the benefits it brings:[8]

> For your sadhana it is necessary first to establish the entire openness of the physical being and stabilise in it the descent of calm, strength, purity and joy with the feeling of the presence and working of the Mother's Force in you.

The change envisaged in the yoga is a radical one, as the entire psychological personality must be reshaped under the influence of deeper and higher spiritual realities. Those attempting self-development on the lines of spirituality must abandon an egoistic, self-centred approach to life. They require a complete reorientation towards life problems and must cultivate a tremendous receptivity to the Divine help. This spiritual approach to life, along with the difficulties which must inevitably rise in the practice of the Integral Yoga, is highlighted in the fourth and final part of the book, which takes up various allied topics such as failures in the sadhana, ways of dealing with difficulties, depression and despondency, reliance on the Divine help, the action of occult hostile forces, and even the causes of madness and hysteria. In the end, the solution to all these problems remains the same, an entire opening to and reliance on the Divine:[9]

> It is the lesson of life that always in this world everything fails a man — only the Divine does not fail him, if he turns entirely to the Divine. It is not because there is something bad in you that blows fall on you, — blows fall on all human beings because they are full of desire for things that cannot last and they lose them or, even if they get, it brings disappointment and cannot satisfy them. To turn to the Divine is the only truth in life.

The letters in this volume illustrate that the work of transformation is a long and assiduous path that requires a tremendous observation, comprehension, and mastery of human nature. The work entails many difficulties and involves numerous dangers. The practice of yoga is not to be taken lightly or in a casual spirit. Success in this endeavour requires a tremendous personal effort, an ultimate reliance on the Divine, and the necessary descent of Divine forces. For the sincere practitioner of the Integral Yoga, these letters provide invaluable guidance and insight.

* * *

28

The Mother with Letters on the Mother

Reading by Gautam Chikermane

I first read *The Mother* as a small 1928 booklet.[1] The impact was profound. This book compresses and captures the core ideas of Sri Aurobindo into a highly concentrated force-field. Despite all six chapters being disparate entities (the first a message, the second a letter to a disciple Motilal Mehta, and the third to sixth, letters to another disciple Punamchand Shah), the final text appears as a single entity. Such is the power contained in these words and so diverse the ways in which devotees read them and sought clarifications on the ideas contained here that it resulted in Sri Aurobindo answering hundreds of letters, an exchange that has expanded and deepened this intense discourse. The result is *The Mother and Letters on the Mother*,[2] a 662-page volume of which the base text, *The Mother*, is just twenty-six pages. The compilation is divided into three parts: the primary text, *The Mother*; letters on *The Mother*, itself broken down into five sections; and translations of the prayers of the Mother from French to English.

This volume takes up complex spiritual themes such as the powers of the Mother,[3] the requirements of doers of divine works,[4] the grace of the Divine Mother and the devotee's faith and surrender,[5] and the sadhak's 'triple labour of aspiration, rejection and surrender', and weaves them into a narrative of truths and advice.[6] With sharp clarity he harmonises the yoga, the yogi and the yogic process—a unification of the Divine, the individual aspirant and the methods followed:[7]

> In Yoga also it is the Divine who is the Sadhaka and the Sadhana; it is his Shakti with her light, power, knowledge, consciousness, Ananda, acting upon the adhara and, when it is opened to her, pouring into it with these divine forces that makes the Sadhana possible.

If it were that simple, why make the effort? Sri Aurobindo provides the answer, '... so long as the lower nature is active the personal effort of the Sadhaka remains necessary'. What is this personal effort? It is a three-stage process consisting of aspiration of the entire being, the rejection of all movements of the lower nature, and a surrender of all of oneself to the Divine.[8]

These are the inner pathways towards a Supramental realization. But on the way, the sadhaka meets several difficulties, the dominant ones being the desire for power, wealth and sex. These three, Sri Aurobindo writes in an intense chapter on money, have 'the strongest attraction for the human ego and the Asura and are most generally misheld and misused by those who retain them'. In other words, the rich and the powerful become instruments of their wealth and their power.

We tend to see both power and money only in their outer manifestations, not live their inner truths. Sri Aurobindo takes money and gives us a spiritual window through which to view it. 'Money,' he writes, 'is the visible sign of a universal force, and this force in its manifestation on earth works on the vital and physical planes and is indispensable to the fullness of the outer life.' The problem is that the money force, like power, has been 'usurped for the uses of the ego or held by Asuric influences and perverted to their purpose'. Hence, most spiritual traditions eschew and leave this force 'in the hands of the hostile forces',[9] from whom it has to be regained, 'To reconquer it for the Divine to whom it belongs and use it divinely for the divine life is the supramental way for the Sadhaka.'[10] Understanding this force in the context of Sri Aurobindo's Integral Yoga rewires the idea in our minds:[11]

> In your personal use of money look on all you have or get or bring as the Mother's. Make no demand but accept what you receive from her and use it for the purposes for which it is given to you. Be entirely selfless, entirely scrupulous, exact, careful in detail, a good trustee; always consider that it is her possessions and not your own that you are handling. On the other hand, what you receive for her, lay religiously before her; turn nothing to your own or anybody else's purpose.

But who or what is the Mother—a person, an entity, a force? Transcendent, she is the original supreme Shakti and stands above the worlds; Universal, she is the cosmic Mahashakti who creates beings and conducts processes and forces; and Individual, she embodies the power of Shakti and Mahashakti and 'mediates between the human personality and the divine Nature'.[12]

Further, she has four aspects or powers using which she deals with the terrestrial play. Masheshwari, wisdom and compassion, who sits above the thinking mind and 'opens us to the supramental infinities and the cosmic vastness, to the grandeur of the supreme Light, to a treasure-house of miraculous knowledge, to the measureless movement of the Mother's eternal forces.'[13] Mahakali, force and strength, the 'Warrior of the Worlds', who is 'intolerant of imperfection', and 'deals roughly with all in man that is unwilling and she is severe to all that is obstinately ignorant and obscure.'[14] Mahalakshmi, who 'lays on men the yoke of the Divine' through love, harmony and beauty.[15] And finally, the youngest of the four, Mahasaraswati, who embodies the Mother's power of work, perfection and order, and 'presides over their detail of organisation and execution, relation of parts and effective combination of forces and unfailing exactitude of result and fulfilment.'[16]

Subsequent letters further explain these four essential aspects as also other forms of the Divine Shakti. Through them we arrive at a subtler understanding of the workings of the Divine Mother. For instance, Maheshwari, Sri Aurobindo explains in a subsequent letter, is one whose 'natural place is in the higher consciousness above mind'.[17] The condition for Mahakali to function 'is a calm inner being'.[18] Durga, not mentioned in the original text, has been elaborated upon in the letters as 'the Mother's power of Protection'.[19] And Mahasaraswati, whose work includes moving 'between the higher consciousness and the heart and through them establish the rule of the Truth in all details of the mind and life and physical nature'.[20] Read together, the text and the letters create vivid images of the various aspects and powers of the Mother that we can identify with, make use of to deepen our sadhana, and discover within ourselves.

Further, Sri Aurobindo identifies the Mother (Mirra Alfassa, his spiritual collaborator) with the Divine Mother:[21]

> There is one divine Force which acts in the universe and in the individual and is also beyond the individual and the universe. The Mother [Mirra Alfassa] stands for all three, but she is working here in the body to bring down something not yet expressed in this material world so as to transform life here — it is so that you should regard her as the Divine Shakti working here for that purpose.

In a 1943 letter, Sri Aurobindo takes up the spiritual unity between the Mother and himself, elaborating what he had written in a 1933 letter, that they are a 'single Power':[22]

> The Mother's consciousness and mine are the same, the one Divine Consciousness in two, because that is necessary for the play. Nothing can be done without her knowledge and force, without her consciousness — if anybody really feels her consciousness, he should know that I am there behind it and if he feels me it is the same with hers. If a separation is made like that (I leave aside the turns which their minds so strongly put upon these things), how can the Truth establish itself — from the Truth there is no such separation.[23]

A consistent theme in Sri Aurobindo's writings is surrender —from *The Life Divine*[24] (See Chapter 18) to *The Synthesis of Yoga*[25] (See Chapter 19) to *Essays on the Gita*[26] (See Chapter 16) to the powerful verses in *Savitri*[27] ('A vast surrender was his only strength,'[28] See Chapter 29). This finds resonance here too:[29]

> There is not much spiritual meaning in keeping open to the Mother if you withhold your surrender. Self-giving or surrender is demanded of those who practise this Yoga, because without such a progressive surrender of the being it is quite impossible to get anywhere near the goal.
>
> The spiritual seeker does not turn aside from the pursuit of realization to mere idealising; not to idealise, but to realise the Divine Truth is always his aim, either beyond or in life also — and in the latter case it is necessary to transform mind and life which cannot be done without surrender to the action of the Divine Force, the Mother.

At a practical level, this surrender expresses itself in day-to-day work, karma. 'Work should be done for the Mother and not for oneself,' Sri Aurobindo writes, 'that is how one encourages the growth of the psychic being and overcomes the ego. The test is to do the work given by the Mother without abhiman or insistence on personal choice or prestige.'[30] In other words, work becomes a sacrifice to a stronger force, a greater ideal, a higher purpose. We have seen this play out in the accomplishments of achievers in battle, in business, in politics, in sports, many of whose common refrains have been going beyond the call of duty and submitting to or moving towards something beyond. In Sri Aurobindo's Integral Yoga, the Mother represents that beyond.

The Mother (Mirra Alfassa) held discussions with sadhakas on various issues. Some of them wrote to Sri Aurobindo for further clarifications. For instance, when the Mother told a sadhaka to concentrate in the heart, the question to Sri Aurobindo was to define concentration and meditation. These are lingering questions for many a seeker who are unable to visualise spiritual terms. Sri Aurobindo's concise answer to this question gives the rest of us greater clarity to power our own sadhana:[31]

> Concentration here means gathering of the consciousness into one centre and fixing it on one object or on one idea or in one condition. Meditation is a general term which can include many kinds of inner activity.

Apart from letters, this volume also carries Sri Aurobindo's translations of twenty-four out of more than 300 prayers of the Mother. A short 1914 prayer holds in itself the promise of the future:[32]

A new light shall break upon the earth,
A new world shall be born,
And the things that were promised shall be fulfilled.

Another inspiring 1928 prayer answers questions about what lies beyond:[33]

> There is a Power that no ruler can command; there is a Happiness that no earthly success can bring; there is a Light that no wisdom can possess; there is a Knowledge that no philosophy and no science can master; there is a Bliss of which no satisfaction of desire can give the enjoyment; there is a thirst for Love that no human relation can appease; there is a Peace that one finds nowhere here, not even in death.
> It is the Power, the Happiness, the Light, the Knowledge, the Bliss, the Love, the Peace that flow from the Divine Grace.

With prayers and contexts covered, there is an entire section on the Mother as Guru and guide.[34] Behind the general principles of the Integral Yoga lie precise guidelines. 'A general principle can be laid down if it is in consonance with the Truth,' writes Sri Aurobindo, 'but its application must be determined by the inner consciousness seeing at each step what is to be done or not done.'[35] This calls for a high degree of alertness that functions within the general, but adapts to the individual, and shows a deep commitment to a sadhaka-specific, non-dogmatic single-fix approach. 'The Guru deals with each disciple in a different way and does not keep one law for all.'[36]

Between the primary text, and the letters that explain and expand it, lies Sri Aurobindo's vision of the Integral Yoga, the Divine and the Supramental realization. The text comprises concentrated first principles, the letters seeker-focussed answers. Read together, they provide a guide to the Mother, her force, her expressions, aspects and powers. And the key to the Integral Yoga—transformation:[37]

> When I speak of the Mother's force, I do not speak of the force of Prakriti which carries on things in the Ignorance but of the higher Force of the Divine that descends from above to transform the nature.

* * *

29

Savitri: A Legend and a Symbol

Reading by Richard Hartz

Savitri: A Legend and a Symbol[1] is set in ancient India and the outline of its story is taken from a well-known episode in the Mahabharata, in which princess Savitri, daughter of King Aswapati, marries a prince named Satyavan, who is prophesied to die early. Eventually, Savitri saves her husband from Yama, the god of death, after a prolonged debate. Sri Aurobindo wrote *Savitri* with his eyes on the future, not on the past. It is the epic of our unfulfilled potentialities. In its exploration of the deepest issues of human life, cosmic existence and the Beyond, it deserves a place among the great philosophical poems of world literature. In the context of the rich spiritual culture of India, it is also a worthy successor to a long line of inspired texts extending as far back as the Veda and Upanishads.

Sri Aurobindo began to write the first known draft of the epic in August 1916. He dictated his last revision of its sixth book, 'The Book of Fate', more than thirty-four years later, in November 1950, only a few weeks before his passing. During the years in between, although he set it aside in the early 1920s and more briefly in the late 1930s, the work he did on *Savitri* far exceeded the attention he gave to any other writing. Meanwhile, the narrative poem he had composed in 1916 expanded into an epic thirty times its original length and much vaster in its scope and significance. In the process, many passages were rewritten dozens of times. The aim of this untiring labour was to capture in every line as far as possible the evocative power of the mantra, in the sense of a 'supreme rhythmic language' bringing out the inmost truths of existence, as explained in *The Future Poetry with On Quantitative Metre*[2] (See Chapter 22).

Even more than Sri Aurobindo's other books, *Savitri* rewards a lifetime of reading and rereading. Only then does the fullness of its meaning gradually reveal itself. As the subtitle, 'A Legend and a Symbol', suggests, the poet relies to a large extent on the power of images and symbols to convey to the sensitive reader a living sense of realities that cannot be adequately expressed in the language of the intellect. We see this in the opening canto itself. Here, dawn, when the decisive events of the poem take place, is described in magical imagery that evokes a splendour that is not of this world:[3]

A wandering hand of pale enchanted light
That glowed along a fading moment's brink,
Fixed with gold panel and opalescent hinge
A gate of dreams ajar on mystery's verge...
The darkness failed and slipped like a falling cloak
From the reclining body of a god.
Then through the pallid rift that seemed at first
Hardly enough for a trickle from the suns,
Outpoured the revelation and the flame...
A message from the unknown immortal Light
Ablaze upon creation's quivering edge,
Dawn built her aura of magnificent hues
And buried its seed of grandeur in the hours.

Savitri itself, one might say, is just such a 'message from the unknown immortal Light', revealed to humankind at the dawn of an age of global seeking and aspiration for change. To derive the utmost benefit from reading it, one must, to whatever degree, be able to open oneself to that Light.

Much of *Savitri* describes things that take place in an inner consciousness or in subtle worlds beyond our normal awareness. The three books of Part One, forming the first half of the epic, are almost entirely of this character. After two opening cantos introducing the heroine's crisis on the morning of the fateful day to which the narrative returns hundreds of pages later in 'The Book of Death', the rest of Part One is a flashback to the spiritual and occult experiences of Aswapati, the king and yogi who is Savitri's father in the legend. These books culminate in a vision of the Divine Mother and her promise of an incarnation who is to bring a new factor into the play of forces upon earth.

In Books Four to Eight the human drama unfolds, from the birth and youth of Savitri to love at first sight when she meets Satyavan in the forest, the heavenly seer Narad's prediction of his death and, a year later, its tragic fulfilment. Savitri's inward journey of self-discovery that prepares her to face this event is the subject of Book Seven, 'The Book of Yoga'. In Books Nine to Eleven, she pursues Death into unseen realms to win back the soul of Satyavan. Finally, Savitri and Satyavan return to earth in a short epilogue that forms Book Twelve.

Although so much of *Savitri* deals with inner experiences or with other planes of existence, there is nothing otherworldly in its message. It is to find the key to a transformation of life *in this world* that the poet explores the invisible and affirms the possibility of deepening, widening and heightening our consciousness beyond its present limits:[4]

In moments when the inner lamps are lit
And the life's cherished guests are left outside,
Our spirit sits alone and speaks to its gulfs.
A wider consciousness opens then its doors…
A tide of mightier surgings bears our lives
And a diviner Presence moves the soul;
Or through the earthly coverings something breaks…
Assured of the Apocalypse to be,
It reckons not the moments and the hours;
Great, patient, calm it sees the centuries pass,
Awaiting the slow miracle of our change
In the sure deliberate process of world-force
And the long march of all-revealing Time.

Many will find such passages to be among the most inspiring to meditate upon as aids to their own inner awakening. But there is much more in *Savitri*. Sri Aurobindo has packed into it his whole philosophy of life and interpretation of the nature and meaning of existence. This includes his explanation of the evolution of consciousness on earth, an emergence which he considers to have reached only a half-way point with the appearance of the human mind. Again and again, such seemingly abstract and artistically unpromising subject-matter is transmuted into the stuff of splendid poetry. In the following lines, for instance, the modern theory of biological evolution is synthesised with the Upanishadic discovery of a principle of delight (Ananda) underlying all existence:[5]

That rapture's smile is secret everywhere;
It flows in the wind's breath, in the tree's sap,
Its hued magnificence blooms in leaves and flowers.
When life broke through its half-drowse in the plant
That feels and suffers but cannot move or cry,

In beast and in winged bird and thinking man
It made of the heart's rhythm its music's beat....
Born strangely in Time from the eternal Bliss,
It presses on heart's core and vibrant nerve.....
All Nature's longing drive none can resist,
Comes surging through the blood and quickened sense;
An ecstasy of the infinite is her cause.

As Sri Aurobindo developed the epic material, he made many significant changes to the source legend. In Part One, he expanded the role of Aswapati until his ascent to the summits of being came to rival in importance the victory of Savitri herself. Yet, her defiance of Fate and her encounter with Death remain central to the epic. The deeper meaning of all that she does, which culminates in her triumph over Death and Satyavan's return to life, cannot be reduced to a simple, allegorical interpretation. Broadly speaking, however, what is signified by Fate, Death and related symbols such as Night and the Abyss is the negation and frustration of the freedom and fulfilment of the human spirit. In 'The Book of Eternal Night', where Death leads away the soul of Satyavan into his own dark kingdom, Savitri follows them undaunted:[6]

The Woman first affronted the Abyss
Daring to journey through the eternal Night...
A curtain of impenetrable dread,
The darkness hung around her cage of sense
As, when the trees have turned to blotted shades
And the last friendly glimmer fades away,
Around a bullock in the forest tied
By hunters closes in no empty night...
On all that claims here to be Truth and God

And conscious self and the revealing Word
And the creative rapture of the Mind
And Love and Knowledge and heart's delight, there fell
The immense refusal of the eternal No.

The ensuing debate and contest of wills between Savitri and the figure of Death who appears before her is a struggle between this all-encompassing negation and her invincible affirmation of the 'everlasting Yes'.[7]

Sri Aurobindo's depiction of this confrontation differs fundamentally from Savitri's encounter with Yama, the God of Death, in the ancient legend in the Mahabharata. Vyasa's Savitri, for all her strength and courage, embodies primarily the virtues of the ideal wife or, more specifically, the dharma of the *kshatriya* (warrior class) woman. Yama is not only the god of Death, but of dharma, the moral and social law. As such, he is pleased by Savitri's learning, eloquence and constancy. He rewards her with boon after boon until, finally, he restores her husband to life.

In Sri Aurobindo's poem, on the other hand, the being Savitri opposes is 'the Spirit of the Void' who claims the world 'for Death and Nothingness'.[8] Here, too, Death represents law, but that of a material nature, not moral and social law. In the Mahabharata, Yama, whose power remains intact, brings Satyavan back to life by granting a boon. But in Sri Aurobindo's epic, the crucial event results from a victory of the spiritual force incarnate in Savitri over everything that restrains and represses the human spirit—even death itself, the thing over which we have least control.

What is at issue in Savitri's long dialogue with Death is nothing less than the whole question of the meaning of our existence. Death argues with devastating logic and a discouraging array of facts that the notion of any intelligible purpose in earthly life, let alone a divine destiny, is a mere delusion. Asserting the irreconcilability of Matter and Spirit, he draws upon scientific materialism and ascetic spirituality alike to make his case for the insignificance and futility of things. In reply, Savitri points out that he is reasoning from the appearances of 'an unfinished world'.[9] Dwelling on the materialistically inexplicable unfolding of life, mind and spirit on this seemingly inanimate and unconscious globe, she claims that the human being is simply God disguised and will one day throw off the disguise. Death responds with contempt:[10]

> "Thy words are large murmurs in a mystic dream.
> For how in the soiled heart of man could dwell
> The immaculate grandeur of thy dream-built God,
> Or who can see a face and form divine
> In the naked two-legged worm thou callest man?..."
> But Savitri replied to the dire God:
> "Yes, I am human. Yet shall man by me,
> Since in humanity waits his hour the God,
> Trample thee down to reach the immortal heights,
> Transcending grief and pain and fate and death.
> Yes, my humanity is a mask of God:
> He dwells in me, the mover of my acts,
> Turning the great wheel of his cosmic work...."

This liberating and empowering knowledge of the divinity within us is the core of the message of *Savitri*. This epic crowns the extraordinary body of writings bequeathed by Sri Aurobindo to humankind. It sums up much of his prose—his yoga, philosophy and vision of the future—and reveals secrets found nowhere else. What most sets it apart is its visionary intensity and the power of its poetry, whose rhythms reverberate in our inner being like those of the Vedic mantra as described in *Savitri* itself, 'Sight's sound-waves breaking from the soul's great deeps.'[11]

* * *

30

Letters on Himself and the Ashram

Reading by Peter Heehs

In the Bhagavad Gita, Arjuna asks Krishna for the signs of a man of settled intelligence (*sthitadhih*). How does he speak, how sit, how walk? Commenting on this verse in *Essays on the Gita*[1] (See Chapter 16), Sri Aurobindo explained that Arjuna, in posing these questions, was 'voicing the average human mind'.[2] Eager to find salvation but confused by the multitude of paths, human beings look for outward signs of perfection in teachers and avatars. In fact, wrote Sri Aurobindo, 'no such signs can be given'.[3] The 'great stamp of the liberated soul' is equality (*samata*), 'and of that equality even the most discernible signs are still subjective'.[4]

Like Arjuna in the epic, many of Sri Aurobindo's disciples asked him questions about his outward life in the hope of finding signs of spiritual greatness. Answering one such inquirer, in a note published in *Letters on Himself and the Ashram*,[5] Sri Aurobindo wrote, 'What matters in a spiritual man's life is not what he did or what he was outside to the view of the men of his time, but what he was and did within; it is only that that gives any value to his outer life at all.' The outer life draws its power from the inner, and 'the inner life of a spiritual man is something vast and full and, at least in the great figures, so crowded and teeming with significant things that no biographer or historian could ever hope to seize it all or tell it.'[6]

This 858-page volume is a collection of letters in which Sri Aurobindo answered questions from disciples and others about his outer and inner life and about the workings of the Sri Aurobindo Ashram. What happened while he was a student in England, an employee and professor in the service of the Maharaja of Baroda, and a revolutionary leader in Bengal? What sort of experiences did he have while practicing yoga in Baroda, Calcutta and Pondicherry? What is the role of the spiritual guru and what is an avatar? What was the nature of his yoga as practised in the Ashram under his and the Mother's guidance? His answers to such questions, collected and arranged by the editors, are published in the first four parts of this book.

Sri Aurobindo's disciples knew he had been a revolutionary leader, but few understood what this entailed. When one disciple suggested (perhaps just to draw him out) that Sri Aurobindo had not 'lived dangerously' during the freedom movement, he replied in mock anger, 'If you don't realise that starting and carrying on for ten years and more a revolutionary movement for independence without means and in a country wholly unprepared for it meant living dangerously, no amount of puncturing of your skull with words will give you that simple perception.'[7] Unlike many political figures, Sri Aurobindo never blew his own trumpet. Even while active in the movement, he was most comfortable working behind the scenes, letting others take credit for successes. If later he offered details about his role, as when he revealed that it was he and not Lokmanya Tilak 'who gave the order that led to the breaking of the [Surat] Congress,'[8] he did so just to set the record straight and not to steal the limelight.

Starting in 1908, Sri Aurobindo had a series of spiritual experiences that changed his outlook on life. Leaving the political field, he gave all of his attention to the practice of yoga. This was a deeply private endeavour. He wrote about his progress in his diary, *Record of Yoga*[9] (See Chapter 8), but he rarely spoke about his inner life, even with the young men who lived with him. As this small group grew into an ashram, the members speculated about his yogic life. They begged him for details about his inner experiences but he rarely obliged. Once, he provided an especially persistent disciple with a summary of his early experiences. When the disciple misinterpreted everything he wrote, Sri Aurobindo exclaimed:[10]

> The Brahman experience came when I was groping for some way, doing no sadhana at all, making no effort because I didn't know what effort to make, all having failed. Then in three days I got an experience which most Yogis get only at the end of a long Yoga, got it without wanting or trying for it, got it to the surprise of Lele [a Maharashtrian yogi he met in 1908] who was trying to get me something quite different. But I don't suppose you are able to understand—so I say no more.

Some of Sri Aurobindo's disciples considered him an avatar without fully knowing what the term implied. If an avatar is an incarnation of God, why couldn't he or she remove all the sadhaks' problems—or even transform the entire world—at a single stroke? This was not a subject Sri Aurobindo liked to get into, but when pressed, he agreed to discuss it in impersonal terms:[11]

> There are two sides of the phenomenon of Avatarhood, the Divine Consciousness behind and the instrumental personality. The Divine Consciousness is omnipotent but it has put forth

> the instrumental personality in Nature, under the conditions of Nature, and it uses it according to the rules of the game — though also sometimes to change the rules of the game. If Avatarhood is only a flashing miracle, then I have no use for it. If it is a coherent part of the arrangement of the omnipotent Divine in Nature, then I can understand and accept it.

One thing that puzzled many of Sri Aurobindo's disciples was the relationship between spiritual experience and work in the world. If a yogi has achieved complete realization, they reasoned, why should he or she take any interest in *samsara*, the cycle of worldly existence? This way of looking at things is based on the idea that the only way to achieve spiritual freedom is to renounce the life of the world. Sri Aurobindo, whose motto was 'All life is Yoga',[12] rejected this approach. It was, he said, perfectly possible to act dynamically on a basis of spiritual calm, 'The proof is that out of an absolute silence of the mind I edited the *Bande Mataram* for four months and wrote 6 volumes of *Arya*, not to speak of all the letters and messages etc. etc. I have written since.' Out of that silence, he 'conducted a pretty strenuous political activity and have also taken my share in keeping up an Asram which has at least an appearance to the physical senses of being solid and material!'[13]

Sri Aurobindo wrote this while spending up to ten hours a day answering letters sent by disciples and others. Why did he devote so much time to this often-thankless task? Because, he explained, he considered correspondence with disciples to be 'an effective instrument towards my central purpose', which was the transformation of consciousness and life. There were, he continued, 'a large number of sadhaks whom it has helped to awake from lethargy and begin to tread the way of spiritual experience, others whom it has carried from a small round of experience to a flood of realizations, some who have been absolutely hopeless for years who have undergone a conversion and entered from darkness into an opening of light'.[14]

Correspondence was a way to open the consciousness of the disciples to the higher energy he and the Mother were trying to bring down into the 'earth-consciousness'.[15] This process took place not on ideal spiritual planes but in the actual world of mind, life and matter, a world filled with contradictions and conflict. The ashram was a local representation of this world, and its members imperfect instruments of the transformation he foresaw. 'The Divine does not act in the void,' he explained in a letter of 1932, 'but through instruments, embodiments or channels. If a new creation is intended'—and Sri Aurobindo was sure that it was—human instruments had 'to be prepared who can be part of the creation and at the same time the means of developing it'.[16]

Because the aim of the Ashram was transformation and not withdrawal from life, it had a different focus from most such institutions, 'This is not an Asram like others,' he wrote to an inquirer, 'the members are not Sannyasis; it is not *moksha* that is the sole aim of the Yoga here. What is being done here is a preparation for a work—a work which will be founded on Yogic consciousness and Yoga-Shakti, and can have no other foundation.'[17]

The preparation for this yogic 'work' involved work in the ordinary sense of the term. Each member had (and has) to spend much of each day working in one of the Ashram's departments: Dining Room, Laundry, Building Services, Library, and so forth. Whatever it involved, work in the ashram was to be regarded 'as a field and an opportunity for the Karmayoga part of the integral Yoga—for learning to work in the true Yogic way—dedication through service, practical selflessness, obedience, scrupulousness, discipline, setting the Divine and the Divine's work first and oneself last, harmony, patience, forbearance etc'.[18]

Most ashrams in India follow conventional Hindu forms of worship and spiritual practice. Not Sri Aurobindo's. Although he received inspiration from Hindu texts such as the Bhagavad Gita and even, as he explained in his Uttarpara Speech, guidance from Sri Krishna himself, he did not want the ashram to become a sectarian institution. 'The Asram has nothing to do with Hindu religion or culture or any religion or nationality,' he wrote in a letter of 1936. 'The Truth of the Divine which is the spiritual reality behind all religions and the descent of the supramental which is not known to any religion are the sole things which will be the foundation of the work of the future.'[19] Caste rules and communal prejudices had no place in the Ashram. In a letter that still resonates eighty-five years after it was written, he said: 'It is to be hoped that in time the present mentality will pass away and both [Hindu and Muslim] communities learn to live as children of the same Mother. If they fight, neither are likely to gain but both to lose, even perhaps giving an opening to a third party as has happened before in their history.'[20]

Because Sri Aurobindo viewed the members of the Ashram as instruments of spiritual change, he took their struggles and sufferings seriously. He encouraged them to write not only about the faltering first steps of their spiritual lives but also the day-to-day problems of their outer existences. Every bout with depression, every attack of illness, every argument with one's neighbour or colleague was an occasion for sadhaks to open themselves to his and the Mother's help. Such help comes in two forms, he explained: 'invisible help' from the inner Divine 'and that which a spiritual guide gives to his disciples.'[21] The first sort is available to all who open themselves to the inner guidance; the second was the special privilege of those who had the opportunity to write to Sri Aurobindo and the Mother and receive their replies.

Readers of the fourth part of *Letters on Himself and the Ashram*, 'The Practice of Yoga in the Ashram and Outside', will find pages and pages of letters Sri Aurobindo wrote about the sadhaks' routine activities, diet, reading, musings, literary efforts, relationships with others, and so forth. Gathered together in a book, they seem rather repetitive. One wonders how Sri Aurobindo managed it. What is remarkable is that he never lost patience and always had a helpful word to offer. This comes out especially in the fifth part of the book, 'Mantras and Messages'. Here is a message Sri Aurobindo wrote for his disciples on 15 August 1929:[22]

> The Divine gives itself to those who give themselves without reserve and in all their parts to the Divine. For them the calm, the light, the power, the bliss, the freedom, the wideness, the heights of knowledge, the seas of Ananda.

* * *

31

Autobiographical Notes and Other Writings of Historical Interest

Reading by Peter Heehs

'Neither you nor anyone else knows anything at all of my life; it has not been on the surface for man to see,' wrote Sri Aurobindo to a disciple who had written an inaccurate account of his life.[1] He rewrote the disciple's attempt and the result was later published as a piece under the title 'Sri Aurobindo: A Life Sketch'.[2] This is the only complete text written by Sri Aurobindo that could be called autobiographical in the ordinary sense of the term. Yet, the collection *Autobiographical Notes and Other Writings of Historical Interest* contains more than a hundred pages of material from Sri Aurobindo's pen that deals with various aspects of his life. Most of it consists of his corrections of statements made by biographers and other writers. There are also a few miscellaneous jottings. Despite the haphazard origin of these notes, they are of considerable interest—not only to historians but also to the general reader.

Arranged chronologically, some notes deal with Sri Aurobindo's years as a student in England, others with his life as an employee and professor in the service of the Maharaja of Baroda. The largest section deals with his activities as a political and revolutionary leader between 1902 and 1910. There are, in contrast, only a handful of notes relating to his activities between 1910 and 1950, when he lived in Pondicherry. An even smaller number are concerned with his inner life—that is, his spiritual development. What was 'not on the surface for man to see' remains largely out of sight.

Sri Aurobindo began to practice pranayama around 1903 and took up regular meditation two years later. He was active as a politician between 1906 and 1910, including a one-year gap when he was in jail. This means his early sadhana overlapped with his political career. Because his way of yoga does not reject the life of action, he experienced 'no conflict or wavering between yoga and politics; when he started yoga, he carried on both without any idea of opposition between them'.[3] During the first phase of his yoga, he explained in one note, he gathered up 'the essential elements of spiritual experience that are gained by the paths of divine communion and spiritual realization followed till now in India'.[4]

Afterwards, he sought to unite and harmonise the two ends of existence, Spirit and Matter. 'Most ways of Yoga,' he wrote, 'are paths to the Beyond leading to the Spirit and, in the end, away from life.'[5] His own path 'rises to the Spirit to redescend with its gains bringing the light and power and bliss of the Spirit into life to transform it.' But how does this process of ascent and descent actually work? 'It is possible by opening to a greater divine consciousness to rise to this power of light and bliss, discover one's true self, remain in constant union with the Divine and bring down the supramental Force for the transformation of mind and life and body. To realise this possibility,' Sri Aurobindo concluded, was the 'dynamic aim' of his yoga.[6]

We learn about the details of Sri Aurobindo's outer life from the 'Letters of Historical Interest' that make up the second part of the book. Before he began his extensive correspondence with disciples in the 1930s, Sri Aurobindo was not an assiduous writer of letters. The few that have survived—to family members, colleagues, political associates, early followers, public figures—are valuable indexes to his thoughts and feelings. From his first attempt to contact his young sister, who could hardly have understood his impeccable Cambridge English, to his note informing Mahatma Gandhi that it was not a good moment for a meeting, the letters provide a wealth of information about his ideas and activities and also give a glimpse of his character—polite without being unctuous, straightforward without being curt.

Many people in positions of authority are called upon to write letters of condolence to bereaved family members. Few such letters ring as truly as one Sri Aurobindo wrote on behalf of the Maharaja of Baroda. The deceased gentleman, Sri Aurobindo wrote, 'was a friend with whom His Highness could always converse and interchange views freely, a thing which is very rare amongst our countrymen'. The Maharaja found him 'prudent, sympathetic and strong, able to withstand influences, which are not uncommon in a palace and surroundings, such as obtain in a Native State. His Highness feels that it would be long before his place can be filled, if indeed it can ever be filled at all.'[7] When active in politics, Sri Aurobindo occasionally wrote letters to influential leaders such as Bipin Chandra Pal and B.S. Moonje. Less important historically, but to me equally striking, is a letter of acknowledgement he wrote in his own hand to a lady who had donated the sum of ten rupees to the National University Fund.[8]

His letters to Motilal Roy, a young man connected with the revolutionary movement in Bengal, straddled the spheres of politics and yoga. In one, written from Pondicherry in 1912, Sri Aurobindo began with details about sending 'Yogini Chakras',[9] apparently a code phrase for revolvers (he could not write openly about such things in a letter that might be opened by the police). He then went on to his own practice of yoga: 'My subjective sadhana may be said to have received its final seal and something like its consummation by a prolonged realization & dwelling in Parabrahman for many hours.' Turning to his plans for future work, he explained it would have four main objects:[10]

1. To reexplain the Sanatana Dharma to the human intellect in all its parts, from a new standpoint.
2. On the basis of Vedic knowledge to establish a Yogic sadhana which will not only liberate the soul, but prepare a perfect humanity & help in the restoration of the Satyayuga.
3. India being the centre [of the spiritual awakening], to work for her restoration to her proper place in the world.
4. A perfect humanity being intended society will have to be remodelled so as to be fit to contain that perfection.

At this point, amid the anticolonial struggle, Sri Aurobindo's focus was, understandably, Indo-centric. By the time independence was achieved thirty-five years later, it had expanded beyond the confines of the nation-state. A statement from the third part of the book, 'Public Statements and Other Communications on Indian and World Events', illustrates this:[11]

> An international spirit and outlook must grow up and international forms and institutions; even it may be such developments as dual or multilateral citizenship and a voluntary fusion of cultures may appear in the process of the change and the spirit of nationalism losing its militancy may find these

> things perfectly compatible with the integrity of its own outlook. A new spirit of oneness will take hold of the human race.

Many of the statements collected here deal with matters that are now of interest only to historians. But some have an eerily contemporary ring. On 28 June 1950, three days after the army of North Korea, supported by its Soviet and Chinese allies, invaded South Korea, a disciple of Sri Aurobindo's who was a newspaper editor wrote to Sri Aurobindo asking for clarification. He replied immediately:[12]

> There is nothing to hesitate about there, the whole affair is as plain as a "pikestaff." It is the first move in the Communist plan of campaign to dominate and take possession first of these northern parts and then of South East Asia as a preliminary to their manoeuvres with regard to the rest of the continent — in passing, Tibet as a gate opening to India. If they succeed, there is no reason why domination of the whole world should not follow by steps until they are ready to deal with America.

An Indian diplomat reported that when United States President John F. Kennedy read an article based on this statement in 1962 (the year China attacked India through Tibet), he remarked, 'You mean to say that a man devoted to meditation and contemplation, sitting in one corner of India, said this about the intentions of Communist China as early as 1950?'[13]

Sri Aurobindo's experience as a politician gave him a clear understanding of the way human beings act in conflict situations. This did not prevent him from remaining optimistic about the future of humanity. In a letter of April 1950, he wrote that 'the dark conditions do not discourage me or convince me of the vanity of my will to "help the world", for I knew they had to come; they were there in the world nature and had to rise up so that they might be exhausted or expelled so that a better world freed from them might be there'. Various things had to be 'cleared out', such as India's friction with Pakistan, but once they were, 'the work for the Divine will become more possible and it may well be that the dream, if it is a dream, of leading the world towards the spiritual Light, may even become a reality'.[14]

The last part of *Autobiographical Notes and Other Writings of Historical Interest* consists of 'Public statements and notices concerning Sri Aurobindo's Ashram and Yoga'. The closing lines of a statement Sri Aurobindo wrote about his Ashram in February 1934, when its existence depended on the good graces of the government of French India, concisely sums up its nature and aim even today:[15]

> The Asram is not a religious association. Those who are here come from all religions and some are of no religion. There is no creed or set of dogmas, no governing religious body; there are only the teachings of Sri Aurobindo and certain psychological practices of concentration and meditation, etc., for the enlarging of the consciousness, receptivity to the Truth, mastery over the desires, the discovery of the divine self and consciousness concealed within each human being, a higher evolution of the nature.

Another statement Sri Aurobindo wrote the same month about his teaching sums up the main argument of *The Life Divine* in a few sentences. The One Being and Consciousness is, he says, 'involved here in Matter'.[16]

> Evolution is the method by which it liberates itself; consciousness appears in what seems to be inconscient, and once having appeared is self-impelled to grow higher and higher and at the same time to enlarge and develop towards a greater and greater perfection. Life is the first step of this release of consciousness;

> mind is the second; but the evolution does not finish with mind, it awaits a release into something greater, a consciousness which is spiritual and supramental. The next step of the evolution must be towards the development of Supermind and Spirit as the dominant power in the conscious being.

Beginning with clarifications about Sri Aurobindo's early life and moving to explanations about the supramental yoga, *Autobiographical Notes and Other Writings of Historical Interest* demonstrates the diversity and depth of both Sri Aurobindo's life and thought.

* * *

Conclusion: Reading Beyond this Book

Devdip Ganguli

On 15 August 2022, India and the world will celebrate the 150th birth anniversary of Sri Aurobindo. This book is our tribute to him. It is also an invitation to you, the reader, to delve deeper into his incredible body of writings. The reasons for doing so are many, and have already been covered in the introduction by my co-editor and initiator of this project, Gautam Chikermane. As editors, our intention and purpose in preparing this book will be fulfilled if we can, in any way, inspire you to pick up the original writings of Sri Aurobindo and discover them for yourself.

I was a student at the Sri Aurobindo International Centre of Education (SAICE), the Ashram school in Pondicherry, when I received my first book by Sri Aurobindo as a Christmas gift. It was a thin booklet titled *The Philosophy of the Upanishads.*[1] I do not know who thought this would be an appropriate gift for a twelve-year-old, but I remain very grateful to this unknown benefactor.

I understood almost nothing of the book. But even then, I was aware I was holding something precious in my hands, some profound wisdom beyond my grasp, expressed in a language I could hardly comprehend. With child-like faith, I believed that reading that text and making even a little sense of those important-sounding words would somehow turn me intelligent! I still have the dog-eared book, numerous paragraphs and sentences marked with a pink highlighter, indications of my struggle with the text as a child.

That early fascination for Sri Aurobindo's writings would eventually grow into an intense desire to read every book of his, to soak in their atmosphere, and spend as much time as possible in the luminous consciousness of the author. It is perhaps not a coincidence that a few years later, as an undergrad, Sri Aurobindo's translations and commentaries on the Upanishads (Volumes 17 and 18) would stir me beyond words, his explanation of the Isha Upanishad (See Chapter 14) open new worlds of knowledge and experience.

It is often said that Sri Aurobindo is too difficult to read, his writings beyond the grasp of even native English speakers. It is true that his literary style of writing, his characteristic long sentences, and a terminology that many are unfamiliar with, can take some getting used to. But the real difficulty is that many of us have lost the habit of dealing with complex ideas.

Sri Aurobindo's approach is integral; he explores issues from multiple standpoints, presenting each perspective fully, before moving towards resolution and synthesis. In a world of shortening attention spans and greater engagement with views and opinions rather than with pure ideas, this approach requires patience. But the fruit of such effort is sublime. Vast vistas of thought open as we read Sri Aurobindo; our minds grow ever more into wideness and Truth. And in the words of the Mother, his spiritual collaborator, 'the door of the future' opens before us.[2]

Some are equally overwhelmed by the sheer breadth of his writings, unsure where to start, what to read. There is no single answer suitable for all. It is best to start with whichever volume appeals to you. Each carries its own unique atmosphere, each leads you along different paths to the same integral vision of the Master. We hope the essays in this book will help you in making a more informed decision as you begin (or continue) your journey into the vast body of his works. But ultimately, the determination must stem from deep within.

Sri Aurobindo's style of writing varied widely, depending on when it was written, the nature of the writing, and its context. His early writings (mostly in *Volume 1*) offer a preview of the genius to come. These pieces read more easily and in them one can discern the lines that Sri Aurobindo will develop in subsequent decades. His political speeches and writings (Volumes 6, 7 and 8) were written for publication in newspapers and journals before his move to Pondicherry in 1910. These pieces tend to be shorter and are formulated with directness and intensity of expression. These, again, are an excellent doorway, for they draw us in as soon as we begin reading them.

The bulk of his writings were written for *Arya*, and these constitute his major works (from Volumes 15 to 26). In these pages, we discover Sri Aurobindo in all his glory and splendour, scaling Himalayas of thought, traversing oceans of existence. The style of writing we most associate with him finds its full efflorescence and impact in these pages. But even among the major works, differences of style can be discerned. Whereas Sri Aurobindo writes for the spiritual seeker in *The Synthesis of Yoga*, *The Life Divine* appeals to the philosophic mind, and the language of his social and political writings in books like *The Human Cycle* addresses the more cosmopolitan reader.

Sri Aurobindo's vast body of letters (*Volumes 27* to *32*, and *Volume 35*) has a more informal air to them. The style of these letters was often dictated by the temperament and needs of the correspondent. The general air of impersonality in his major works is replaced here with a sense of the Divine Person reaching down to meet humanity to help it lift beyond itself. Many readers will find these volumes more approachable than his major works, and a good place to begin their acquaintance with his writings.

Savitri: A Legend and a Symbol in Volumes 33 and 34 stands apart as a universe in itself. Considered the longest epic poem in blank verse in the English language, it draws us into a world of symbols and profound mysteries that mirrors the yoga of Sri Aurobindo and the Mother. Some find it impossible to read, others are drawn to it with an inexplicable attraction. With time and steady effort, the wonder of *Savitri* reveals itself. On the other hand, for an easier entry into his poetic creations, his *Collected Poems* in *Volume 2* is a delightful book. The sonnets, especially, are short and a perfect introduction to spiritual poetry.

But ultimately, whichever book you choose to start from, your discovery of Sri Aurobindo's writings will proceed along lines unique to you, dictated by your questions, needs and temperament.

Another question that is often asked is, given the profound nature of his work, how best to read Sri Aurobindo. While speaking about the right way to read such books, the Mother commented, '...you must be able to read it in the mind's silence; you must wait and let the expression go deep inside you into the region where words are no more and from there come slowly back to your exterior consciousness and its surface understanding… There can be no perfect understanding unless you are in union with the unexpressed mind that is behind the centre of expression.'[3]

And more specifically, when asked by a youngster about the right way of reading Sri Aurobindo, the Mother replied:[4]

> I advise always to read *a little* at a time, keeping the mind as tranquil as one can, without making an effort to understand,

> but keeping the head as silent as possible, and letting the *force contained in what one reads enter deep within.* This force received in the calm and the silence will do its work of light and, if needed, will create in the brain the necessary cells for the understanding. Thus, when one re-reads the same thing some months later, one perceives that the thought expressed has become much more clear and close, and even sometimes altogether familiar.
>
> It is preferable to read regularly, a little every day, and at a fixed hour if possible; this facilitates the brain-receptivity (emphasis in the original).

Regular readers of Sri Aurobindo's works will attest to the common experience of a progressive and growing comprehension after repeated readings of the same text.

It would not be out of place here to mention that the Mother too has a number of published writings, letters and conversations. The *Collected Works of the Mother* run into seventeen volumes that offer those interested in the Integral Yoga an easier understanding and a direct entry into its practice. These volumes are equally revelatory in their import, and are an excellent companion to many of Sri Aurobindo's works—her commentaries and answers to questions on many of Sri Aurobindo's books are of immense value. The Mother's writings also offer an insight into the incredible scope of her action in Pondicherry: from guiding disciples, to developing the Sri Aurobindo Ashram, to establishing the Ashram school (SAICE) and a new approach to education, and finally, the founding of the experimental township of Auroville in the last years of her life.

All the books of Sri Aurobindo and the Mother can be ordered online, either as individual books or as full sets. We recommend SABDA, the Sri Aurobindo Ashram's own book distribution agency for its high quality of printing, its subsidised pricing, and to ensure the most up-to-date editions. You may access it here: https://www.sabda.in.

The *Complete Works of Sri Aurobindo* and the *Collected Works of the Mother* are also available as free PDF downloads on the Sri Aurobindo Ashram's official website, https://www.sriaurobindoashram.org.

A number of disciples have published books that are of immense help in further discovering Sri Aurobindo. Among them, A.B. Purani, Amal Kiran (K.D. Sethna), Jugal Kishore Mukherjee, Kireet Joshi, Manoj Das, Nirodobaran, Nolini Kanta Gupta, and Pavitra, are some names we can strongly recommend. Their books may also be purchased from SABDA.

As editors, we believe that in the years to come Sri Aurobindo will be read ever more widely. In the measure that humanity seeks more ardently for solutions to fundamental problems of existence, the value of his writings and of his yoga will become more evident. His works contain in them a compelling understanding of the ills that plague us individually and collectively, as also the solutions that can lead us towards a fundamental transformation of human nature and life. To read Sri Aurobindo is a privilege and a life-changing experience, and we join all our contributors in welcoming you as you embark on your own 'adventure of consciousness and joy'.[5]

***

Acknowledgements

Reading Sri Aurobindo is not a moment in time; it is the coming together of knowledge-rivers and soul-journeys across time. There are several boats that have sailed in these rivers, all which have poured themselves into the great ocean of Sri Aurobindo's yoga. This pouring is a work in progress in the larger scale of humanity's material-spiritual evolution. As a start, therefore, we consider ourselves privileged to have received directions from souls and institutions that have carried this evolution from the past till today and to those who will cart it to a golden tomorrow.

We are grateful to Sri Aurobindo Ashram, Pondicherry, for undertaking the publication of the Complete Works of Sri Aurobindo (CWSA), a gift for humankind for all time to come. The Ashram has made these writings available to general readers via their subsidized price in beautifully printed editions, while PDF editions are available for free on the Ashram website. The editions brought out by the Ashram have gone through the rigour of line-by-line checks, and we consider them the only authentic source for reading and citing their work. In addition, we are grateful to the Copyright Department of the Ashram for permissions to reproduce rare manuscripts and photographs of Sri Aurobindo, and extracts from his writings.

This book has been made possible only because of the work of the Sri Aurobindo Ashram Archives and Research Library in Pondicherry, which painstakingly compiled Sri Aurobindo's writings and speeches in thirty-six volumes; two more volumes, a *Reference Volume* and a *Glossary to the Record of Yoga* are still underway. We are glad that three members of the editorial team for the CWSA volumes—Richard Hartz, Peter Heehs, and Matthijs Cornelissen—are also contributors to this book.

Our gratitude also to the nineteen other writers who have contributed to this book. They have brought decades of studying the works of Sri Aurobindo into each chapter, with commitment and consecration. Each of them has approached this project with knowledge and devotion. We are humbled by their trust and their offering.

Over the years, several Ashramites and devotees have added layers of knowledge to our reading of Sri Aurobindo. In no particular order, we are grateful to Nirodbaran, Manoj Das Gupta, Partho, Jugal Kishore Mukherjee, Neeltje Huppes, Hriday Narayan, Chinmayee Maheshwari, Prapanna Randall Smith, and Matriprasad (also a contributor).

The Ashram's Grace Office provided us the platform for, and has been witness to, several conversations about and around this book. In addition to its charged atmosphere, Grace offered us countless coffees. A special mention to Foxy, who with her warm eyes and friendly wags of her tail added a silent but soulful presence to our work.

In Penguin we found the perfect partner for this book. Milee Ashwarya made the book happen, from idea to bookstores. Even editors need editors, and Dipanjali Chadha and Shreya Mukherjee tightened the chapters. Due credit to Gunjan Ahalwat who worked with us patiently to deliver the final cover. We thank Rishi Agrawal and Ishani Sarkar for bringing the editors' faces on the book with the photographs of Gautam and Devdip.

Finally, we would like to thank the contribution and encouragement of our families to this project. They are well-acquainted with the works of Sri Aurobindo and, as a result, we received insightful suggestions on various aspects of the book. Our special gratitude to Karuna and Sandip Ganguli, Monika Halan and Meera Chikermane, both for ideas and expressions.

And advance gratitude to you, dear reader. It is because of you that this book has materialized. You are indeed the most important person here, and we thank you for deciding to read this book. All royalty proceeds of this book are going to the Sri Aurobindo Ashram—so buy one copy and gift ten!

We look forward to hearing from you as you sail your own boat in your own river that will join the great ocean of Sri Aurobindo's Integral Yoga.

* * *

List of Contributors

Readers' profiles

Anirban Ganguly, PhD, is honorary director, Dr. Syama Prasad Mookerjee Research Foundation. He is also a Member of the Bharatiya Janata Party's National Executive Committee. Anirban had his early education at Sri Aurobindo International Centre of Education in Pondicherry, holds a Master's degree in international relations (Annamalai University), a PG Diploma in mass communication and journalism (Jadavpur University), and a Ph.D. in education (Jadavpur University). He has authored numerous books and articles on culture, politics, and India's freedom movement.

Anshul Sinha is an alumnus of the Sri Aurobindo International Centre of Education, Pondicherry, completed his Master's degree in philosophy from the Pondicherry University, and intends to pursue a Ph.D. Though his primary interest is to understand consciousness through Indian psychology, the opportunities to research on the subject are sparse within an academic setting. He hopes to establish Indian philosophy and psychology as relevant subjects within that setting.

Anuradha Choudry is an alumnus of Sri Aurobindo International Centre of Education, Pondicherry, and faculty at the Department of Humanities and Social Sciences, the

Centre of Excellence for Indian Knowledge Systems and a member of the Rekhi Centre of Excellence for the Science of Happiness at the Indian Institute of Technology, Kharagpur. A coordinator for the Indian Knowledge Systems at AICTE, she is a multilingual Sanskritist, and works in the areas of yoga psychology, philosophy and culture.

Anuradha Agrawal has been working in the field of Integral Education and Integral Yoga since 1986. She is the co-founding trustee of The Gnostic Centre. Her work includes teaching, designing and facilitating workshops and courses for school teachers, university students and faculty. She has written extensively on issues relevant for personal and social change, based on the Integral Yoga philosophy. Anuradha holds a Master's degree in international education (University of Sussex).

Debashish Banerji, PhD, is the Haridas Chaudhuri Professor of Indian philosophies and cultures and the Doshi Professor of Asian art at the California Institute of Integral Studies, San Francisco. His academic interests lie in postcolonial, cross-cultural and posthuman approaches to Indian philosophy, psychology and culture. He has authored and edited books on major figures, including Rabindranath Tagore and Abanindranath Tagore. His last book was *Meditations on the Isha Upanishad* (Sri Aurobindo Samity and Maha Bodhi Publishers, 2019).

Devdip Ganguli teaches undergraduate students at the Sri Aurobindo International Centre of Education, Pondicherry, where he offers courses on the social and political philosophy of Sri Aurobindo, as well as on ancient Indian history, art and culture. He is frequently invited to speak in Universities in India and abroad on topics related to Sri Aurobindo's writings.

He also works in one of the administrative departments of Sri Aurobindo Ashram.

Gautam Chikermane is a writer. Currently, vice president at Observer Research Foundation, he has worked in leadership positions at India's top newspapers and magazines, including *Hindustan Times*, *The Indian Express* and *Outlook*. His areas of interest are economic policy and international relations. His last book was *India 2030* (Penguin, 2021) and his next book is *Reform Nation* (HarperCollins, 2022). He has been studying the works of Sri Aurobindo since 2000.

Georg Stollenwerk is co-director of the Sri Aurobindo Center, Berlin and, since 2006, board member of Auroville International, Germany. His primary research focuses on the manifold facets of the evolution of consciousness through the material universe and man. He gives talks on areas related to the Integral Yoga and the collective development of mankind according to Sri Aurobindo's vision and has published a short introduction on *Savitri* as well as a booklet on *The Evolution of Matter*.

Karen Ecke was born and raised in the US but found her spiritual home in India when she met the Mother in 1971. She joined Auroville the following year and worked at the Matrimandir and at Aurobrindavan for eighteen years. In 1990 she taught degree-level courses based on the pedagogy of the Brazilian educator Paolo Friere at the US. She finally returned to the Sri Aurobindo Ashram in 2005, where she does editorial work for the publication department.

Larry Seidlitz is a devotee and scholar of Sri Aurobindo's yoga and philosophy, residing near and informally associated with the Sri Aurobindo Ashram and Auroville. A research psychologist in the US, he has worked with the Sri Aurobindo Centre for

Advanced Research since 2004. He has written three books on Sri Aurobindo's yoga and philosophy and articles for various journals. He edits books for other Sri Aurobindo scholars, and was editor of the journal 'Collaboration' from 2004 to 2019.

Matriprasad completed his studies at Sri Aurobindo International Centre of Education in 1975, and thereafter joined Sri Aurobindo Ashram, Pondicherry. Currently, he assists the trustees of the Ashram in their administrative responsibilities. He also teaches the social and political philosophy of Sri Aurobindo at the undergraduate level. He has a keen interest in English, French, Sanskrit and Urdu poetry, the classical arts, and Hindustani classical music.

Matthijs Cornelissen was born in The Netherlands and studied medicine and psychology in Amsterdam. At the age of twenty-seven, he relocated to India and helped with the creation of Mirambika, a school in Delhi. He also assisted the publication of *The Complete Works of Sri Aurobindo*, and was the founding director of the Indian Psychology Institute (IPI). Matthijs teaches psychology and Sri Aurobindo's writings at the Sri Aurobindo International Centre of Education, Pondicherry.

Monika Halan works the areas of media, public policy and financial education. She is the founder of Dhan Chakra Financial Education and author of the bestselling book, *Let's Talk Money*. An M.A. in economics from the Delhi School of Economics, in journalism from University of Wales, and a Yale World Fellow (2011), Monika is an adjunct professor at National Institute of Securities Markets, Indian Institute of Corporate Affairs, and Banasthali University.

Patrick Beldio, PhD, is a professor of comparative theology and religion at Marymount University and George Washington University in the Washington, DC metro area. His current book project features the Mother and her contribution to the Integral Yoga. He is also a professional sculptor with a studio at the Franciscan Monastery in Washington. He has been a student of the Mother and Sri Aurobindo since the early 1990s.

Payal Adhikari has been teaching in both urban and rural schools in Pondicherry and Auroville for the past twenty years. Her primary work is with teenagers, with a focus on creating an enriching classroom experience and a holistic learning environment for children, based on the principles of Integral Education. Payal also holds administrative responsibilities in the Handmade Paper Factory, a small-scale cottage industry setup associated with the Sri Aurobindo Ashram.

Peter Heehs was born and educated in the US, and has been based in Pondicherry since 1971. He has been a member of the Sri Aurobindo Ashram Archives and Research Library since its founding, and is currently part of the editorial team of *The Complete Works of Sri Aurobindo* project. He is the author or editor of twelve books, including *The Lives of Sri Aurobindo* (Columbia University Press, 2008), and *Spirituality without God* (Bloomsbury Academic, 2018).

Pranjal Garg, Ph.D, is an assistant professor at the Department of History, in Central University of Tamil Nadu. He specializes in ancient Indian history, culture and archaeology. Graduating from the Sri Aurobindo International Centre of Education, Pondicherry, and inspired by Sri Aurobindo's writings, he was motivated to take up Vedic and Indic studies to better understand symbolism and esoteric concepts in Indian culture. His doctoral research was in Harappan studies in Classical Archaeology.

Richard Hartz studied philosophy at Yale University, and South Asian languages and literature at the University of Washington. He has lived since 1980 in Pondicherry, India, where he works in the Sri Aurobindo Ashram Archives and teaches at the Sri Aurobindo International Centre of Education. He is one of the editors of *The Complete Works of Sri Aurobindo* and the author of *The Clasp of Civilizations* (D.K. Print World, 2015).

Sampadananda Mishra, PhD, is a professor at Rashtram School of Public Leadership, Rishihood University. An author and researcher in Sanskrit and Indian culture, he has written several books and articles. He was Associate Editor of the *Collected Works of Vasishtha Kavyakantha Ganapati Muni* published in twelve volumes and is the recipient of the President of India award (Maharshi Badarayna Vyasa Samman 2011) and Kendra Sahitya Akademi Bala Puraskar (2018).

Thirthankar Chakraborty, PhD, is assistant professor in the Department of Liberal Arts at the Indian Institute of Technology (IIT) Bhilai, India. He holds a doctorate in comparative literature from the University of Kent, UK, and has graduated from the Sri Aurobindo International Centre of Education, Pondicherry. His research interests focus around comparative and world literature, modernism and literary theory, and he has published several articles and book chapters on these topics.

Uday Arya returned to India in 2017 after fourteen years in New York and Paris, working in various capacities in investment banking. His principal areas of formal expertise are structured finance, risk management and value investing. He is co-founder of BlueLotus Ventures, an India-based VC firm that invests in highly promising early-stage start-ups. He currently teaches Critical Thinking and History at Sri Aurobindo International Centre of Education, Pondicherry.

Notes

Introduction: The Supramental Sage

1. The Mother, *Collected Works of the Mother, Volume 16* (Sri Aurobindo Ashram Trust, 2004), p. 312.
2. The Mother, *Collected Works of the Mother, Volume 12* (Sri Aurobindo Ashram Trust, 2002), p. 116.
3. Sri Aurobindo, *Complete Works of Sri Aurobindo, Volume 26* (Sri Aurobindo Ashram Trust, 1997), p. 218.
4. Sri Aurobindo, *Complete Works of Sri Aurobindo, Volume 12* (Sri Aurobindo Ashram Trust, 1997), p. 302.
5. Sri Aurobindo, *Complete Works of Sri Aurobindo, Volume 32* (Sri Aurobindo Ashram Trust, 2012), p. 10.
6. Sri Aurobindo, *Complete Works of Sri Aurobindo, Volume 13* (Sri Aurobindo Ashram Trust, 1998), p. 57.
7. Mona Sarkar, Sri Aurobindo Circle No. 32 (Sri Aurobindo Ashram Trust, 1967), pp. 1–6.
8. Sri Aurobindo, *Complete Works of Sri Aurobindo, Volumes 33 & 34* (Sri Aurobindo Ashram Trust, 1997), pp. 1–2.

1. Early Cultural Writings

1. Sri Aurobindo, *The Complete Works of Sri Aurobindo, Volume 1* (Sri Aurobindo Ashram Trust, 2003), pp. 351–427.
2. Ibid., pp. 81–351.
3. Ibid., pp. 429–754.

4. Ibid., pp. 3–7.
5. Ibid., pp. 415–27.
6. Ibid., pp. 612–13.
7. Ibid., p. 383.
8. Ibid., pp. 383–85.
9. Ibid., p. 384.
10. Ibid., p. 384.
11. Ibid., p. 385.
12. Ibid., p. 385.
13. Ibid., p. 426.
14. Ibid., p. 427.
15. Ibid., pp. 146–47.
16. Ibid., p. 146.
17. Ibid., p. 147.
18. Ibid., pp. 277–344.
19. Ibid., pp. 345–50.
20. Ibid., p. 294.
21. Ibid., p. 299.
22. Ibid., p. 304.
23. Ibid., p. 306.
24. Ibid., p. 306.
25. Ibid., pp. 305–06.
26. Ibid., pp. 694–721.
27. Ibid., p. 716.
28. Ibid., p. 714.
29. Ibid., p. 766.

2. Collected Poems

1. Sri Aurobindo, *The Complete Works of Sri Aurobindo, Volume 5* (Sri Aurobindo Ashram Trust, 1999).
2. Sri Aurobindo, *The Complete Works of Sri Aurobindo, Volume 9* (Sri Aurobindo Ashram Trust, 2017).
3. Sri Aurobindo, *The Complete Works of Sri Aurobindo, Volumes 33 and 34* (Sri Aurobindo Ashram Trust, 1997).

4. Sri Aurobindo, *The Complete Works of Sri Aurobindo, Volume 25* (Sri Aurobindo Ashram Trust, 1997), p. 9.
5. Ibid., p. 607.
6. Ibid., p. 621.
7. Ibid., p. 201.
8. Ibid.
9. Ibid., pp. 295–308.
10. Ibid., pp. 303–04.
11. Ibid., pp. 655–60.
12. Ibid., p. 363.
13. Ibid, p. 364.
14. Ibid., p. 477.
15. Sri Aurobindo, *The Complete Works of Sri Aurobindo, Volume 5* (Sri Aurobindo Ashram Trust, 2009), p. 9.
16. William Shakespeare, *A Midsummer Night's Dream*, ed. Barbara A. Mowat and Paul Werstine (Simon & Schuster, 2016), p. 143.

3. Collected Plays and Stories I and II

1. Sri Aurobindo, *The Complete Works of Sri Aurobindo, Volumes 3 and 4* (Sri Aurobindo Ashram Trust, 1998).
2. Ibid., pp. 1–183.
3. Ibid., pp. 185–324.
4. Ibid., pp. 325–528.
5. Ibid., pp. 529–617.
6. Ibid., pp. 619–745.
7. Sri Aurobindo, *The Complete Works of Sri Aurobindo, Volumes 6 and 7* (Sri Aurobindo Ashram Trust, 2002).
8. Ibid., pp. 749–75.
9. Ibid., pp. 783–844.
10. Ibid., pp. 745–927
11. Ibid., pp. 685.
12. Ibid., pp. 845–927.
13. Ibid., p. 528.
14. Ibid., pp. 86–87.

15. Ibid., p. 410.
16. Ibid.
17. Ibid., p. 353.
18. Ibid., pp. 991–95.
19. Ibid., pp. 777–82.
20. Ibid., p. 783
21. Ibid., p. 793.
22. Ibid., p. 459.
23. Ibid., pp. 953–64.
24. Ibid., pp. 965–86.
25. Sri Aurobindo, *The Complete Works of Sri Aurobindo, Volumes 33 and 34* (Sri Aurobindo Ashram Trust, 1997).

4. Translations

1. Sri Aurobindo, *The Complete Works of Sri Aurobindo, Volume 1* (Sri Aurobindo Ashram Trust, 2003), p. 240.
2. Sri Aurobindo, *The Complete Works of Sri Aurobindo, Volumes 14, 15 and 16* (Sri Aurobindo Ashram Trust, 2016, 1998, 2013).
3. Sri Aurobindo, *The Complete Works of Sri Aurobindo, Volumes 17 and 18* (Sri Aurobindo Ashram Trust, 2003, 2001).
4. Sri Aurobindo, *The Complete Works of Sri Aurobindo, Volume 32* (Sri Aurobindo Ashram Trust, 2011), pp. 631–647.
5. Sri Aurobindo, *The Complete Works of Sri Aurobindo, Volume 9* (Sri Aurobindo Ashram Trust, 2017), pp. 281–289, 312–320, 331–333, 348–351, 360–376.
6. Sri Aurobindo, *The Complete Works of Sri Aurobindo, Volume 2* (Sri Aurobindo Ashram Trust, 2009).
7. Sri Aurobindo, *The Complete Works of Sri Aurobindo, Volumes 3 and 4* (Sri Aurobindo Ashram Trust,1998).
8. Ibid., p. 252.
9. Sri Aurobindo, *The Complete Works of Sri Aurobindo, Volume 5* (Sri Aurobindo Ashram Trust, 1999), pp. 121–225.
10. Ibid., p. 191.

11. Sri Aurobindo, *The Complete Works of Sri Aurobindo, Volume 1* (Sri Aurobindo Ashram Trust, 2003), p. 246.
12. Sri Aurobindo, *The Complete Works of Sri Aurobindo, Volume 5* (Sri Aurobindo Ashram Trust, 1999), p. 421.
13. Ibid., pp. 469–524.
14. Ibid., pp. 637–638.
15. Ibid., pp. 496–498.
16. Ibid., pp. 465–468.
17. Ibid., p. 587.
18. Sri Aurobindo, *The Complete Works of Sri Aurobindo, Volume 2* (Sri Aurobindo Ashram Trust, 2009), 333–473.
19. Sri Aurobindo, *The Complete Works of Sri Aurobindo, Volume 5* (Sri Aurobindo Ashram Trust, 1999), p. 604.
20. Sri Aurobindo, *The Complete Works of Sri Aurobindo, Volume 12* (Sri Aurobindo Ashram Trust, 1997), p. 100.

5. Bande Mataram: Political Writings and Speeches, 1890–1908

1. Henry W. Nevinson, *The New Spirit in India* (London-New York: Harper & Brothers, 1908), p. 222.
2. Sri Aurobindo, *The Complete Works of Sri Aurobindo, Volume 36* (Sri Aurobindo Ashram Trust, 2006), p. 56.
3. Ibid., p. 81
4. Ibid.
5. A.B. Purani, *The Life of Sri Aurobindo*, (Sri Aurobindo Ashram Publication Department), p. 90.
6. Cited in Manoj Das, *Sri Aurobindo: the Life and Times of the Mahayogi (The Pre-Pondicherry Phase)* (Sri Aurobindo International Centre of Education, 2020), pp. 260–261.
7. Sri Aurobindo, *The Complete Works of Sri Aurobindo, Volume 36* (Sri Aurobindo Ashram Trust, 2006), p. 78.
8. Ibid., p. 79.

9. Sri Aurobindo, *The Complete Works of Sri Aurobindo, Volume 36* (Sri Aurobindo Ashram Trust, 2006), p. 54.
10. Peter Heehs, *Sri Aurobindo: a Brief Biography* (Oxford University Press, 1989), p. 41.
11. Sri Aurobindo, *The Complete Works of Sri Aurobindo, Volume 36* (Sri Aurobindo Ashram Trust, 2006), p. 79.
12. Manoj Das, *Sri Aurobindo: the Life and Times of the Mahayogi (The Pre-Pondicherry Phase)* (Sri Aurobindo International Centre of Education, 2020), p. 260.
13. Sri Aurobindo, *The Complete Works of Sri Aurobindo, Volume 36* (Sri Aurobindo Ashram Trust, 2006), p. 79
14. Sri Aurobindo, *The Complete Works of Sri Aurobindo, Volumes 6 & 7* (Sri Aurobindo Ashram Trust, 2002), p. 298
15. Ibid., pp. 265–303.
16. Peter Heehs, *Sri Aurobindo: a Brief Biography* (Oxford University Press, 1989), p. 44.
17. Sri Aurobindo, *The Complete Works of Sri Aurobindo, Volumes 6 & 7* (Sri Aurobindo Ashram Trust, 2002), p. 272.
18. Ibid., p. 276.
19. Ibid., p. 357.
20. Ibid., p. 1106.
21. Ibid., pp. 656–657.
22. Ibid., pp. 818–819.

6. Karmayogin: Political Writings and Speeches, 1909–1910

1. Sri Aurobindo, *The Complete Works of Sri Aurobindo, Volume 8* (Sri Aurobindo Ashram Trust, 1997), p. 24.
2. Ibid., p. 4.
3. Ibid., p. 4.
4. Ibid., p. 11.
5. Ibid., p. 12.
6. Ibid., p. 277.

7. Ibid., p. 277.
8. Ibid., p. 169.
9. Ibid., p. 164.
10. Ibid.
11. Sri Aurobindo, *The Complete Works of Sri Aurobindo, Volume 2* (Sri Aurobindo Ashram Trust, 2009), p. 202.
12. Sri Aurobindo, *The Complete Works of Sri Aurobindo, Volume 36*, (Sri Aurobindo Ashram Trust, 2006), p. 255.

7. Writings in Bengali and Sanskrit

1. Sri Aurobindo, *The Complete Works of Sri Aurobindo, Volume 9* (Sri Aurobindo Ashram Trust, 2017).
2. Ibid., pp. 1–2.
3. Ibid., p. 2.
4. Sri Aurobindo, *Bengali Writings translated into English* (Sri Aurobindo Ashram Trust, 1991), p. 4
5. Sri Aurobindo, *The Complete Works of Sri Aurobindo, Volume 9* (Sri Aurobindo Ashram Trust, 2017), pp. 7–73.
6. Ibid., p. 16.
7. Sri Aurobindo, *Bengali Writings translated into English* (Sri Aurobindo Ashram Trust, 1991), p. 272–73
8. Sri Aurobindo, *The Complete Works of Sri Aurobindo, Volume 9* (Sri Aurobindo Ashram Trust, 2017), pp. 77–94.
9. Ibid., pp. 124.
10. Sri Aurobindo, *Bengali Writings translated into English* (Sri Aurobindo Ashram Trust, 1991), p. 224
11. Sri Aurobindo, *The Complete Works of Sri Aurobindo, Volume 9* (Sri Aurobindo Ashram Trust, 2017), pp. 95–141.
12. Ibid., pp. 143–240.
13. Ibid., pp. 114–15.
14. Sri Aurobindo, *Bengali Writings translated into English* (Sri Aurobindo Ashram Trust, 1991), pp. 221–22.

15. Sri Aurobindo, *The Complete Works of Sri Aurobindo, Volume 9* (Sri Aurobindo Ashram Trust, 2017), p. 252.
16. Sri Aurobindo, *Bengali Writings translated into English* (Sri Aurobindo Ashram Trust, 1991), p. 171.
17. Sri Aurobindo, *The Complete Works of Sri Aurobindo, Volume 19* (Sri Aurobindo Ashram Trust, 1997).
18. Sri Aurobindo, *The Complete Works of Sri Aurobindo, Volume 9* (Sri Aurobindo Ashram Trust, 2017), pp. 259–324.
19. Sri Aurobindo, *The Complete Works of Sri Aurobindo, Volume 9* (Sri Aurobindo Ashram Trust, 2017), p. 276.
20. Sri Aurobindo, *Bengali Writings translated into English* (Sri Aurobindo Ashram Trust, 1991), pp. 99–100.
21. Sri Aurobindo, *The Complete Works of Sri Aurobindo, Volume 9* (Sri Aurobindo Ashram Trust, 2017), p. 327–76.
22. Ibid., pp. 379–391.
23. Ibid., pp. 566–568.
24. Ibid., p. 586.
25. Sri Aurobindo, *Bengali Writings translated into English* (Sri Aurobindo Ashram Trust, 1991), p. 447.
26. Sri Aurobindo, *The Complete Works of Sri Aurobindo, Volume 9* (Sri Aurobindo Ashram Trust, 2017), pp. 687–693.
27. Ibid., pp. 699–700.
28. Ibid., pp. 696–698.
29. Ibid., pp. 694–695.
30. Ibid., p. 687.
31. Sri Aurobindo, श्रीअरविन्दोपनिषद् (Sanskrit Karyalaya, Sri Aurobindo Ashram Trust, 3rd edition, 2000).
32. Ibid., p. 3
33. Sri Aurobindo, *The Complete Works of Sri Aurobindo, Volume 9* (Sri Aurobindo Ashram Trust, 2017), p. 708.

8. Record of Yoga

1. Sri Aurobindo, *The Complete Works of Sri Aurobindo, Volumes 10 and 11* (Sri Aurobindo Ashram Trust, 2001).

2. Sri Aurobindo, *The Complete Works of Sri Aurobindo, Volume 35* (Sri Aurobindo Ashram Trust, 2011), p. 78.
3. Sri Aurobindo, *The Complete Works of Sri Aurobindo, Volume 10* (Sri Aurobindo Ashram Trust, 2001), pp. 173–74.
4. Sri Aurobindo, *The Complete Works of Sri Aurobindo, Volume 36* (Sri Aurobindo Ashram Trust, 2006), p. 290.
5. Sri Aurobindo, *The Complete Works of Sri Aurobindo, Volume 10* (Sri Aurobindo Ashram Trust, 2006), p. 222–223.
6. Sri Aurobindo, *The Complete Works of Sri Aurobindo, Volume 19* (Sri Aurobindo Ashram Trust, 1997).
7. Ibid., p. 549.
8. Sri Aurobindo, *The Complete Works of Sri Aurobindo, Volume 10* (Sri Aurobindo Ashram Trust, 1999), pp. 307–308.
9. Sri Aurobindo, *The Complete Works of Sri Aurobindo, Volume 24* (Sri Aurobindo Ashram Trust, 1999), pp. 607–904.
10. Sri Aurobindo, *The Complete Works of Sri Aurobindo, Volume 10* (Sri Aurobindo Ashram Trust, 1999), p. 647.
11. Ibid., p. 135.
12. Sri Aurobindo, *The Complete Works of Sri Aurobindo, Volume 23* (Sri Aurobindo Ashram Trust, 1999), p. 8.

9. Essays Divine and Human

1. Sri Aurobindo, *The Complete Works of Sri Aurobindo, Volume 12* (Sri Aurobindo Ashram Trust, 1997).
2. Ibid., pp. 221.
3. This was the monthly philosophical review authored by Sri Aurobindo between 1914 and 1920 in which most of what are now known as his major works were published.
4. Sri Aurobindo, *The Complete Works of Sri Aurobindo, Volumes 21 and 22* (Sri Aurobindo Ashram Trust, 2005).
5. Sri Aurobindo, *The Complete Works of Sri Aurobindo, Volumes 23 and 24* (Sri Aurobindo Ashram Trust, 1999).

6. Sri Aurobindo, *The Complete Works of Sri Aurobindo, Volumes 28, 29, 30 and 31* (Sri Aurobindo Ashram Trust 2012, 2013, 2014 and 2014 respectively).
7. Sri Aurobindo, *The Complete Works of Sri Aurobindo, Volume 12*, (Sri Aurobindo Ashram Trust, 1997), pp. 38–45.
8. Ibid., pp. 41.
9. Ibid., pp. 41.
10. Ibid., pp. 45.
11. Sri Aurobindo, *The Complete Works of Sri Aurobindo, Volume 12* (Sri Aurobindo Ashram Trust, 1997), pp. 33–37.
12. Ibid., pp. 50–58.
13. Ibid., pp. 59–63.
14. Ibid., p. 63.
15. Ibid., pp. 177–373. The entire Part Two of this volume captures this theme.
16. Sri Aurobindo, *The Complete Works of Sri Aurobindo, Volumes 33 and 34* (Sri Aurobindo Ashram Trust, 1997), p. 77.
17. Sri Aurobindo, *The Complete Works of Sri Aurobindo, Volumes 33 and 34* (Sri Aurobindo Ashram Trust, 1997).
18. Sri Aurobindo, *The Complete Works of Sri Aurobindo, Volume 12* (Sri Aurobindo Ashram Trust, 1997), p. 144.
19. Ibid., p. 188.
20. Ibid., pp. 271–326.
21. Ibid., p. 323.
22. Ibid., pp. 423–500.
23. Sri Aurobindo, *The Complete Works of Sri Aurobindo, Volume 13* (Sri Aurobindo Ashram Trust, 1998), p. 217.
24. Sri Aurobindo, *The Complete Works of Sri Aurobindo, Volumes 33 and 34* (Sri Aurobindo Ashram Trust 1997), p. 259.
25. Ibid., p. 65.
26. The Mother, *The Collected Works of The Mother, Volume 10* (Sri Aurobindo Ashram Trust 1977), p. 333.
27. Sri Aurobindo, *The Complete Works of Sri Aurobindo, Volume 12* (Sri Aurobindo Ashram Trust, 1997), p. 432.

28. Ibid., p. 490.
29. The Mother, *The Collected Works of The Mother, Volume 10* (Sri Aurobindo Ashram Trust, 1977).
30. Ibid., pp. 8–9.
31. Ibid., pp. 96.
32. Sri Aurobindo, *The Complete Works of Sri Aurobindo, Volume 29* (Sri Aurobindo Ashram Trust, 2013), pp. 322–323.
33. Sri Aurobindo, *The Complete Works of Sri Aurobindo, Volume 13* (Sri Aurobindo Ashram Trust, 1998), p. 221.
34. Sri Aurobindo, *The Complete Works of Sri Aurobindo, Volumes 33 and 34* (Sri Aurobindo Ashram Trust, 1997), p. 660.

10. Essays in Philosophy and Yoga

1. Sri Aurobindo, *The Complete Works of Sri Aurobindo, Volume 13* (Sri Aurobindo Ashram Trust, 1998), p. 585.
2. Ibid., pp. 201–07.
3. Ibid., p. 201.
4. Ibid., p. 585.
5. Sri Aurobindo, *The Complete Works of Sri Aurobindo, Volumes 21 and 22* (Sri Aurobindo Ashram Trust, 2005), p. 6.
6. Sri Aurobindo, *The Complete Works of Sri Aurobindo, Volume 13* (Sri Aurobindo Ashram Trust, 1998), p. 503.
7. Sri Aurobindo, *The Complete Works of Sri Aurobindo, Volumes 21 and 22* (Sri Aurobindo Ashram Trust, 2005), pp. 200–09.
8. Ibid., Volume 13, p. 473.
9. Ibid.
10. Swami Jyotirmayananda, Ed, *Vivekananda: His Gospel of Man-making with A Garland of Tributes and A Chronicle of His Life and Times with Pictures*, All India Press (1988) p. 59.
11. Ibid., Volume 13, pp. 57–59.
12. Ibid., p. 57.
13. Ibid., p. 59.

14. Sri Aurobindo, *The Complete Works of Sri Aurobindo, Volumes 23 and 24* (Sri Aurobindo Ashram Trust, 1999).
15. Ibid., p. 316.
16. Sri Aurobindo, *The Complete Works of Sri Aurobindo, Volume 19* (Sri Aurobindo Ashram Trust, 1997).
17. Ibid., p. 440.
18. Sri Aurobindo, *The Complete Works of Sri Aurobindo, Volume 29* (Sri Aurobindo Ashram Trust, 2013).
19. Ibid., pp. 149–50.
20. Ibid., Volume 13, pp. 101.
21. Ibid., p. 211.
22. Ibid.
23. Ibid.
24. Ibid., p. 50.
25. Ibid., p. 6.
26. Ibid., p. 147.
27. Ibid., p. 60.
28. Ibid., p. 317.
29. Sri Aurobindo, *The Complete Works of Sri Aurobindo, Volume 12* (Sri Aurobindo Ashram Trust, 1997).

11. Vedic and Philological Studies

1. Sri Aurobindo, *The Complete Works of Sri Aurobindo, Volumes 21 and 22* (Sri Aurobindo Ashram Trust, 2005).
2. Sri Aurobindo, *The Complete Works of Sri Aurobindo, Volume 25* (Sri Aurobindo Ashram Trust, 1997).
3. Sri Aurobindo, *The Complete Works of Sri Aurobindo, Volume 26* (Sri Aurobindo Ashram Trust, 1997).
4. Sri Aurobindo, *The Complete Works of Sri Aurobindo, Volume 15* (Sri Aurobindo Ashram Trust, 1998).
5. Sri Aurobindo, *The Complete Works of Sri Aurobindo, Volume 16* (Sri Aurobindo Ashram Trust, 2013).

6. Sri Aurobindo, *The Complete Works of Sri Aurobindo, Volume 14* (Sri Aurobindo Ashram Trust, 2016).
7. Ibid., pp. 1–196.
8. Sri Aurobindo, *The Complete Works of Sri Aurobindo, Volume 15* (Sri Aurobindo Ashram Trust, 1998), p. 36.
9. Sri Aurobindo, *The Complete Works of Sri Aurobindo, Volume 14* (Sri Aurobindo Ashram Trust, 2016), pp. 20–23. The title of this essay has been supplied by the editors, in the absence of a title in the manuscript.
10. Sri Aurobindo, *The Complete Works of Sri Aurobindo, Volume 15* (Sri Aurobindo Ashram Trust, 1998), pp. 253–56.
11. Sri Aurobindo, *The Complete Works of Sri Aurobindo, Volume 14* (Sri Aurobindo Ashram Trust, 2016), p. 20.
12. Ibid., p. 21. For the translation of the Kena Upanishad, see Sri Aurobindo, *The Complete Works of Sri Aurobindo, Volume 18* (Sri Aurobindo Ashram Trust, 2001), pp. 5–11.
13. Sri Aurobindo, *The Complete Works of Sri Aurobindo, Volume 14* (Sri Aurobindo Ashram Trust, 2016), pp. 22–23.
14. Sri Aurobindo, *The Complete Works of Sri Aurobindo, Volume 35* (Sri Aurobindo Ashram Trust, 2011), p. 78.
15. Sri Aurobindo, *The Complete Works of Sri Aurobindo, Volume 14* (Sri Aurobindo Ashram Trust, 2016), p. 98.
16. Ibid., p. 526.
17. Ibid., p. 552.
18. Ibid., p. 559.
19. Ibid., p. 563.
20. Sri Aurobindo, *The Complete Works of Sri Aurobindo, Volume 26* (Sri Aurobindo Ashram Trust, 1997), pp. 14–15.
21. Sri Aurobindo, *The Complete Works of Sri Aurobindo, Volume 14* (Sri Aurobindo Ashram Trust, 2016), p. 543.
22. Ibid., p. 526.
23. Sri Aurobindo, *The Complete Works of Sri Aurobindo, Volume 32* (Sri Aurobindo Ashram Trust, 2012), p. 22.

12. The Secret of the Veda

1. Sri Aurobindo, *The Complete Works of Sri Aurobindo, Volume 15* (Sri Aurobindo Ashram Trust, 1998), p. 3.
2. Ibid., p. 45.
3. Ibid., pp. 52–53.
4. Ibid., p. 54
5. Ibid., p. 52
6. Ibid., p. 53–54
7. Ibid.
8. Ibid.
9. Ibid., p. 76
10. Ibid., p. 61
11. Ibid., pp. 65–66
12. Ibid., p. 66
13. Ibid., p. 76
14. Ibid.
15. Ibid., p. 80
16. Ibid.
17. Ibid., p. 83
18. Ibid., p. 73
19. Ibid., p. 380
20. Ibid.
21. Ibid., p. 87
22. Ibid., p. 92
23. Ibid., p. 92
24. Ibid., p. 96
25. Ibid.
26. Ibid., p. 83
27. Ibid., p. 131
28. Ibid., p. 134
29. Ibid., pp. 253–360
30. Ibid., p. 384.
31. Ibid., p. 596
32. Ibid., pp. 368–69

13. Hymns to the Mystic Fire

1. Sri Aurobindo, *The Complete Works of Sri Aurobindo, Volume 17* (Sri Aurobindo Ashram Trust, 2003).
2. Sri Aurobindo, *The Complete Works of Sri Aurobindo, Volume 15* (Sri Aurobindo Ashram Trust, 1998), p. 66.
3. Sri Aurobindo, *The Complete Works of Sri Aurobindo, Volume 16* (Sri Aurobindo Ashram Trust, 2013).
4. Ibid., p. 747.
5. Ibid., Publisher's Note.
6. Ibid., p. 754.
7. Ibid., Publisher's Note.
8. Ibid., p. 9.
9. Ibid., p. 10
10. Ibid., p. 22.
11. Ibid., p. 760.
12. Ibid., p. 756.
13. Ibid., p. 9.
14. Ibid., p. 26.
15. Ibid., p. 748.
16. Ibid., p. 451.
17. Ibid., p. 452.
18. Ibid., p. 461.
19. Ibid., p. 20.
20. Ibid., p. 26.
21. Ibid., p. 118.
22. Ibid., p. 18.
23. Ibid., p. 735.
24. Ibid., p. 122.
25. Ibid., p. 122.

14. Isha Upanishad

1. Sri Aurobindo, *The Complete Works of Sri Aurobindo, Volume 17* (Sri Aurobindo Ashram Trust, 2003).

2. *Sri Aurobindo, The Complete Works of Sri Aurobindo, Volume 18* (Sri Aurobindo Ashram Trust, 2001).
3. Ibid., Volume 17, p. 71.
4. Ibid., pp. 303–05.
5. Ibid., pp. 95–99.
6. Ibid., pp. 95–98.
7. Ibid., p. 98.
8. Ibid., pp. 101–67.
9. Purani, A.B. Ed., *Evening Talks with Sri Aurobindo Complete in One Volume* (Sri Aurobindo Ashram Trust, 1982), p. 591. The injunction from Ramakrishna was received in a session of automatic writing which Sri Aurobindo seems to have taken seriously, though he later reinterpreted its sense to mean, building a temple to God within oneself.
10. Sri Aurobindo, *The Complete Works of Sri Aurobindo, Volume 6 and 7* (Sri Aurobindo Ashram Trust, 2002), p. 79.
11. Ibid., *Volume 17,* p. 101.

    The word "arya" should not be confused with the pejorative understanding it has developed in the common mind of our times due to its racist distortions under German Nationalist Socialism in the third and fourth decades of the 20th century.
12. Ibid., p. 101.
13. Ibid., p. 112–17.
14. Ibid., p. 103. The word *vasyam* is interpreted as dress or robe by Shankara. Sri Aurobindo follows this interpretation here but by his final translation (Part One) he takes vasyam to mean "habitation" and contests Shankara's interpretation. See Ibid., p. 5, fn. 1.
15. Ibid., pp. 48–50.
16. Ibid., pp. 65–75.
17. Ibid., pp. 48, 71–73.
18. Ibid., pp. 169–301.
19. Ibid., p. 5.
20. Ibid., pp. 199–205.

21. Ibid., pp. 8–9.
22. Ibid., pp. 311–49.
23. Ibid., pp. 361–90.
24. Sri Aurobindo, *The Complete Works of Sri Aurobindo, Volume 15* (Sri Aurobindo Ashram Trust, 1998).
25. Sri Aurobindo, *The Complete Works of Sri Aurobindo, Volume 18* (Sri Aurobindo Ashram Trust, 2001).
26. Sri Aurobindo, *The Complete Works of Sri Aurobindo, Volume 19* (Sri Aurobindo Ashram Trust, 1997).
27. Sri Aurobindo, *The Complete Works of Sri Aurobindo, Volumes 21 and 22* (Sri Aurobindo Ashram Trust, 2005), pp. 543–72.
28. Sri Aurobindo, *The Complete Works of Sri Aurobindo, Volume 17* (Sri Aurobindo Ashram Trust, 2003), pp. 330–36.
29. Ibid., p. 368.
30. Ibid., pp. 367–68.
31. Ibid., p. 588.
32. Ibid., pp. 584–90
33. Ibid., p. 596.
34. Ibid., pp. 13–15.
35. Ibid., pp. 71–72.

15. Kena and Other Upanishads

1. Sri Aurobindo, *Complete Works of Sri Aurobindo, Volume 21* (Sri Aurobindo Ashram Trust, 2005), p. 3.
2. Sri Aurobindo, *Complete Works of Sri Aurobindo, Volume 20* (Sri Aurobindo Ashram Trust, 1997), p. 204.
3. Sri Aurobindo, *Complete Works of Sri Aurobindo, Volume 18* (Sri Aurobindo Ashram Trust, 2001), p. 241.
4. Sri Aurobindo, *Complete Works of Sri Aurobindo, Volume 18* (Sri Aurobindo Ashram Trust, 2001).
5. Sri Aurobindo, *Complete Works of Sri Aurobindo, Volume 8* (Sri Aurobindo Ashram Trust, 1997).
6. Ibid., pp. 345–399.

7. Ibid., p. 345.
8. Ibid., p. 273.
9. Ibid., p. 274.
10. Ibid., p. 273.
11. Ibid., p. 274.
12. Ibid., p. 278.
13. Ibid., p. 274.
14. Ibid., p. 5.
15. Ibid., p. 275.
16. Ibid., p. 401.
17. Ibid., p. 417.
18. Ibid., p. 349.
19. Ibid., p. 311.
20. Ibid., p. 410.
21. Ibid., p. 423.
22. Ibid., p. 275.

16. Essays on the Gita

1. Sri Aurobindo, *The Complete Works of Sri Aurobindo, Volume 19* (Sri Aurobindo Ashram Trust, 1997).
2. Ibid., p. 571.
3. Ibid., pp. 3–11.
4. Ibid., pp. 12–19.
5. Ibid., pp. 29–38.
6. Sri Aurobindo, *The Complete Works of Sri Aurobindo, Volume 19* (Sri Aurobindo Ashram Trust, 2003), p. 33.
7. Ibid., p. 366.
8. Sri Aurobindo, *Essays on the Gita with Sanskrit Text and Translation of the Gita* (Madanlal Himatsinghka, 1972).
9. Ibid., pp. 57–67.
10. Ibid., pp. 463–76.
11. Ibid., p. 572.

17. The Renaissance in India with a Defence of Indian Culture

1. In 1953 many of these essays were put together and published in New York under a title given by the editors of the book: "The Foundations of Indian Culture". Volume 20 of the Complete Works of Sri Aurobindo puts together all the essays on the topic, and has been renamed using Sri Aurobindo's own titles to two of the principal series of essays.
2. Sri Aurobindo, *The Complete Works of Sri Aurobindo, Volume 20* (Sri Aurobindo Ashram Trust, 1997), pp. 3–40.
3. Ibid., pp. 43–52.
4. Ibid., pp. 55–93.
5. Ibid., pp. 97–444.
6. James H. Cousins & Margaret E. Cousins, *We Two Together* (Ganesh & Co. Ltd., Madras, 1950), p. 364.
7. Ibid., p. 394.
8. Sri Aurobindo, *The Complete Works of Sri Aurobindo, Volume 20* (Sri Aurobindo Ashram Trust, 1997), p. 447.
9. Ibid., p. 39.
10. Ibid., p. 13.
11. Ibid., 16.
12. Ibid., p. 22.
13. Ibid., pp. 41–52.
14. Ibid., p. 49.
15. Ibid., pp 53–93.
16. John Woodroffe, *Is India Civlised?,* (Ganesh & Co. Ltd., Madras, 1918).
17. William Archer, *India and the Future,* (Hutchinson & Co., London, 1917).
18. Ibid., p. 38.
19. Sri Aurobindo, *The Complete Works of Sri Aurobindo, Volume 20* (Sri Aurobindo Ashram Trust, 1997), p. 91.
20. Ibid., 95–444.

21. Ibid., pp. 97–99.
22. Ibid., pp. 106–107.
23. Ibid., p. 217.
24. Ibid., pp. 140–143.
25. Ibid., pp. 162–166.
26. Ibid., p. 170.
27. Ibid., p. 168.
28. Ibid. pp. 193–195.
29. Ibid. p. 195.
30. Ibid., pp. 196–213.
31. Ibid., pp. 270–284.
32. Ibid., pp. 285–297.
33. Ibid., pp. 298–313.
34. Ibid., pp. 314–328.
35. Ibid., pp. 329–341.
36. Ibid., pp. 342–353.
37. Ibid., pp. 354–367.
38. Ibid., pp. 368–383.
39. Ibid., 384–444.
40. Ibid., p. 215.
41. Ibid., p. 216.
42. Ibid., p. 216.

18. The Life Divine

1. Sri Aurobindo, *The Complete Works of Sri Aurobindo, Volumes 21 and 22* (Sri Aurobindo Ashram Trust, 2005).
2. Ibid., p. 695.
3. Ibid., p. 3.
4. Sri Aurobindo, *The Complete Works of Sri Aurobindo, Volumes 33 and 34* (Sri Aurobindo Ashram Trust, 1997).
5. Ibid., p. 313.
6. Ibid., Volume 21, p. 11.
7. The most significant exception is Sankhya.

8. Yoga in the broad sense of a practice that leads to union with the Divine.
9. Here, the main exception is Tantra and one could argue that from among the Indian systems, Kashmiri Shaivism comes, at least in this respect, closest to Sri Aurobindo's.
10. Sri Aurobindo, *The Complete Works of Sri Aurobindo, Volume 35* (Sri Aurobindo Ashram Trust, 2011).
11. Ibid., p. 249.
12. Sri Aurobindo published *The Life Divine* originally in the *Arya*, a monthly journal he brought out between 1914 and 1920. In 1939–40, he published a second, extensively revised edition in book form.
13. Ibid., p. 1107.

19. The Synthesis of Yoga

1. Sri Aurobindo, *The Complete Works of Sri Aurobindo, Volumes 21 and 22* (Sri Aurobindo Ashram Trust, 2005).
2. Sri Aurobindo, *The Complete Works of Sri Aurobindo, Volumes 23 and 24* (Sri Aurobindo Ashram Trust, 1999).
3. Ibid., pp. 32–33.
4. Ibid., pp. 5–6.
5. Ibid., pp. 6–8.
6. Ibid., pp. 31–40.
7. Ibid., pp. 41–43.
8. Ibid., pp. 44–45.
9. Sri Aurobindo, *The Complete Works of Sri Aurobindo, Volume 17* (Sri Aurobindo Ashram Trust, 2003).
10. Sri Aurobindo, *The Complete Works of Sri Aurobindo, Volume 19* (Sri Aurobindo Ashram Trust, 1997).
11. Ibid., *Volume 17*, pp. 8, 51–59.
12. Ibid., *Volumes 21 and 22*, pp. 543–572.
13. Ibid., *Volumes 23 and 24*, pp. 44–45.

14. Sri Aurobindo, *The Complete Works of Sri Aurobindo, Volume 19* (Sri Aurobindo Ashram Trust, 1997), pp. 263–277.
15. Ibid., *Volumes 23 and 24*, p. 44.
16. Ibid., pp. 45–46.
17. Ibid., p. 47.
18. Ibid., p. 47.
19. Ibid., p. 57.
20. Ibid., p. 61.
21. Ibid., p. 53.
22. Sri Aurobindo, *The Complete Works of Sri Aurobindo, Volumes 10 and 11* (Sri Aurobindo Ashram Trust, 2001), pp. 409, 53, 74, 153, 157, 168, 236, 258, 289, 297, 336, 347.
23. Sri Aurobindo, *The Complete Works of Sri Aurobindo, Volume 35* (Sri Aurobindo Ashram Trust, 2011), p. 432.
24. Sri Aurobindo, *The Complete Works of Sri Aurobindo, Volume 8* (Sri Aurobindo Ashram Trust, 1997), pp. 5–8.
25. Ibid., p. 5.
26. Sri Aurobindo, *The Complete Works of Sri Aurobindo, Volumes 10 and 11* (Sri Aurobindo Ashram Trust, 2001).
27. Ibid., pp. 3–29.
28. Sri Aurobindo, *The Complete Works of Sri Aurobindo, Volumes 23 and 24* (Sri Aurobindo Ashram Trust, 1999), p. 913.
29. Sri Aurobindo, *The Complete Works of Sri Aurobindo, Volumes 28, 29, 30 and 31* (Sri Aurobindo Ashram Trust, 2012, 2013, and 2014).
30. Sri Aurobindo, *The Complete Works of Sri Aurobindo, Volume 32* (Sri Aurobindo Ashram Trust, 2012).

20. The Human Cycle

1. Sri Aurobindo, *The Complete Works of Sri Aurobindo, Volume 25*, Sri Aurobindo Ashram Trust (1997).
2. Ibid., p. 687.
3. Ibid.

4. Ibid., p. 72.
5. Ibid., p. 10.
6. Ibid., p. 11.
7. Ibid.
8. Ibid., p. 15.
9. Ibid., p. 29.
10. Ibid., pp. 124–35.
11. Ibid., p. 235.
12. Ibid., p. 182.
13. Ibid., pp. 182–83.
14. Ibid., p. 249.
15. Ibid., p. 265.
16. Ibid., p. 263.
17. Sri Aurobindo, *The Complete Works of Sri Aurobindo, Volumes 33 and 34* (Sri Aurobindo Ashram Trust, 1997), p. 724.

21. The Ideal of Human Unity; and War and Self-Determination

1. Sri Aurobindo, *The Complete Works of Sri Aurobindo, Volume 25* (Sri Aurobindo Ashram Trust, 1997), pp. 5–269.
2. Ibid., pp. 279–595.
3. Ibid., pp. 599–681.
4. Sri Aurobindo, *The Complete Works of Sri Aurobindo, Volume 35* (Sri Aurobindo Ashram Trust, 2011), p. 51.
5. Ibid., p. 279.
6. Ibid., p. 688.
7. Ibid., p. 423.
8. Ibid., p. 577.
9. Ibid., pp. 569–570.
10. Ibid., p. 600.
11. Ibid., p. 611.
12. Ibid., p. 621.
13. Ibid., p. 663.

22. The Future Poetry with On Quantitative Metre

1. Sri Aurobindo, *The Complete Works of Sri Aurobindo, Volume 26* (Sri Aurobindo Ashram Trust, 1997).
2. Sri Aurobindo, *The Complete Works of Sri Aurobindo, Volumes 21 and 22* (Sri Aurobindo Ashram Trust, 2005), pp. 18.
3. Ibid., p. 18.
4. Ibid., *Volume 26*, p. 270.
5. Ibid., pp. 399–400.
6. Ibid., pp. 205–06.
7. Ibid., p. 301.
8. Ibid., pp. 400.
9. Ibid., Volume 26, p. 17.
10. Ibid., p. 10.
11. Ibid., p. 19.
12. Ibid., p. 26.
13. Ibid., pp. 41–45.
14. Ibid., pp. 110–11.
15. Ibid., pp. 163–68.
16. Ibid., p. 191.
17. Ibid., p. 201.
18. Ibid., p. 172.
19. Ibid., p. 222.
20. Ibid., p. 247.
21. Ibid., p. 225.
22. Ibid., p. 264.
23. Ibid., p. 281.
24. Ibid., p. 286.
25. K.D. Sethna, *The Poetic Genius of Sri Aurobindo* (Clear Ray Trust, Pondicherry, 2008).
26. Ibid., *Volume 26*, pp. 266–67.

23. Letters on Poetry and Art

1. Sri Aurobindo, *The Complete Works of Sri Aurobindo, Volume 26* (Sri Aurobindo Ashram Trust, 1997).
2. Ibid., p. 26–27.
3. Ibid., p. 5.
4. Ibid.
5. Ibid., p. 22.
6. Ibid., p. 61.
7. Ibid., p. 27.
8. Ibid., p. 20.
9. Sri Aurobindo, *The Complete Works of Sri Aurobindo, Volume 32* (Sri Aurobindo Ashram Trust, 2012), pp. 20–22.
10. This phrase is important to Sri Aurobindo. We find it ten times in this volume: pp. 17, 45, 71–75, 185, 194, and 211, and eighteen other times throughout *The Complete Works of Sri Aurobindo: Volumes 10 and 11:* 188; *Volume 13:* 210, 534; *Volume 19:* 299, 581, and 589; *Volumes 23 and 24:* 470, 498, 785, 810; *Volume 29:* 471; *Volume 31:* 659; and *Volume 32:* 23, 96, 255, 423.
11. Ibid., p. 100.
12. Ibid., p. 50.
13. Ibid., p. 63.
14. Ibid., 567–568.
15. Sri Aurobindo, *The Complete Works of Sri Aurobindo, Volumes 33 and 34* (Sri Aurobindo Ashram Trust, 1997).
16. Ibid., Volume 32, p. 6.
17. Ibid., Volume 27, p. 261.
18. Ibid., p. 271.
19. Ibid.
20. Sri Aurobindo uses this phrase in several letters: Ibid., pp. 17, 45, 71, 73, 74, 75, 185, 194, and 211.
21. Ibid., p. 272.
22. Ibid., Volume 27, p. 715.
23. Ibid., p. 723.
24. Ibid., p. 71.

24. Letters on Yoga I: Foundations of the Integral Yoga

1. Sri Aurobindo, *The Complete Works of Sri Aurobindo, Volume 28 (*Sri Aurobindo Ashram Trust, 2012).
2. Ibid., p. 7.
3. Ibid., p. 257.
4. "Important Dates in the Ashram," Sri Aurobindo Ashram Trust, https://www.sriaurobindoashram.org/darshan/dates.php.
5. Ibid., p. 346.
6. Ibid., pp. 338–339.
7. Ibid., p. 485.

25. Letters on Yoga II

1. Sri Aurobindo, *The Complete Works of Sri Aurobindo, Volume 29* (Sri Aurobindo Ashram Trust, 2013).
2. Ibid., pp. 1–202
3. Ibid., pp. 203–367.
4. Ibid., pp. 368–511.
5. Ibid., p. 69.
6. Sri Aurobindo, *The Complete Works of Sri Aurobindo, Volumes 23 and 24* (Sri Aurobindo Ashram Trust, 1999).
7. Sri Aurobindo, *The Complete Works of Sri Aurobindo, Volume 31* (Sri Aurobindo Ashram Trust, 2014).
8. Ibid., Volume 29, p. 207.
9. Ibid., p. 242.
10. Ibid., pp. 281–282.
11. Ibid., pp. 283–285.
12. Ibid., pp. 290–294.
13. Ibid., p. 297.
14. Ibid., p. 302.

15. Ibid.
16. Ibid., p. 310.
17. Ibid., p. 311.
18. Ibid., p. 336.
19. Ibid.
20. Ibid., p. 339.
21. Ibid., p. 350.

26. Letters on Yoga III: Experiences and Realizations in the Integral Yoga

1. Sri Aurobindo, *The Complete Works of Sri Aurobindo, Volume 30* (Sri Aurobindo Ashram Trust, 2014).
2. Ibid., pp. 1–81.
3. Ibid., pp. 83–188.
4. Ibid., pp. 189–313.
5. Ibid., pp. 315–497.
6. Ibid., p. 47.
7. Ibid., p. 70.
8. Ibid., p. 91.
9. Ibid., p. 112.
10. Ibid., p. 138.
11. Ibid., p. 211.
12. Ibid., p. 268.
13. Ibid., pp. 295–307.
14. Ibid., p. 303.
15. Ibid., pp. 295–296.
16. Ibid., p. 361.
17. Ibid., p. 380.
18. Ibid., p. 380.
19. Ibid., p. 411.

27. Letters on Yoga IV: Transformation of Human Nature in the Integral Yoga

1. Sri Aurobindo, *The Complete Works of Sri Aurobindo, Volume 31* (Sri Aurobindo Ashram Trust, 2014), p. 5.
2. Ibid., p. 187.
3. Ibid., p. 145.
4. Ibid., p. 300.
5. Ibid., p. 365.
6. Ibid., p. 569.
7. Ibid., p. 611.
8. Ibid., p. 362.
9. Ibid., p. 625.

28. The Mother with Letters on the Mother

1. Sri Aurobindo, *The Mother* (Sri Aurobindo Ashram, 1928).
2. Sri Aurobindo, *The Complete Works of Sri Aurobindo, Volume 32* (Sri Aurobindo Ashram Trust, 2011).
3. Ibid., p.14.
4. Ibid., p. 12.
5. Ibid., p. 8.
6. Ibid., p. 6.
7. Ibid.
8. Ibid.
9. Ibid., p. 10.
10. Ibid.
11. Ibid., p. 11.
12. Ibid., p. 14.
13. Ibid., p. 18.
14. Ibid., p. 19.
15. Ibid., p. 21.
16. Ibid., p. 22.
17. Ibid., p. 66.

18. Ibid., p. 67.
19. Ibid., p. 69.
20. Ibid., p. 72.
21. Ibid., p. 50.
22. Ibid., p. 79.
23. Ibid.
24. Sri Aurobindo, *The Complete Works of Sri Aurobindo, Volumes 21 and 22* (Sri Aurobindo Ashram Trust, 2005).
25. Sri Aurobindo, *The Complete Works of Sri Aurobindo, Volumes 23 and 24* (Sri Aurobindo Ashram Trust, 1999).
26. Sri Aurobindo, *The Complete Works of Sri Aurobindo, Volume 19* (Sri Aurobindo Ashram Trust, 1997).
27. Sri Aurobindo, *The Complete Works of Sri Aurobindo, Volumes 33 and 34* (Sri Aurobindo Ashram Trust, 1997).
28. Ibid., p. 315.
29. Ibid., *Volume 32*, p. 141.
30. Ibid., p. 413.
31. Ibid., p. 610.
32. Ibid., p. 634.
33. Ibid., p. 644.
34. Ibid., pp. 345–73.
35. Ibid., p. 346.
36. Ibid., p. 351.
37. Ibid., p. 193.

29. Savitri: A Legend and a Symbol

1. Sri Aurobindo, *The Complete Works of Sri Aurobindo, Volumes 33 and 34* (Sri Aurobindo Ashram Trust, 1997).
2. Sri Aurobindo, *The Complete Works of Sri Aurobindo, Volume 26* (Sri Aurobindo Ashram Trust, 1997), p. 218.
3. Ibid., *Volume 33*, pp. 3–4.
4. Ibid., *Volume 33*, pp. 47–48.
5. Ibid., p. 139.

6. Ibid., *Volume 34*, pp. 582–83.
7. Ibid., *Volume 33*, p. 310.
8. Ibid., *Volume 34*, p. 717.
9. Ibid., p. 623.
10. Ibid., p. 634.
11. Ibid., p. 383.

30. Letters on Himself and the Ashram

1. Sri Aurobindo, *The Complete Works of Sri Aurobindo, Volume 19* (Sri Aurobindo Ashram Trust, 1997).
2. Ibid., p. 102.
3. Ibid.
4. Ibid.
5. Sri Aurobindo, *The Complete Works of Sri Aurobindo, Volume 35* (Sri Aurobindo Ashram Trust, 2011).
6. Ibid., p. 6.
7. Ibid., p. 26.
8. Ibid., p. 26.
9. Sri Aurobindo, *The Complete Works of Sri Aurobindo, Volumes 10 and 11*, (Sri Aurobindo Ashram Trust, 2001).
10. Ibid., pp. 237–38.
11. Ibid., p. 414.
12. Sri Aurobindo, *The Complete Works of Sri Aurobindo, Volumes 23 and 24* (Sri Aurobindo Ashram Trust, 1999), p. 1.
13. Ibid., *Volume 35*, pp. 346–47.
14. Ibid., p. 452.
15. Ibid., p. 155.
16. Ibid., p. 598.
17. Ibid., p. 590.
18. Ibid., p. 750.
19. Ibid., p. 701.
20. Ibid., p. 679.
21. Ibid., p. 439.
22. Ibid., p. 837.

31. Autobiographical Notes and Other Writings of Historical Interest

1. Sri Aurobindo, *The Complete Works of Sri Aurobindo, Volume 36* (Sri Aurobindo Ashram Trust, 2006), p. 11.
2. Ibid., pp. 5–10.
3. Ibid., p. 110.
4. Ibid., p. 10.
5. Ibid.
6. Ibid., pp. 9–10.
7. Ibid., p. 161.
8. Ibid., p. 166.
9. Ibid., p. 177.
10. Ibid., p. 177–78.
11. Ibid., p. 477.
12. Ibid., p. 507.
13. Sudhir Ghosh, *Gandhi's Emissary* (Rupa and Co., 1967), pp. 314–15.
14. Sri Aurobindo, *The Complete Works of Sri Aurobindo, Volume 36* (Sri Aurobindo Ashram Trust, 2006), pp. 506–07.
15. Ibid., p. 531.
16. Ibid., p. 547.

Conclusion: Reading Beyond this Book

1. Sri Aurobindo, *Complete Works of Sri Aurobindo, Volume 18* (Sri Aurobindo Ashram Trust, 2001), pp. 345–99.
2. The Mother, *Collected Works of the Mother, Volume 12* (Sri Aurobindo Ashram Trust, 2002), p. 214.
3. The Mother, *Collected Works of the Mother, Volume 3* (Sri Aurobindo Ashram Trust, 2003), p. 65.
4. The Mother, *Collected Works of the Mother, Volume 12* (Sri Aurobindo Ashram Trust, 2002), p. 203.
5. Sri Aurobindo, *Complete Works of Sri Aurobindo, Volumes 33 and 34* (Sri Aurobindo Ashram Trust, 1997), p. 2.